FOOD LOVERS'
GUIDE TO
MANHATTAN

FOOD LOVERS' SERIES

FOOD LOVERS'
GUIDE TO®
MANHATTAN

The Best Restaurants, Markets
& Local Culinary Offerings

1st Edition

Alexis Lipsitz Flippin

Guilford, Connecticut

Editor: Amy Lyons
Project Editor: Lynn Zelem
Layout Artist: Mary Ballachino
Text Design: Sheryl Kober
Illustrations by Jill Butler with additional art by Carleen Moira Powell and MaryAnn Dubé
Map: Alena Joy Pearce © Morris Book Publishing, LLC

ISBN 978-0-7627-8424-0

Printed in the United States of America

All the information in this guidebook is subject to change. We recommend that you call ahead to obtain current information before traveling.

Contents

Downtown

Midtown

Uptown

Recipes, 207

Appendices, 231

About the Author

Alexis Lipsitz Flippin was born and raised in the small-town South. Her Baptist mother prepared exemplary Southern classics and her Jewish grandmother cooked state-of-the-art chopped liver and potato latkes and, in the fashion of the day, dabbled in Cantonese-American specialties—her chicken chow mein was built from scratch. So to grow up in sun-dappled kitchens where three wondrous cuisines commingled and perfumed the air was a pretty powerful culinary apprenticeship of sorts. It's little wonder that the biggest topic of conversation at the Lipsitz family table was the next meal.

Now living in downtown New York, Alexis is the author of *Frommer's New York Day by Day, Frommer's New York City with Kids, Frommer's Turks & Caicos,* and *Frommer's St. Maarten/St. Martin, Anguilla & St. Barts* and coauthor of *Frommer's 500 Extraordinary Islands, Frommer's Caribbean,* and *Frommer's Carolinas & Georgia.* She has written for numerous magazines and webzines including CNN.com, MSNBC.com, AARP.com, Away.com, and the *Wall Street Journal,* and is a former Senior Editor at Frommer's travel guides.

Acknowledgments

First off, I'd like to thank my uncles and aunts who live in and around the city: Betty and Lee Rout; Hilary and Ethel Lipsitz; and Steve and Barbara Lipsitz. It was through their generosity and boundless passion for food that I was introduced to such wondrous spots as Canton in Chinatown; Gallagher's steakhouse near Times Square; Teachers and Teachers Too on the Upper West Side; and Dominick's in the Bronx. Second, I'd like to thank those chefs who so magnanimously gave of their time and their expertise—emblematic of the overall spirit of goodwill in the Manhattan community of chefs. Lastly, I'd like to thank the best restaurant companions a girl could have: my husband, Royce, and my daughter, Maisie.

Introduction

For sheer sizzle and razzle-dazzle, few cities on the planet can rival the Big Apple in all its chest-puffing self-promotion (okay, Vegas is a contender and Dubai is not far behind). And when it comes to dining out, New York works hard to outdazzle just about anyone else. But in this noisy culinary cauldron, where the chessboard moves of top chefs are breathlessly noted in the blogosphere, and a certain crowd is always chasing the hottest new thing—and yes, in a city where everyone's a critic—it can be challenging to separate the hype from the genuine, to find those places, as *New York Times* writer Pete Wells put it, where "the razzle-dazzle is on the plate."

I myself am hardly immune to razzle-dazzle and readily acknowledge the prowess of a theatrical showplace. And sometimes, if the food's all right, that's enough for a good night out. But at the end of the day it's really about, well, what's on the plate. While *Food Lovers' Guide to Manhattan* includes plenty of places where the design makes the spirit soar, my goal is to point you to the city's most memorable culinary experiences and most flavorful food. I've found that if you can fight your way past the hype and the din and the chattering cognoscenti, with fork and knife in hand you'll discover in Manhattan one of the richest, most satisfying dining scenes in the world.

Trends, 'Hoods & Mini Empires

The Manhattan food scene is soaring again, following a dark recessionary period that saw the folding of too many mom-and-pop eateries and the scaling back of many grand endeavors. Today, even though big is

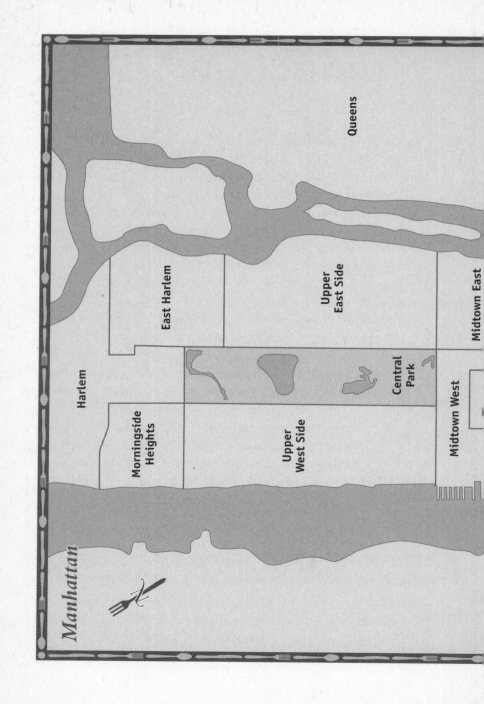

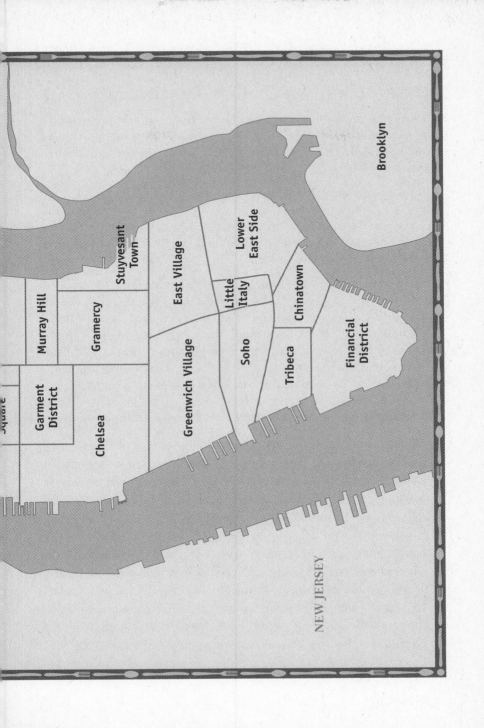

DINING THE WORLD, ONE CUISINE AT A TIME

Serendipity in Manhattan is stumbling upon an ethnic pocket so steeped in another culture that you're not sure for a moment where you've landed. Here are some of the borough's distinctly ethnic enclaves, where food is often the main draw.

Chinatown. Manhattan has one of the country's largest Chinatowns, a bustling sprawl of restaurants, noodle shops, bakeries, and produce and seafood markets. Most restaurants offer dim sum during the day and full menus at night, and the food for the most part is good and inexpensive.

Little Italy. Manhattan's Little Italy has been shrinking for decades, but the streets between Mulberry and Grand are still wall-to-wall restaurants, cafes, and Italian markets. The tourist trade is the bread and butter of Little Italy, with red-sauce cuisine, Olde Italy decor, and touts beckoning diners with flowery "buon giornos." Although menus for the most part stick to formulaic Italian-American standards, the food is good quality and often delicious.

definitely back, it's lost its glitzy frivolity. A great deal of thought goes into the opening of a new restaurant—and "new" just for the sake of new is so passé. In other developments, the artisanal-food movement has tunneled in from Brooklyn, and Manhattan menus proudly carry many MADE IN BROOKLYN foodstuffs. Nutritious, ingredient-driven eating has eased into the mainstream (notwithstanding the fact that steak houses and burger joints have never been more popular), and it's comforting to know that New York's french fries, doughnuts, cupcakes, and even movie popcorn are healthier—Bloomberg's ban on trans fats has been an unqualified success. In fact, sustainable and eco-conscious "farm-to-table" dining is in full flower—the city now hosts 55 active Greenmarket farmers' markets (grownyc.org). "Mayberry bucolic" has

Koreatown. Located in the low 30s between Sixth and Madison Avenues, Koreatown is filled with barbecue restaurants, *mandoo* dumpling shops, and karaoke lounges. The busiest street is 32nd Street between Fifth Avenue and Broadway, with neon signs and billboards in Korean and a handful of hotels.

Little Tokyo. Japanese restaurants, stores, and sake bars are congregated around 9th and 10th Street between First and Third Avenues in the East Village. Expect to find sake bars, soba shops, ramen counters, and *robata* (grill) restaurants.

Little India. Manhattan has two different Little Indias. "Curry Hill," around Lexington Avenue from 26th to 29th Streets, offers restaurants, grocery stores, and sari shops. The block-long Little India in the East Village, along 6th Street between First and Second Avenues, has a lineup of Bengali restaurants where the food is cheap, and you may be serenaded by sitar or raga music.

Little Brazil. Brazilian specialties such as *feijoada* (a bean and meat stew) are found in Brazilian restaurants along West 45th and 46th Streets between Fifth and Sixth Avenues.

even become a growing design motif, with the influx of sunny, whitewashed, flowerpot spots that would be right at home in Berkeley or Nantucket plunked down on gritty, car-choked streets. A number of enterprising chefs have even taken to growing vegetables and herbs on restaurant roofs (including Jean-Georges's ABC Kitchen, which grows herbs and microgreens 10 stories up). Rosemary's, a bucolic Italian in the West Village, has a chicken coop—and the rarefied roof of the Waldorf Astoria is now home to a beehive making silky "Waldorf Honey."

Manhattan truly does bring a world of food to its citizens. It may lack the sheer breadth of ethnic eateries you find in, say, Astoria, Queens, or

Brooklyn, but the borough can claim a substantial Chinatown; a shrinking Little Italy; and a small but kicking Koreatown (blocks in the low 30s btw. Madison and Sixth Aves.), Little Brazil (West 45th and 46th Sts. btw. Fifth and Sixth Aves.), Little Tokyo (East Village, along and around 9th and 10th Sts. btw. Second and Third Aves.), and Little India (two strongholds: "Curry Hill," on and around Lexington Ave. from 26th to 29th Sts. and the one-block stretch of East 6th St. btw. First and Second Aves.). There's a sturdy enclave of Szechuan restaurants in and around the 30s in Midtown. You can't throw a cat without hitting a tapas joint, and sushi remains ever popular.

Meanwhile mini-empires march on, with star chefs such as Daniel Boulud setting up exemplary dining rooms in all corners of Manhattan and powerhouse teams like the Torrisi clan (fomenting an Italian renaissance downtown) making smart, judicious, and often thrilling forays into the restaurant fray. New York has no dearth of ambitious statement restaurants from world-beating chefs who make you really think about what you are eating. Any foodie would be remiss if he or she did not sample such a place when visiting—this is where big ideas are ignited and delivered right on the plate. But don't discount the powerful embrace of those unsung neighborhood restaurants, reliable as rain and often much more than that. In this city of neighborhoods, locals claim a tribal allegiance to the little community around them. Many of these neighborhood spots are emblematic of the people around it; others offer a highly refined sense of place; still others express a longing for a home far, far away. Here you may find the beating heart of the Manhattan dining food scene and very often serendipity on a plate.

How to Use This Book

Food Lovers' Guide to Manhattan is separated into three sections: Downtown, Midtown, and Uptown, and within those sections are neighborhood chapters. Inside those chapters are the following categories:

Foodie Faves

These are our favorite places to dine in Manhattan, running the spectrum from high end to economical, formal to casual, trendy to off-the-radar, and special occasion to roll-up-your-sleeves down and dirty.

Landmarks & Old-School Faves

Manhattan wouldn't be Manhattan without its iconic landmark restaurants and vintage neighborhood favorites. This category lists those landmarks and old-school faves that have stood the test of time but continue to deliver a solid—and often ethereal—culinary experience.

Specialty Stores, Markets & Producers

Bringing a world of food to Manhattan Island are these specialty purveyors, niche markets, and farmstand faves. The list includes gourmet-food emporiums, sweets shops, butchers, seafood slingers, roasters, and bakeries, among others.

Price Code

We've given each restaurant a dollar-sign price code that is a rough approximation of the cost of a meal. All restaurant prices are based on the following general guidelines for an appetizer, entree, and dessert for one person (using the average menu prices), before drinks, tax, and tip. As a general rule, double the figure to estimate the cost of a three-course meal with a glass or two of wine, tax, and tip.

$	under $20
$$	$20 to $40
$$$	$40 to $60
$$$$	$60 and over

Saving Money on Meals

The Big Apple has some of the most expensive dining in the world. Manhattan is an island, after all, and a pretty congested one at that, without so much as an inch of space for growing and cultivating crops. Food must be transported in daily by road, train, and air. Storage is at a premium, so the roadways and airways in and out of the city are always jammed with trucks and planes bringing the goods: foodstuffs for the hungry masses, exotica for prickly gourmands, and farm-fresh produce to sate the city's growing Greenmarket clientele. Sky-high rents mean that restaurants, delis, and markets must charge inflated prices: It's no wonder food is sold at a premium! That said, savvy diners can find ways to mitigate the spending agony. Here are a few tips on saving money on meals in Manhattan.

Look for prix-fixe multicourse deals. Many restaurants offer nightly prix-fixe meals that represent good value. Tasting menus are often good values as well, and offer a chance to sample a chef's repertoire in one sitting.

If you're determined to sample New York's priciest spots, dine at lunch. Lunch prices run considerably lower than nighttime menus.

Sign up for deal-of-the-day websites for discounted restaurant deals. Join the New York version of deal-of-the-day websites like

Getting Around

It's amazing that so many people can congregate on this little island and move around it, but truth be told: Gridlock is a way of life in Manhattan. The quickest way to get from here to there is the subway. Yes, the subway system is an antique; it's smelly and crowded and loud. But when things are humming along, it's fast. New cars and new electronic signage that lets you know how many minutes you have to wait for the

Groupon.com, GiltCity.com, and BlackboardEats.com to snag coupons, discounts, and deals on Manhattan restaurants—many with certificates for popular restaurants for as much as 30 to 50 percent off. Note that the certificates have expiration dates, so snap up your deals with timing in mind.

Find a hotel that includes breakfast or has self-catering capabilities—a kitchen or kitchenette—to save on meals by having breakfast or lunch in, for example (bagels from the local deli, fresh orange juice) so you can eat out for dinner.

Have Chinese for lunch. Most Chinese restaurants offer gut-busting lunch specials: entrees plus soup or other appetizer, including rice, for under $10.

Have a slice. Do what many thrifty New Yorkers do and have a slice and a drink for lunch. A number of $1-a-slice pizza joints have opened up around town, and the pizza's not half bad and is guaranteed to fill you up.

Grab picnic fixings at a farmers' market. The Union Square Greenmarket, open 4 days a week year-round, has plenty of picnic fare, from farm-made goat cheese, bread, and focaccias to apple cider, fresh fruit, and even smoked fish.

next train have made things even more palatable down under. Consider buying multiride MetroCards for subway discounts and bonus rides (mta.info/nyct; or call 511). Buses are great for sightseeing, but they lumber along in traffic, and taxis creep along on busy thoroughfares at rush hours in the morning and early evening. But if you have the time, the best, cheapest, and most appealing way to experience the city New York is on foot. This is one of the great walking cities of the world, and for foodies, the scent of New York street food is even more incentive to stroll. You'll experience a lot more by walking than you will if you ride beneath the street in the subway or fly by in a cab—and serendipitous food finds are all over Manhattan. So pack your most comfortable shoes and hit the pavement for prime food foraging.

Keeping Up with Food News

Buzz doesn't get any buzzier than that which drives the restaurant business in New York City. Whether it comes via overcaffeinated PR mavens, food blogs, or word-of-mouth, breaking restaurant news is rarely under the radar. We find that it's best to stay away from a hot new restaurant until the hype has died down and the dust settles, but ah, then we're not on many VIP lists. So how do you know if a place is really worth your money? Taste is subjective, of course, but look to the following sources for smart, thoughtful critical takes and a broader perspective. We tend to scan the user-generated content sites (Yelp, TripAdvisor) with a somewhat skeptical eye, although the reviews can be valuable for discerning common threads and getting a general sense of what to expect—especially when a place is a disaster. We do, however, highly recommend getting opinions on the ground once you arrive. Talk to the locals—people who are passionate about food, and that would be just about any New Yorker with a pulse, aren't likely to steer you wrong.

PUBLICATIONS

The *New York Times*. In a city awash in hyperbole, the *Times* is an oasis of measured reason and critical acuity. The Wednesday *New York Times* has a terrific Dining section with an always eagerly anticipated restaurant review by the *Times* critic du jour—as of this writing, the estimable Pete Wells—not to mention the latest food news, recipes, and feature-length articles. If you miss Wednesday's paper, you can get it all and more by checking out the *Times's* online Dining

& Wine section (nytimes.com) with a Diner's Journal and a backlog of restaurant reviews. Also look for food columnist Mark Bittman's passionate features and editorials on food safety, sustainable farming, and responsible eating.

The *New York Post*. Like the *New York Times,* the *New York Post* has a Wednesday Dining section, albeit a small one, with a review or two and a smattering of food news. It's the domain of savvy and ofttimes sour food critic Steve Cuozzo, who suffers no fools in his dining escapades as the *Post's* food columnist (since 1998).

New York. *New York* magazine is one of the city's best sources for unvarnished restaurant reviews and the latest food news. The magazine covers the Manhattan food scene with excellent weekly restaurant reviews (Adam Platt and the Underground Gourmet team) and yearly "Best of New York" and "Cheap Eats" issues. But the most helpful is the collection of smart, engaging online reviews (nymag.com) of just about every Manhattan eatery, updated regularly with pertinent info.

Time Out New York. *Time Out*'s online food information is plenty exhaustive: foodie features, reviews, and a slew of "Best" roundups (Best Pizza, Best Burgers, Best Steak Houses, etc.) along with guides to best restaurants by neighborhood. Like *New York* magazine, *Time Out* magazine features weekly restaurant reviews and yearly "Best of New York" food issues.

WEBSITES/BLOGS

Chowhound.com (Manhattan discussion). Of all the user-generated

Foods We Love:
Our Favorite Grab-and-Go Addictions

In Manhattan, you don't have to sit down and dine to sample gourmet treats. Here are some of our favorite grab-and-go foods.

Sea-salt chocolate-chip cookie, Sweet Corner Bakeshop (Greenwich Village), p. 83

Square slice zucchini, mushroom, and mozzarella pizza, Farinella Bakery (Upper East Side), p. 126

Peppercorn catfish sandwich, Num Pang (multiple locations), p. 72

Fresh loaf of *foccacia fino,* Il Buco Alimentari (NoHo), p. 40

Cheese biscuits, Amy's Bread (multiple locations), p. 109

Cup of classic hot chocolate, Jacques Torres (Hudson Square and other locations), p. 46

Gaspé nova on bagel, Russ & Daughters (Lower East Side), p. 61

Pizze zucchini, Sullivan St. Bakery (Midtown West), p. 110

Pretzel croissant, City Bakery (Union Square/Flatiron), p. 87

Lobster roll, Luke's Lobster (multiple locations), p. 60

content sites, this is by far the best and most legitimate, with a passionate coterie of regular contributors who really know and live the Manhattan food scene. It's largely used for asking for restaurant recommendations, such as where to eat brunch in the East Village or best places to get Szechuan food.

Eater.com. A smart, opinionated website with updated restaurant news, recommended restaurants by neighborhood, and a regularly updated "Eater's 38 Top Restaurants."

Gothamist.com. Mixed into this bubbling stew of news about daily life in 21st-century Manhattan are sassy, well-curated "Best of" food and restaurant lists and slide shows.

GrubStreet.com. *New York* magazine's spirited, smartly designed blog culls the latest food news, openings, rivalries, and more from sources near and far.

OpenTable.com. What once started as an online restaurant reservation service is now a full-service food site, with reviews, reader-generated reviews, and photos. It's great for making reservations, however, and if the restaurant is not available you can plug in your choice of neighborhood and cuisine and OpenTable algorithmically divines other options.

SeriousEats.com. Ed Levine, passionate food writer (*New York Eats*) and one of the legends of the New York food world, is the founder of this James Beard Award–winning website, a smorgasbord of food news, tips, features, recipes, and "Best of" lists.

TastingTable.com. Coming on strong is this newcomer, the local edition of which is a savvy, well-written, and reliable source for restaurant openings and interesting features. It looks great, too.

January

Restaurant Week (Jan–Feb and June), nycgo.com/restaurantweek. Twice a year some of the best restaurants in town offer three-course prix-fixe meals at almost affordable prices. (Restaurant Week is a bit of a misnomer; the deals often go for 20 days or so, and in summer, the deals can last into Labor Day.) Lunch is $25, while dinner is $38. It's a great way to sample the menus at some of New York's most heralded restaurants (and not break the bank doing it).

February

Chinese New Year, explorechinatown.com or betterchinatown.com. The dates vary every year, but that doesn't keep the party from slowing down. Chinatown rings in its own New Year (based on a lunar calendar) in late winter with 2 weeks of celebrations, including parades with dragon and lion dancers, and food, food, food. Most every Chinese restaurant has a special Chinese New Year menu, all with some kind of lucky noodle dish.

April

New York Travel Festival, nytravfest.com. Brand-new in 2013, this proudly proclaims itself as the cool alternative to the behemoth *New York Times* Travel Show held annually in the Javits Center. Besides keynote speeches, debates, and tours, the New York Travel Fest has food and drink—from moonshine made in upstate New York to regionally made honey and chocolates.

May

Ninth Avenue International Food Festival, ninthavenue foodfestival.com. The year 2013 marked the 40th anniversary of one of New York's best and most venerable street fairs. You can spend the whole day sampling Italian sausages, clams, and oysters on the half shell, homemade pierogi, spicy curries, and other ethnic dishes. Street musicians, bands, and vendors add to the festive atmosphere stretching along Ninth Avenue from 37th to 57th Streets.

Taste of Tribeca, tasteoftribeca.com. This outdoor food festival in the heart of TriBeCa has been a hit since it started 20 years ago. It traditionally gets strong participation from the neighborhood's best restaurants, including Locanda Verde, Gigino, Tribeca Grill, and Bouley, among others. Festival-goers can buy "tastings" of each restaurant's signature dishes at tables set up on the street.

June

Big Apple Barbecue Block Party, bigapplebbq.org. One of the biggest and most anticipated food events in Manhattan, the Big Apple Barbecue brings a number of the nation's top barbecue pitmasters to Madison Square Park for genuine smoked barbecue, foot-stomping music, a beer garden, and more.

Restaurant Week (see January, p. 14).

Taste of Times Square, timessquarenyc.org. Sponsored by the Times Square Alliance, this outdoor food and music festival serves up food from some of the neighborhood's top restaurants. Festival-goers can buy "tastings" of each restaurant's signature dishes from tables set up on the street.

July

French Restaurant Week, frenchrestaurantweek.com. To coincide with Bastille Day, participating French restaurants around the city offer special "restaurant week" prix-fixe menus.

August

Blues Barbecue Festival, hudsonriverpark.org. This Saturday-afternoon Hudson River Park festival combines blues and roots music with smoked barbecue from Dinosaur BBQ and Brother Jimmy's BBQ. It's at Pier 84 on the Hudson River.

September

Feast of San Gennaro, sangennaro.org. Filling the streets of Little Italy with carnival booths and Italian food stands for 11 days around the saint's day, San Gennaro is crowded but fun.

October

Food Network's New York City Wine & Food Festival, nycwff.org. Moving to Midtown along the Hudson River on Pier 92 and Pier 94 in 2013, the NYC Wine & Food Festival also pops up at various other venues around town.

November

New York Chocolate Show, chocolateshow.com. This 4-day event devoted to chocolate takes place each year about 2 weeks before Thanksgiving and is open to the public. The event features booths representing more than 50 of the world's best chocolate makers, tastings, demonstrations, and activities for children.

Downtown

Financial District, Battery Park, Chinatown & Little Italy

An area still rebounding from the devastation of 9/11 was no match for the winds and waves of Hurricane Sandy, which sent an 8-foot wall of seawater deep into the labyrinthine streets of downtown on a long, dark night in October 2012. At press time, the area was still in recovery mode, especially the South Street Seaport waterfront and Battery Park. But big changes are afoot. Spirits in the Seaport were raised by the dogged persistence of the New Amsterdam Market and the entry of the **Brooklyn Flea** (see p. 24) onto the downtown food scene. The barren food wasteland that is Battery Park City will change overnight when a $250-million makeover of the World Financial Center is expected to transform the Winter Garden waterfront esplanade into a European-style marketplace with retail wings and a humongous second-floor dining terrace/food hall. (And a new name: Brookfield Place.) If you build it, will they come? For a still-transitional area buffeted by tragedy and natural disaster, only time will tell. But with the incredible popularity of the nearby 9/11 Memorial and the much-ballyhooed 2014 opening of the 9/11 Museum—and those sumptuous Hudson River views, the sun glinting off the water and the Statue of Liberty reflected in the mighty harbor—plenty of high rollers are betting on it.

The canyons of Wall Street have no lack of fine-dining temples targeted at deep-pocketed finance types. Many are quite good, but few are truly destination spots. A handful have a historic patina; this is, after all, where the European colonists first settled—all the development in the city radiated northward from Manhattan's seafaring southern "boot."

New York's Chinatown is always bustling with industry, and food is central to the people who live here. All day, it seems, you can see Chinese women toting orange plastic bags of fresh vegetables, fish, and meat. Many places offer dim sum all week long from around 11 a.m. to 3 p.m., and the chatter around big round tables in cavernous Hong Kong–style banquet halls can be deafening on weekends, when dim sum mid-day meals become a family affair for locals. Chinatown has for years been busting its seams, while its neighbor to the north, Little Italy, just gets smaller and smaller. The tourist trade is the bread and butter of this little enclave. More than a few Manhattanites turn up their noses at the cornball touristic vibe of Little Italy—where Frankie Sinatra croons night and day and the mustachioed touts put a little too much bounce in their buona sera. The menus sometimes feel like an Italian-American template—expect rivers of red sauce—but hey, competition keeps the kitchens sharp, and most of the food is pretty decent. Kids love the "O Sole Mio" tableau. During the summer, Mulberry Street is closed off to traffic from Friday at 6 p.m. to Sunday night, and it's a pasta party under the stars.

Foodie Faves

Angelo's of Mulberry St., 146 Mulberry St., btw. Grand and Hester Sts.; (212) 966-1277; angelosofmulberryst.com; Subway: N,

Q, R, W, 6 to Canal St.; Italian; $$. One of the most durable spots in Little Italy is this Mulberry Street oldie, established in 1902. Yes, that would be an Olde Italy mural on the wall, and the bow-tied, world-weary waitstaff is part of the shtick. But Angelo's does the classics straight up and delicious, and the Neapolitan food has a homemade freshness.

The Butcher's Daughter, 19 Kenmare St., at Elizabeth St.; (212) 219-3434; thebutchersdaughter.com; Subway: 6 to Spring St. or M, N, R, Z, 6 to Canal St.; Vegan/Organic; $. The kind of place that would look right at home on a leafy street in Berkeley, this windowed, whitewashed newcomer on the gritty edges of the Bowery and China-town is defiantly sunny and open. All butcher-block wood and big windows and flower boxes, the Butcher's Daughter peddles house-made organic juices and creative vegetarian fare like raw pesto linguine, beet tartare, and a PB & Raw J (a flavorful mashup of nut butters with sliced grapes or banana). The kale salad comes with a sunflower-seed tahini, green apples, avocado, and a smoked sea salt, and a root potato salad consists of roasted veggies with a whole-grain mustard aioli. At night, wine and beer are served with bar snacks.

Nom Wah Tea Parlor, 13 Doyers St., off Pell St.; (212) 962-6047; Subway: J, M, N, R, Z, 6 to Canal St.; Chinese; $. The oldest dim sum parlor in Manhattan sits on the the city's "crookedest street," Doyers St., also known as the Bloody Angle for the blood spilled during the Tong Wars fought in the early 20th century. Opened at 13-15 Doyers St. in 1920, Nom Wah started as a tea parlor and bakery. Even when it moved to its current location in 1968 the menu remained unchanged. For years Nom Wah sort of ambled along in an early-20th-century time capsule. But in 2010 a young nephew took over the family business, brightening up the decor,

CHEAP EATS: PROSPERITY DUMPLINGS

Can the city of the $50 designer burger coexist with the cheap (and good) dumpling? Seems to, swimmingly. **Prosperity Dumpling** (46 Eldridge St., btw. Canal and Hester Sts.; 212-343-0683) is one of a handful of Chinatown dumpling storefronts where you can get five hot-off-the-wok pork and chive dumplings for a mere $1. There's a reason a line snakes out the front door: These dumplings are good.

updating the kitchen, and making dim sum to order rather than letting it sit in steam carts for hours. The place still looks like a colorful time capsule from a hundred years ago, but now the fresh, tasty food makes it really worth a stop.

Oriental Garden, 14 Elizabeth St., btw. Bayard and Canal Sts.; (212) 619-0085; orientalgardenny.com; Subway: J, M, N, R, Z, 6 to Canal St.; Chinese; $$–$$$. Next door, the dim sum palace Jing Fong serves hundreds of people a day in a cacophonous room the size of a football field. But here in the Oriental Garden's vastly more intimate space you can dine in serenity on some of Chinatown's most delicious Cantonese food, including dim sum delicacies made to order. The room has a white-tablecloth crispness, and tanks of live seafood. The Cantonese dishes are fresh-tasting and flavorful, without the cloying oiliness of other Chinatown spots, and vegetables come to the table with color and snap.

Peking Duck House, 28 Mott St., near Pell St.; (212) 227-1810; pekingduckhousenyc.com; Subway: J, M, N, R, Z, 6 to Canal St.; Chinese; $$$–$$$$. The minimalist, monochromatic decor sets the Peking Duck House apart from its fellow Chinatown restaurants, the fancier of which favor gilt-flecked red lacquer. It's a little more formal than most in every way, and pricier, too, and sometimes the waitstaff can seem, well, a tad dour. But the food is generally top-notch, and the house specialty, Peking duck, is still one of the best dishes in town, served in thin pancakes with scallions and hoisin sauce. Seafood dishes are exemplary as well. There's also a Midtown location (236 E. 53rd St., btw. Second and Third Aves.; 212-759-8260).

P.J. Clarke's on the Hudson, 4 World Financial Center, at North End Ave.; (212) 285-1500; pjclarkes.com; Subway: N, R to Cortlandt St. or E to World Trade Center; American; $$–$$$. The Downtown iteration of one of Manhattan's storied old-timers, this P.J. Clarke's has what the original never had: views, in this case, expansive Hudson River panoramas to go with the restaurant's classic burger. Set on the harborside of the World Financial Center, with extensive seating out on the waterfront terrace, it's a fine place to watch boats go by and count the billionaires' yachts bobbing in the yacht basin. P.J. Clarke's classic burger doesn't look like much—it's thin and slightly wan, slapped inside a decidedly unpuffy bun—but more than a few folks think it's the bomb. The menu is upscale saloon, with typical chophouse fare (iceberg wedge with blue cheese, classic Caesar salad, Black Angus steaks) supplemented by classics like chicken pot pie, a slow-braised beef stew, fish-and-chips. Everything is prepared with a sure hand. Shockingly, the island of Manhattan, surrounded as it is by water, has few places to dine with water views. This is one of the bright spots of an anemic food zone, and wowsa, those views . . .

The Royal, 103 Mott St., near Canal St.; (646) 392-4236; Subway: 6 to Spring St. or M, N, R, Z, 6 to Canal St.; Chinese; $. By 11 a.m. daily, this may be the busiest place in Chinatown, maybe all of downtown. The vast banquet-hall space is packed to the gills, and a man with a microphone calls out the name of the next group to be seated over the din of chattering Chinese families and businesspeople (and a smattering of tourists). Carts carrying steaming dim-sum delicacies rumble through the aisles. As busy dim-sum palaces go, this one offers little in the way of decor—white and red walls have a minimum of adornment other than TVs showing Chinese television shows—but the bustle tells the real story. The dim sum—served from 8 a.m. till 3 p.m. every day of the week—is some of the freshest in Chinatown, and the menu has some winners as well, including house-made shrimp rice noodles and lobster Cantonese. The Royal is located on the Little Italy (north) side of Canal Street.

Landmarks & Old-School Faves

Harry's, 1 Hanover Square, corner of Pearl and Stone Sts.; (212) 785-9200; harrysnyc.com; Subway: 2, 3 to Wall St.; American/Steak House; $$$$. Harry's handsome steak house, restaurant, and cafe are located on the lower floors of the old India House, a Florentine brownstone built in the 1850s. Harry's is all gleaming wood, but not in the shabby-rustic way of colonial taverns. This place has a moneyed burnish, with clubby leather banquettes, a copper ceiling and the charred perfume of grilled New York strip. Rooms unfold onto candlelit nooks and crannies where the bones of the old house are revealed in whitewashed brick, all that's left of the original 1751 home of merchant Nicholas Bayard. Unlike some of the neighborhood's other "vintage" restaurants, which either fetishize its history or scrub out imperfections with a lurid Disney makeover, Harry's is a thoroughly 21st-century chophouse.

The Old and Not So Old

Manhattan's southern "toe" has seen so much physical change since Henry Hudson sailed into the harbor, it's a wonder anything has survived from the days of Olde New York. But artifacts remain, pieces here and there, despite fires, storms, neglect, and the bulldozing of whole neighborhoods of early European architecture. The South Street Seaport survives thanks to some early preservationists, and beautifully shows the scale of what was, back in colonial times, a bustling maritime district. Alas, few of the old dining places from centuries past survive, and those that remain have been greatly altered, with the exception of the **Bridge Cafe** (see sidebar p. 26). There's little that's original at **Fraunces Tavern** (54 Pearl St.; 212- 968-1776; frauncestavern.com), the colonial-era tavern where George Washington famously gave his farewell speech in 1783. Upstairs is a museum; downstairs is the Porterhouse Brewing Co., a genuinely atmospheric spot with wood plank floors and muskets hanging over fireplaces. It looks colonial, by golly, and feels period (except for the dissonant

Specialty Stores, Markets & Producers

Brooklyn Flea at the Seaport, 11 Front St., at Fulton St., South Street Seaport; brooklynflea.com; Subway: A, C, J, Z, 2, 3, 4, 5 to Fulton St.; Food Market. Nowhere in the city has the artisanal food movement been more an essential element of the fiber and fabric of everyday life than in Brooklyn. So it's hoped that the enormously successful Brooklyn Flea/Smorgasburg in Williamsburg and DUMBO will rub off on the imported Seaport franchise, where a dozen or so artisanal food and beverage vendors park their carts on the pedestrian plaza on the Seaport's Front Street daily from late May to late October.

rock music pumped into dining rooms and the den of smirking banker boys at the Speakeasy Bar), but the tavern was in such lousy shape in the early 1900s that it was largely rebuilt. The decent menu is a nod to the tavern's heyday, serving up plump oysters on the half-shell, Fraunces Tavern Pot Pie, and Jefferson's Cobb salad (with pecan bacon) to a daily influx of tourists. Fast forward to the 19th century, when **Delmonico's** (56 Beaver St. at South William St.; 212-509-1144; delmonicosrestaurantgroup.com) pampered high rollers in a triangular-shaped brownstone building in the canyons of Wall Street. This is where scene-stealing dishes like baked Alaska and lobster Newberg (see recipe on p. 222) originated. Delmonico's elegant circa-1837 exterior is unchanged from those days, with a lamplit rotunda supported by Pompeiian pillars. Inside, a sweeping Gilded Age fantasy is sheathed in polished mahogany and plush carpet—except that little original remains, other than a hand-carved staircase or two. But it's still a hoot to dine among the ghosts of Wall Street on lobster Newberg, baked Alaska, and Delmonico's fat, juicy steak.

It's a humongous step up from the nearby South Street Seaport Food Court, where the soaring views are blunted by a lame lineup of insipid mall franchisees. At press time, Brooklyn Flea vendors included Red Hook Lobster Pound (Maine lobster rolls, shrimp rolls), Brooklyn Oyster Party (fresh-shucked oysters), Milk Truck Grilled Cheese (handcrafted grilled-cheese sandwiches), Pizza Moto (wood-fired pizzas), and Blue Marble Ice Cream—plus a full bar inside a shipping container. Yay!

Caffè Roma, 385 Broome St., at Mulberry St.; (212) 226-8413; Subway: 6 to Spring St. or M, N, R, Z, 6 to Canal St.; Coffee Shop/ Pastries. In the heart of shrinking Little Italy, this family-owned pastry shop still conveys the flavor of the old neighborhood. With its vintage tile floors and original pressed-tin ceiling, Caffè Roma is a wonderful

A Long Run, Interrupted

Even though it sits on a rise two blocks up from the South Street Seaport waterfront, one of the city's most venerable old-timers was no match for Hurricane Sandy in October 2012, when a record storm surge caused the East River to overflow its banks. Storm waters swamped the **Bridge Cafe** (279 Water St., at Dover St.; bridgecafenyc.com; 212-227-3344), flooding the dining room and kitchen in the saloon/restaurant—in operation since 1794—with 4 feet of churning East River seas (the basement was completely inundated). It's taken longer than expected to clean up the mess and preserve 200-year-old water-saturated wood beams and a burnished oak bar, but it's hoped that the city's oldest commercial wood-frame building will be back in business by summer 2014. A onetime brothel, the Bridge Cafe long ago left its rakish days behind. What remains—and what has been sorely missed—is a warmly welcoming neighborhood cafe whose latest menus trended toward aspirational bistro (hanger steak with a shallot reduction; wild Pacific salmon in a wasabi-avocado cream). Here's hoping the Bridge Cafe can continue its long, impressive run in the old Seaport.

place to sample Italian cookies or cannoli and a cappuccino or espresso, made the classic way. Go now, before someone comes in and scrubs the century-old patina away; it's one of the last of a breed.

Di Palo's Fine Foods, 200 Grand St., at Mott St.; (212) 226-1033; dipaloselects.com; Subway: 6 to Spring St. or M, N, R, Z, 6 to Canal St.; Italian Food Market. Only a handful of markets selling Italian foodstuffs are left in Little Italy, and this has an old-world feel. It should: It opened in 1925 as a traditional *latteria* (dairy shop) by the daughter of Savino Di Palo, a Southern Italian cheesemaker who immigrated to America the early 1900s. Now in its fifth generation of Di

Palos and newly expanded in 2014, the shop offers a formidable selection of Italian cheeses as well as *salumi,* sauces, pasta, bread, olives, and prepared foods. Next door the family *enoteca* sells Italian wines.

New Amsterdam Food Market, the Old Fulton Fish Market, South St. between Beekman St. and Peck Slip; (212) 766-8688; newamsterdammarket.org; Subway: A, C, J, Z, 2, 3, 4, 5 to Fulton St.; Food Market. A self-styled reinvention of the city's public markets, the New Amsterdam Food Market is an award-winning weekend market where local and regional food purveyors, farmers, and cooks sell an amazing array of artisanal foods and gourmet foodstuffs—including hand-crafted breads, apple cider, seafood, and much more. It's set in the Old Fulton Fish Market, which closed this landmark location in 2005 when the seafood sellers and distributors moved to Red Hook, Brooklyn. At press time, the market was in danger of losing its space as part of a proposed mall/hotel/condo expansion by the Howard Hughes Corporation, the mega-developer responsible for the Seaport's Pier 17. For now, the New Amsterdam Market is open from 11 a.m. to 5 p.m. on designated Sundays from late spring through mid-December.

New York Marts, 128 Mott St., btw. Grand and Hester Sts.; (212) 680-0566; Subway: 6 to Spring St. or M, N, R, Z, 6 to Canal St.; Food Market. Chinatown has some of the best and cheapest seafood and vegetable markets in the city, and this one is a doozy. It's not for the faint-hearted, as much for the crowded aisles as for such exotica as conch, lionfish, and barrels of fist-size bullfrogs (very much alive). Enter on Mott Street to a seafood emporium, which leads to aisles piled high with vegetables, many of them staples in Chinese dishes (bok choy, Chinese broccoli, *sing gua*). Another room contains shelves of sauces, vinegars, and oils, freezers filled with ready-made dumplings, and refrigerator cases of fresh wonton wrappers and tofu. Prices are considerably cheaper all around than

STONE STREET: DINING ALFRESCO WITH THE GHOSTS OF WALL STREET

For an immersion in old New York, head to the cobbled alleyways of Stone Street and adjoining Coenties Slip. Stone Street looks much as it did in its heyday in the 18th century, and even more so when it transforms into a car-free zone from April to November. That's when the conglomeration of fashionably laid-back eateries moves right on the old cobblestoned streets. During the week, these two blocks of real estate host a buzzing happy hour crowd of Wall Street types, jackets off and ties askew. Join them with a classic burger or fish-and-chips at the **Stone Street Tavern** (52 Stone St.) or thin-crust pizza at **Adrienne's PizzaBar** (54 Stone St.). Sip a frosty beer at the **Dubliner** (45 Stone St.), **Ulysses Folk House** (95 Pearl St., with seating on Stone St.), or **Vintry Wine & Whiskey** (57 Stone St.). More food is available at little takeout joints along connecting Coenties Slip (**Pizza Pizza, Golden Chopsticks, Ruben's Empanadas**).

those charged at most Manhattan grocery chains, so it's a great place to stock up on Chinese condiments.

Pasanella and Son Vintner, 115 South St., btw. Beekman St. and Peck Slip; (212) 233-8383; pasanellaandson.com; Subway: A, C, J, Z, 2, 3, 4, 5 to Fulton St.; Wine Shop. The labor of love that is this wonderful Seaport wine shop is the work of Marco Pasenella and his wife, Becky. In 2006, Pasanella abandoned his accomplished career as an architect and designer (he designed the interiors of the Maritime Hotel, among others) to open a wine store on the ground floor of the couple's five-story 1839 Federal townhouse. The travails of their remarkable adventures in wine are told in Pasanella's captivating book, *Uncorked* (Clarkson Potter, 2012). With a baby-blue 1964 Fiat as the store's buoyant centerpiece, Pasanella and Son is that rare big-city find, an old-fashioned mom-and-pop wine store where the owners are intimately involved in every aspect of the business, from sourcing wines to store design to hosting events in the romantic tasting room in back, with bluestone floors and a private garden. Be sure to take home a bottle or two of the Pasanella-brand house red or white, a flavorful quaff and terrific bargain at $10.99. (And have Marco show you where the waters from Hurricane Sandy crested in 2012.)

Tribeca

The cobblestone streets are paved in gold in this sprawling downtown enclave just south of SoHo, where media moguls, filmmakers, and hedge funders occupy industrial lofts that once housed dry goods, textile manufacturers, and dairy markets and later, of course, artist studios. Tribeca—the acronym for Triangle Below Canal—may be one of the country's priciest zip codes, but it's also one of the city's most liveable neighborhoods. The sidewalks are wide, parks are green and spacious, and restaurants have a corresponding luxury of outsized space, all lofty ceilings and picture windows—a grand tableau for cigar-chomping world-beaters and their families. Tribeca was on the front lines of the devastation of 9/11, but it's come back in a big way, with help from folks like resident Robert DeNiro, cofounder of the Tribeca Film Festival. Some of the city's most esteemed chefs are well established here. Both David Bouley and Nobu Matsuhisa opened pioneering restaurants in the area in the eponymous Bouley and Nobu, respectively, both still exemplary dining experiences. You can eat high on the hog in Tribeca, but you can also dine quite well in a range of laid-back mid-priced spots. In any case, the general vibe is one of casual, cosseted well-being.

Bubby's, 120 Hudson St., at North Moore St.; (212) 219-0666; bubbys.com; Subway: 1 to Franklin St. or A, C, E to Canal St.; New American; $$. This Tribeca restaurant trucks quite successfully in old-fashioned hominess, with whitewashed wainscoting, handsome wood floors, and a picket fence outside (overseen by a big papier-mâché cow). The food is big on Americana comfort classics, lots of meat loaf, buttermilk biscuits, and mac 'n' cheese, a trope that would be slightly grating to non-nostalgists if everything weren't so incredibly fresh and flavorful. Expect a great selection of delicious Grandma-style pies (it started as a wholesale pie company), plus breakfast food served until 4 p.m. The Saturday and Sunday brunch is hugely popular, and you will likely have to wait in line for a table. But know that you'll be waiting behind the daddy moguls of Tribeca, doing their weekend kid duty and getting some Bubby's love.

Ecco, 124 Chambers St., between Church St. and Broadway; (212) 227-7074; eccorestaurantny.com; Subway: A, C, E to Chambers St.; Italian; $$$. This handsome Italian saloon, tucked behind a burgundy façade on Chambers Street, has a seductive antique charm, with vintage tile floors and a wine-colored tin ceiling. Its old New York ambience is palpable, and no wonder: This was a lively spot known as the Fritz Cafe in the early 1900s. The wooden bar, an old pharmacy cabinet, runs the length of the front of the house. Ecco is a warm place to be on a cold New York night, when all you want to do is share a libation with friends and tuck into some familiar Italian favorites, in this case a lineup of nicely executed standards from the Italian-American school. This neighborhood classic is celebrating 25 years in Tribeca.

Locanda Verde, 377 Greenwich St., at North Moore St.; (212) 925-3797; locandaverdenyc.com; Subway: 1 to Franklin St. or A, E

to Canal St.; Italian; $$$–$$$$. Sitting pretty in the heart of Tribeca in a warm, high-ceilinged room, this self-styled "Italian tavern" is joined at the hip to the Greenwich Hotel. In spite of its relaxed ambience, this is one hot ticket, where the deceptively casual Italian cuisine of Andrew Carmellini shares the stage with media bigs, Wall Street whippersnappers, and the chattering masses. Foodies are here too, less for the chirping cacophony than for the earthy, transcendent dishes. Start with the (already classic) lamb meatball sliders and marinated beets with herbed goat cheese. The pastas are terrific and reasonably priced and owe more than a nod to old-school Italian cooking—how can you turn down Carmellini's grandmother's meaty ravioli, ladled with a glistening tomato sauce and a dash of Parm? On warm days, the big doors are opened and tables spill out onto the wide, sun-splashed sidewalks, and you feel as if you're at the center of the Tribeca universe.

Sarabeth's Tribeca, **339 Greenwich St., at Jay St.; (212) 966-0421; sarabethstribeca.com; Subway: 1, 2 to Franklin St.; New American; $$$.** Sarabeth's was doing upscale comfort food way back in 1983, when the current buzzmeisters were in pantaloons. Each of the five Sarabeth's locations has an artfully polished design, but this beautiful downtown outpost may be the most lush looking of them all. Set in the heart of Tribeca in what was the Bazzini nut factory and store, the high-ceilinged warehouse space is sheathed in a hue of elegant cream, with towering flower arrangements and mustard-brown banquettes. There's a soothing luxury of space and materials, where the cool granite floor meets the soft, suffused light of old-fashioned lamp sconces. The menu is the standard Sarabeth lineup of nutritious, impeccably prepared comfort foods, including stuffed scrambled egg popovers, seafood cobb salad, rosemary roasted chicken, and jumbo shrimp risotto. It's a reliable spot to eat well, and in these soaring environs, a destination restaurant.

Scalini Fedeli, 165 Duane St., near Hudson St.; (212) 528-0400; scalinifedeli.com; Subway: A, C, 1, 2, 3 to Chambers St.; Italian; $$$$. This operatic space is a throwback to old-world dining rooms of vaulted ceilings and velvet draping. Butter yellow walls are lit with the faintest of lamplight and candles cast flickering shadows throughout. Opened in 2000 in the space formerly occupied by the legendary Bouley, this may be expense-account central for high-living suits, but it's also one of the city's most highly rated Northern Italians among food lovers. It's set in an 1892 Romanesque Revival building that was once a coconut factory. Chef Michael Cetrulo gives the space some serious competition with a prix-fixe menu of meticulous refinement.

Tamarind Tribeca, 99 Hudson St., at Franklin St.; (212) 775-9000; tamarindrestaurantsnyc.com; Subway: 1 to Franklin St. or A, E to Canal St.; Indian; $$$. Tamarind's second location in Manhattan (the Flatiron branch closed in 2013) in a landmark Art Deco building is sprawlingly spacious (11,000 square feet), light-filled, and airy. It's a wow kind of space, a fitting match for a neighborhood of Texas-size loft apartments and the media titans who inhabit them. In spite of its double-level grandeur, Tamarind has an inviting feel thanks to clubby banquettes, teak floors, and a most hospitable staff. It caters to business folks with a very reasonable 3-course "Executive Lunch" menu and a smart and expansive wine list, but Tamarind is on the radar of a wide range of New Yorkers, many of whom think this is the best Indian restaurant in town. It even has a Michelin star to prove it. The chefs have a way with seafood, as in the *kolambi pola,* prawns sauteed in coconut, lemongrass, and dried chiles, or a lobster masala. The classics are masterfully done, from a Goan fish curry to a chicken tandoor perfumed with ginger, garlic, and garam masala.

Tiny's, 135 West Broadway, near Duane St.; (212) 374-1135; tinys nyc.com; **Subway: A, C, 1, 2, 3 to Chambers St.; New American; $$.** This little gem is tucked into two floors of an 1810 Federal town house, its brick façade a peachy pink. The intimate scale, the candlelit nooks, crumbling 19th-century brick walls and salvaged furnishings give the place a Dickensian texture (the groovy clientele notwithstanding). When you're sitting on vintage drafting chairs sipping a pint beneath Tiny's tin ceiling, it's not hard to imagine yourself set down on the cobblestoned streets of early Manhattan. The owner/managers sourced circa-1900s wallpaper for the downstairs walls, and the fireplace blazes in winter. But this is no time-travel slumming. The kitchen has more-than-respectable cooking chops, serving up smart, flavorful American bistro food like grilled hanger steaks, pan-seared scallops, duck, and hake.

Landmarks & Old-School Faves

The Odeon, 145 W. Broadway, at Thomas St.; (212) 233-0507; theodeonrestaurant.com; **Subway: A, C, 1, 2, 3 to Chambers St.; American; $$$.** The Odeon opened its dazzling Art Deco doors in 1980 in a desultory wasteland that one writer described as "peopled by hardscrabble artists, muggers, crack dealers, and nightcrawlers." The makeover of the 1930s-era Tower Cafeteria was minimal; the McNally brothers slapped some red leather on the green banquettes and scrubbed the original terrazzo floor. Up went snazzy wooden blinds and a wooden Deco bar from an old joint in Midtown, and voilà! The old cafeteria became the toast of the town, its neon sign pictured on the cover of Jay McInerney's iconic eighties novel, *Bright Lights, Big City,* in which the protagonist famously describes the Odeon's look as "luncheonette-via-Cartier Deco." Today, the eighties crowd is long gone, but the old gal can still vamp it up with the best of them. Even better, this

BOULEY'S WORLD

The exacting standards of one of the city's greatest chefs continue apace in the little two-block area of Tribeca that is more or less Bouley World. Since 1985, when the world beat a path first to Montrachet and then to his eponymous Bouley to dine on the chef's ethereal French-American cuisine, David Bouley has been at the epicenter of the neighborhood food scene, opening restaurants, markets, and cafes—all, we can attest, dazzling experiments in taste and ever on the forefront of sustainable, artisanal, farm-to-table eating. Today the French-trained chef (an apprentice to Paul Bocuse, among others), farmer, nutritionist, and culinary philosopher is still the cook in the Bouley kitchen at 163 Duane Street. (He also oversees the Japanese kaiseki cuisine at Brushstroke, around the corner at 30 Hudson Street.) But his influence extends to restaurants all over the city helmed by Bouley acolytes and apprentices. Look, there are maybe a handful of chefs of his caliber actually behind the stove these days, so do yourself a favor: Snag a table at Bouley today (davidbouley.com).

sexy, streamlined looker has matured into the very epitome of a great neighborhood restaurant, delivering delicious bistro food and more than occasionally a sizzling dining experience. It's even a local family favorite (kids love getting a ticket from the cafeteria's original "Takacheck" out front), and it's easily our default choice when friends come to town. The modest menu specializes in brasserie classics like hanger steak, roast chicken, and *moules-frites,* but also skates the trends with deft versions of shrimp and grits, tuna burger, and miso-glazed salmon.

Duane Park Patisserie, 179 Duane St., near Greenwich St.; (212) 274-8447; duaneparkpatisserie.com; Subway: A, C, 1, 2, 3 to Chambers St.; Patisserie. On a street that not so long ago bustled with dairy and egg markets, this handsome, high-ceilinged patisserie is set in a former stable, with the rare door that opens outward. Inside the bakery case are fruit pies and berry tarts, not to mention an assortment of cakes. It's a great place to stop for breakfast croissants, scones, Danishes, and muffins in the morning or an afternoon snack of freshly baked cookies or cupcakes and homemade lemonade.

Mulberry & Vine, 73 Warren St., btw. Greenwich St. and West Broadway; (212) 791-6300; mulberryandvine.com; Subway: A, C, 1, 2, 3 to Chambers St.; Organic/Takeout. Filling a void in Tribeca is this "Eat Local, Cook Global" spot offering tasty, healthy prepared foods (takeout or eat-in) with a "local, seasonal, organic, pesticide-free, hormone-free, and antibiotic-free" calling. When you can do all that, *and* make it delicious, we're there. The daily selection of grains includes red rice with cucumber in a soy-shallot vinaigrette and a kicky Southwestern-style quinoa with corn, avocado, chipotle, and cumin seeds. Locally raised meats are also on the menu, like rosemary roast chicken and turkey Bolognese. Mulberry & Vine has daily soups and salads, as well as healthy breakfasts and house-made juices and smoothies. It's a great-looking spot to boot, with a creamy white façade and an airy and spacious interior of industrial lines, wood floors, and lofty ceilings.

SoHo, Hudson Square, NoHo & Nolita

The landmark district of SoHo ("South of Houston") is composed of industrial lofts with fanciful 19th-century cast-iron façades and streets of Belgian cobblestone. But at street level it's all about the bustle and hustle of 21st-century industry: the 24/7 peddling of consumer goods. Forty years ago the pioneering province of artists who used the big lofts of abandoned manufacturing buildings as studios, SoHo is now an atmospheric mega mall. Granted, it does have a few interesting places to wine and dine, and you can see charming intimations of its village roots in the blocks west of West Broadway. Just to the east is the quaint little nabe of Nolita ("North of Little Italy"), where 19th-century tenements and cobblestone streets were once a thriving part of Little Italy. Today hipster shops, cafes, and coffee bars form a low-rise constellation around the original St. Patrick's Cathedral, a circa-1868 behemoth that absorbs an entire block. To the northeast the more compact and condensed area known as NoHo ("North of Houston") was just yesterday a haven for Bowery bums and punk rockers. In its new incarnation, NoHo is lousy with restaurants, and quite a few high-caliber ones. To the west of SoHo, Hudson Square is the newly minted brand for a mixed-use area that includes the car-choked arteries leading to the Holland Tunnel and top media and tech companies. Nevertheless, the vast district (stretching from the Hudson to Sixth Avenue and roughly Canal Street north to Morton) still feels somewhat raw, with spurts of interesting industrial architecture and sleepy, untrodden streets. A historic 2013 rezoning means that all will likely change, and soon, making Hudson Square catnip for restaurant teams on the hunt for new spaces.

Foodie Faves

Back Forty West, 70 Prince St., at Crosby St.; (212) 219-8570; backfortynyc.com; Subway: N, R to Prince St.; New American; $$–$$$. For more than 20 years, pioneering locavore Peter Hoffman and his wheelbarrow bike have been a ubiquitous presence on Greenmarket days in Union Square. Not long after Hoffman closed his farm-to-table jewel box, Savoy, in 2011, he opened Back Forty West in the same 19th-century brick townhouse (Back Forty East is Hoffman's East Village burger joint). It was time, Hoffman told the *New York Times,* for a "reimagining" of the space and the business. Back Forty West would offer "good food in an unpretentious atmosphere" and at lower costs. The atmosphere has changed, all right; the downstairs cafe has a gritty minimalism and a bigger bar to quench the thirst of the younger crowd feeding on grilled pea pods, seasoned with glistening bits of bacon, and a nice grass-fed burger. Upstairs the vibe is more sedate—you can feel the bones of the old building here—and in winter a fireplace gives it peaceful rusticity. The menu has switched oft-elegant New American food for something simpler: grilled fish, smoked chicken or pork shoulder, and plenty of flavorful sides, like roasted beets with crispy quinoa or a basket of airy rosemary fries. Even in its new incarnation, Back Forty West doesn't stray from Hoffman's farm-to-table mantra.

Old-School French Is New Again

After years of taking a backseat to an army of nouveau Italian, Asian, and American eateries, French is back. The opening of several newfangled brasseries may be less about the second coming of highfalutin' spots like Lutèce than a longing for the classic French repertoire and the coming of age of innovative chefs who learned classic French technique from legends like David Bouley. Some of the biggest new names include Andrew Carmellini's **Lafayette** (380 Lafayette St.; lafayetteny.com; see p. 42), which opened in NoHo in the lofty landmark space last occupied by Chinatown Brasserie. It's been completely repurposed as a "grand cafe and bakery" in the classic French style—and it's been humming since the day it opened. A block away is the more sedate and contemplative environs of **Le Philosophe** (55 Bond St.; lephilosophe.us), which gets raves for its self-assured menu of French throwbacks (frogs' legs, *blanquette de veau*). In the East Village, **Calliope** (84 E. 4th St.; calliopenyc.com) is sardine-packed nightly, as much for its Parisian-brasserie good looks (classic tile floor, Deco mirrors) as for the chef's dynamic way with traditional French bistro cuisine.

Balthazar, 80 Spring St., at Crosby St.; (212) 965-1414; balthazar ny.com; Subway: 6 to Spring St.; French Brasserie; $$$–$$$$. Pure celebration, Balthazar has managed to outlast those critics who derided the "inauthenticity" of Keith McNally's meticulous replication of a Parisian brasserie. Just step inside the shimmering space and try not to be seduced. This is no Paris manqué, not with all the yammering Yanks and unlovely location on a traffic-choked street. Inside, the former warehouse off Lower Broadway is wrapped in gleaming Deco hardware and smoky mirrors. It's smart and glamorous, from the glossy zinc bar to the amber glow. Balthazar fizzes night or day, and at 20 years old, it's still a hot ticket. But a trendy scene can keep a place aloft only so long in this city; let us now praise the exemplary bistro food: *moules-frites,* say, or a *côtes de boeuf* for two. Grand seafood platters, icy tiers of *fruits de mer* holding briny oysters on the half shell, lobster, shrimp, and crab, practically require a bottle of bubbly. Ever on trend, Balthazar even serves a kale salad, here with dried currants, pinenut *socca,* and spiced yogurt, and daily specials include a Friday bouillabaisse.

Costata, **206 Spring St., btw. Sixth Ave. and Sullivan St.; (212) 334-3320; costatanyc.com; Subway: 6 to Spring St.; Steak House; $$$–$$$$.** This upscale chophouse brings Chef Michael White back to the kind of cooking that helped make him a big name in Manhattan food circles. We have fond memories of a gargantuan and perfectly charred *bistecca Fiorentina* at White's Tudor Village restaurant, Convivio, back in the day. Sure enough, Costata has its own, a succulent 40-ounce porterhouse. Set in the old Fiamma space on Spring Street's western edge, Costata at press time was still fairly new, but it was getting lots of love for its dry-aged meats, as well as what might be considered a greatest-hits selection from Chef White's considerable repertoire. You can get sparkling *crudo,* à la Marea (fluke, with olives and a tomato confit), solid Italian-tinged salads, à la Ai Fiori (romaine *cacio e pepe*), and state-of-the-art fresh pasta and risotto, à la Osteria Morini (spaghetti *vongole,* garganelli with prosciutto and peas in a truffle cream). Frankly, that works for us. It's all delicious.

Il Buco, **47 Bond St., btw. the Bowery and Lafayette St.; (212) 533-1932; ilbuco.com; Subway: 6 to Bleecker St.; Italian/Mediterranean; $$$.** The evolution of Il Buco from antiques store to transcendent farm-to-table trailblazer is a tale of happy circumstance, befitting a labor of love. Donna Lennert and her partner, Alberto Avalle, set up shop selling Americana on gritty Bond Street 20 years ago, and everything that followed, says Lennert, was "pure serendipity." The couple went from inviting customers in for a lunchtime *pranzo* to serving impeccably sourced Mediterranean meals in what feels like an incandescent countryside retreat in the Umbrian hills. The farmhouse tables, copper bar, chandelier of pear-shaped bulbs, and flickering candlelight: A meal at Il Buco is a transporting experience unlike any other in the city. For Chef Joel Hough, the commitment to fresh and seasonal means sourcing from such far-flung places as the Santa Monica Farmers' Market. It means buying fresh wahoo hooked off the Carolina coast or flavorful pork from rare heritage breeds raised upstate. The menu changes daily and seasonally; on a recent spring day diners were sampling garganelli with English peas, fava beans, and fresh ricotta; tagliolini with a spicy sauce of peekytoe crab and fresh chiles; and an Umbrian *porchetta* panino on fresh ciabatta bread. It's little wonder that Il Buco is always booked; reserve your spot now. (See Chef Joel Hough's recipe for **Artichoke & Arugula Salad** on p. 215.)

Il Buco Alimentari & Vineria, 53 Great Jones St., btw. the Bowery and Lafayette St.; (212) 837-2622; ilbucovineria.com; Subway: 6 to Bleecker St.; Italian/Market/Vineria; $$$. Unlike its progenitor, Il Buco, which developed in a circuitous, organic fashion, this baby came into the world with plenty of forethought. In fact, few restaurants in New York have been given the kind of loving, meticulous attention to detail that you seen in Alimentari, as in none, probably. The copper ceiling is from Florence, Italy; the blue tile is from Umbria, as is the russet-hued terracotta floor. Owner Donna Lennert scoured flea markets to find the cafe chairs. The wood-fired stove in the open kitchen—where Chef Justin Smillie deftly roasts meats, among other things—was shipped from Modena, Italy. White pine reclaimed from the Great Jones Lumber Supply, the restaurant's previous occupant, has been reborn as tables, bars, you name it. "Customers ask where can they get this or that fixture,

but I just shake my head," says Chef Smillie. "This isn't Pottery Barn."
Where Il Buco is all rusticated elegance, Alimentari is casual Italian with
a kicky modern sheen. It's a dynamo both upstairs and down, where
what *Bon Appétit* magazine called a "village's worth of food-makers"
bustle about curing meat, soaking olives, making gelato, baking bread.
Master baker Kamel Saci starts his day in the basement around 3 a.m.
fashioning artisanal bread that crackles so musically it practically sings
as it comes out of the oven. (Tip: Don't leave without buying a loaf or
two of Saci's ethereal *foccacio fino* in the market.) All that attention to
detail has paid off: The *New York Times* gave Il Buco Alimentari a three-
star review in its rookie season. Order up a plate of the daily house
salumi, along with the roasted house-made gnocchi with foraged mushrooms or a nice lasagnette, and then finish with a salt-baked branzino
or a spit-roasted rabbit. Even if you don't dine in, you can take home
the restaurant's bread, cured meats, gelato, olives, and more from the
market/cafe at the front. (See Chef Justin Smillie's recipe for **Roasted
Harissa Chicken with Avocado, Sea Beans & Preserved Meyer Lemon**
on p. 217.)

**Lafayette, 380 Lafayette St., at Great Jones St.; (212) 533-3000;
lafayetteny.com; Subway: B, F, D, M to Broadway/Lafayette; Modern
French; $$$.** A smash hit when it opened, Chef Andrew Carmellini's
foray into French brasserie territory just gets better and better. The
high-ceilinged "grand café" space alone is a revelation; whereas the
former tenant, Chinese Brasserie, had a Chinese bordello opaqueness,
Lafayette is all sunlit transparency, with glass windows unshrouded to
let in the light and a fresh nursery palette of blue-tile columns and
honey-white walls. The food is just terrific, with
Damon Wise at the helm as chef de cuisine.
Breezy versions of brasserie classics look as
good as they taste. Start with the exemplary
salad Niçoise or the frisée salad with the house
bacon and topped with an organic egg. Entrees

include a Provencal-styled short-rib *daube* or the duck au poivre. Don't miss the silky, elegant desserts, including a chestnut mousse cake and the divine apple tart for two topped with crème fraîche.

The Smile, 26 Bond St., near Lafayette St.; (646) 329-5836; the smilenyc.com; Subway: 6 to Bleecker St.; Mediterranean. $$. With the cafe look du jour—industrial farmhouse mashup, with artfully scuffed wood floors and exposed pipes—this appealing spot has a boho rusticity. On the garden level of an 1830s townhouse, wood tables, exposed brick, Parisian cafe chairs, and a soothing Brazilian jazz weave a chill vibe. In back, scattered Oriental rugs and candles in fireplaces give the place a sexy tavern feel during the heated-up night scene. It would all be a tad contrived if not for the purity of the menu and the heady scent of rosemary and thyme. Executive Chef Melia Marden (daughter of the painter Brice Marden) spent summers growing up in Hydra, Greece, and her thoughtful "Manhattan Mediterranean" menu is an expression of those golden summers. It's the clean, simple food of Italy and Greece, where quality ingredients are paired with good sea salt, olive oil, and fresh herbs, and seasonality is a religion. Sample fava bean crostini in the spring and plum crostini in the summer, and dishes like minted sugar snap peas, roasted trout with fennel, and spaghetti in lemon cream throughout the year.

Westville Hudson, 333 Hudson St., at Charlton St.; (212) 776-1404; westvillenyc.com; Subway: 1, 9 to Houston St.; American; $$. Westville, it seems, is a state of mind, an idealized ode to Mayberry down-hominess, where screen doors, handmade signs, and white-washed wainscoting mirror a menu of handcrafted American comfort food. That ethos is vividly expressed at the Westville franchise's three older locations. But this newish branch in the Hudson Square neighborhood has gone rogue. It's roomy and high-ceilinged, with a cool elegance. Fortunately, the food hasn't followed a similar minimalist trajectory. The Hudson branch still offers Westville's deftly prepared, market-driven American classics. Look for hearty soups and nutritious salads, smoky mac 'n' cheese, burgers, beer-battered cod, and a big selection of daily veggies.

Landmarks & Old-School Faves

Emilio's Ballato, 55 E. Houston St., near Mott St.; (212) 274-8881; Subway: 6 to Bleecker St. or B, D, F, V to Broadway/Lafayette; Italian; $$–$$$. A sprightly red awning fronting car-choked Houston Street leads to this handsome old-school Italian, which has been serving food in this space since 1956. The narrow main dining room has high ceilings and walls that are artfully distressed, hung with antique mirrors and amber sconces. The big dining room in back is very private, great for paparazzi-avoiding celebs. But it's newish and feels it; we prefer the vintage ambience up front. The food is old-school Italian-American as well, but the kitchen has such a sure hand and ingredients are so fresh that each preparation is almost revelatory. Fried zucchini and fried calamari have almost a tempura lightness, grease at a blessed minimum. Pastas are just the way you like 'em, and isn't that a wonder?

Phil's Pizza, 226 Varick St., at W. Houston St.; (212) 243-8629; Subway: 1, 9 to Houston St.; Pizza; $–$$. On the right-hand wall of this bustling little hole in the wall is a timeline of photos following the travails of the fellow who would be Phil, from the smiling young man behind the pizza counter in the 1970s to today's salt-and-pepper-bearded Phil, who also happens to be zipping around behind the counter in crisp white cap and white apron. Phil has been making pizza in this very spot for 41 years, and his pizza can stand up to any slice joint's in town; he also makes solid versions of Sicilian and Grandma's pizzas.

Dean & DeLuca, 121 Prince St., at Broadway; (212) 226-6800; deandeluca.com; Subway: N, R to Prince St.; Specialty Grocery. Opening its doors in SoHo in 1977, Dean & DeLuca was a pioneer that brought the gourmet/artisanal food concept to downtown. The company's flagship store moved to this location, a cavernous 10,000-square-foot warehouse space stretching from Broadway to Crosby Street, in 1986, selling imported cheeses and *salumi,* Italian pastas, fresh arugula, and other culinary exotica. Today this vast gourmet emporium looks as smart as it did 25 years ago, with marble floors and neoclassical columns and a ceiling that reaches into the stratosphere. Head to the prepared-foods department for solid soups, pasta dishes, grilled meats, and salads, or sip an espresso at the coffee bar. Is it all a wee bit overpriced? Always has been, but the quality of what you get here rarely slips.

Despaña SoHo, 408 Broome St., at Center St.; (212) 219-5050; despanabrandfoods.com; Subway: 6 to Spring St.; Spanish Food & Wines. This handsome gourmet food shop sells the food and wine of Spain, including hand-carved meats (Serrano and Ibérico ham), sandwiches, cheeses, and an array of Spanish condiments and olive oils, vinegars, olives, and vegetable and fruit preserves. It also includes a tapas cafe selling fresh-made tapas (small plates of ham, *boquerones* (marinated anchovies), mussels, Spanish omelettes, soups, and *bocadillos* (sandwiches) fashioned with ciabatta bread. The next-door wine shop has a bountiful selection of Spanish wines.

Jacques Torres Chocolate Shop, 350 Hudson St., at King St.; (718) 875-9772; mrchocolate.com; Subway: 1, 2 to Houston St.; Chocolate. This Hudson Square ode to chocolate is the domain of the former pastry chef at Le Cirque, and Torres's hot chocolate is our hands-down favorite in the city, rich and dark and chocolaty. You can sample a steaming cup at the shop's elegant little chocolate bar or buy a tin of the classic hot chocolate to take home. (There's also a "wicked" variety that gets its kick from allspice, cinnamon, sweet ancho chile peppers, and hot chipotle peppers.) The variations of chocolate at Torres's shops are staggering and include chocolate peanut brittle, chocolate-covered Cheerios, and Champagne truffles. Torres also has three other Manhattan locations: Chelsea Market (75 Ninth Ave.; 212-414-2462); Rockefeller Center (30 Rockefeller Plaza; 212-664-1804); and 285 Amsterdam Ave. (at 73rd St.; 212-787-3256).

Kee's Chocolates, 80 Thompson St., near Spring St.; (212) 334-3284; keeschocolates.com; Subway: A, C, E to Spring St./Sixth Ave. Chocolate. In this little Thompson Street shop, owner Kee Ling Tong makes some of the city's best handmade chocolates and macaroons.

East Village & Lower East Side

Despite ongoing blasts of gentrification, the East Village still has a patina of grit and a whiff of anarchist bluster. When it comes to dining out, this is one of Manhattan's least-expensive zip codes, making it a go-to dining destination for young careerists and matriculating types. (Well, that and the industrial-strength bar scene.) The neighborhood has long been a petri dish for some of the city's most interesting food trends. And because rents are traditionally cheaper here, it's also been a launching pad for up-and-coming chefs. You'll find them commandeering space-challenged venues with artistically peeling paint and rooms dripping with candlewax. The boho, dining-down-a-rabbit-hole vibe continues in the East Village's colorful neighbor to the south, the Lower East Side. Its ramshackle 19th-century tenements once housed thousands of European immigrants. An influx of hipster bars, clubs, art galleries, and cafes in the 1990s made the neighborhood a hot destination; billionaire high-rises and boutique hotels are the latest to join the party. The upshot: The LES is a late-night crush most weekends. But it's also a place that offers some seriously good food—so if nightcrawling isn't your thing, hit your favorites on the early side or reserve for weekdays.

Angelika Kitchen, 300 E. 12th St., near Third Ave.; (212) 228-2909; angelicakitchen.com; Subway: 4, 5, 6 to Union Square. Vegan; $–$$. One of the city's vegan pioneers, Angelika still has plenty of creative juice after nearly 40 years in business and plenty of fans devoted to its truly savory take on "organic plant-based cuisine." The restaurant is located in a casual, sun-filled spot right next door to its little takeout store. Expect a range of daily soups, salads, veggies, and gluten-free basics, all fresh and flavorful. On a recent visit, the soup of the day was a creamy zucchini-arugula and the salad a crispy Yukon gold potato–vegetable salad tossed in dill dressing. A white bean stew came loaded with vegetables—grilled zucchini, sweet potatoes and turnips, carrots and lima beans—and was served with a cracked-black-pepper biscuit. It's easy to see why plenty of non-vegans make this a regular pit stop; if you're one of them, don't leave without Angelika staples like fresh-made wheat-free cornbread and miso-tahini spread.

Antibes, 112 Suffolk St.; btw. Rivington and Delancey Sts.; (212) 533-6088; antibesbistro.com; Subway: F, J, M, Z to Essex St./ Delancey St.; Provençal; $$. Just yards away from east Delancey Street, where traffic rumbles on and off the Williamsburg Bridge, is this peaceful little pocket of Provence. The restaurant lies in the shadow of a handsome former public school (now a Latino arts and cultural center) built in 1898. With a rustic Steampunk-meets-Provence ambience—wood floors, whitewashed brick, Edison bulbs, sprigs of dried lavender—an appealing Mediterranean menu, and gentle prices, this is a serendipitous special-occasion choice for underfinanced urbanites. The unfussy, flavorful dishes have an elegant presentation. Truffle-roasted asparagus comes with a sauté of wild mushrooms and a scrim of crème fraîche. Grilled jumbo shrimp are balanced by an avocado mousse and tomato compote. A house-made cavatelli is tossed with a savory sauce of roasted tomatoes, broccoli rabe, ricotta, and poached figs. Hearty meat entrees include a chicken roasted under a brick and Guinness-braised short ribs.

Boukiés, 29 E. 2nd St., at Second Ave.; (212) 777-2502; boukies restaurant.com; Subway: 6 to Astor Place; Greek; $$–$$$. This gleaming space has an indoor-outdoor breeziness, with beige banquettes, black-and-white tile floors and blond-wood farm tables; when the big glass doors are opened onto the sidewalk, Second Avenue feels like summer. Boukiés celebrates the food of Greece with an emphasis on *mezes,* or small plates. You can get finely wrought Greek classics like phyllo stuffed with spinach and cheese and a rich chickpea-eggplant casserole, or you can go simple, with seafood marinated or drizzled in good olive oil, served with roasted tomatoes or seasonal greens, and char-grilled. It's the Mediterranean diet in all its uncomplicated glory set down on the streets of the East Village.

Dirt Candy, 430 E. 9th St., btw. First Ave. and Ave. A; (212) 228-7732; dirtcandynyc.com; Subway: 6 to Astor Place; Vegetarian/ Vegan; $$. Tiny and narrow, this spunky little space is the domain of Chef Amanda Cohen, who spins vegan magic with fresh, seasonal vegetables, what she calls "candy from the dirt." Chef Cohen combines a sure touch and a sense of whimsy. In spring, that might mean an appetizer of fennel and sunflower soup, dotted with pickled mustard seeds and a mustard green pesto, or a Chinese kohlrabi salad with purple cabbage wontons and Szechuan walnuts. Dirt Candy main courses might be parsnip pillows or smoked broccoli "dogs" with broccoli kraut.

Empellón Cocina, 105 First Ave., near 6th St.; (212) 780-0999; empellon.com/cocina; Subway: 6 to Astor Place; Mexican; $$–$$$. Alex Stupak got into cooking, he says, because "I made something for my mom once and it made her smile." Building on that gentle note of encouragement, Stupak let his inner child fly and today is reaping the rewards with a James Beard nomination and packed houses nightly. And he's not much past 30. "Alex is a genius," said a fellow New York chef. "I had a discussion with him about cream soda that went on for three hours." Where Stupak's West Village location, Empellón Taqueria, has a celebrative night-out fizz, the monochrome, pared-down environs of Cocina are where the former pastry chef drills deep but also soars. Pastrami tacos? You bet. A spring taco of English peas, green onions, and ricotta? Oh, *yeah!* The margaritas are state of the art, but you shouldn't leave without sampling the yuzu margarita, a heady wonder marrying the fire of tequila with the floral perfume of the yuzu, a Japanese citrus fruit. The pistachio guacamole has a nutty snap, and the seven salsas—from smoky mild to searing—are perfect for sharing. Both guacamole and salsas come with house-made masa chips, coarsely textured and thrillingly addictive. Sample from the "hot" and "cold" menus, but don't pass up the roasted carrots, a deceptively simple wonder tossed with mole poblano, yogurt, and toasted sesame seeds (see recipe on p. 211).

Freemans, end of Freeman Alley, off Rivington St., btw. the Bowery and Christie St.; (212) 673-3209; freemansrestaurant.com; Subway: F, V to Second Ave. or J, M, Z to Bowery; New American; $$$. We were all ready to write this place off—it felt like the restaurant equivalent of the hipster fedora. Even the name of its clothing store next door, Freemans Sporting Club, seemed too clever by half; for those who don't get the motif, deer antlers on the walls and a retro collegiality drive it home. In truth, Freeman's is a design triumph—quite simply, it's dreamy, someone's notion of a Victorian hunting lodge or a fancy (read: Madeline) orphanage. You dine in big candlelit rooms on wooden farm tables; a lucky few diners are given romantic little nooks off the big rooms. Get there early on weekends if you're the retiring type, but if you crave a fizzy scrum, dine later, when the place is rocking with youngsters on an LES prowl. The kitchen is cooking, literally and figuratively, sending out remarkably tasty, refined food to hundreds of diners nightly. Don't pass up the smashing artichoke dip or perfectly wrought devils on horseback (bacon-wrapped dates). Trout is grilled with a simple schmear of garlic and lemon (and a dash of thyme). The panfried pork schnitzel is a menu staple with a knowing nod to the neighborhood's old-world heritage.

Han Dynasty, 90 Third Ave., btw. 12th and 13th Sts.; (212) 390-8685; handynasty.net; Subway: 6 to Astor Place or Union Square/14th St.; Szechuan; $$. The warm, russet-hued room is the antithesis of every dreary-looking Chinese restaurant we've eaten in in Manhattan, and we've dined in a few. Walls are painted a soothing mustard, black banquettes stretch along the wall, and low-hanging lamps with Edison bulbs give it a spritz of Steampunk. The look at Han Dynasty invites you in, but the smells wafting from the kitchen don't let you go. We hope this is a sign that the Chinese oeuvre is being revitalized in Manhattan; it's clear to see that Szechuan cuisine is definitely having a moment. This particular Szechuan arrived from Philadelphia, where it garnered acclaim for its fire and freshness (CNN named it one of the top Chinese restaurants in America). Now it's landed in the East Village and is very much worth a detour from wherever you are for the signature dan dan noodles; dumplings in chile oil; and pork, beef, chicken or seafood mains offered in a range of styles (dry pepper, garlic sauce, cumin, and more), with a numbered heat index. For those who love fiery Szechuan and bemoan the lack of good Chinese in the city, Han Dynasty is reason to celebrate.

Hearth, 403 E. 12th St., at First Ave.; (646) 602-1300; restaurant hearth.com; Subway: L at 14th St./First Ave.; Italian; $$$–$$$$. In a space that manages to feel both modern and warmly bucolic, Hearth hasn't missed a beat since it opened to foodie acclaim 10 years ago. One of the city's most genial presences, Chef Marco Canora is still happily behind the stove most nights, and his cooking at Hearth embodies what he and his partner Paul Grieco like to describe as "American cooking with Italian influences." Those influences include an Italian mama whose simple but ethereal recipes were once featured in the *New York Times* but also extend to the kind of dedicated farm-to-table sustainability proudly exhibited on the menu's detailed list of regional purveyors. The food is both soulful and assured, with an emphasis on Greenmarket seasonality; we recommend the seven-course tour of the Hearth menu, which might include house-made charcuteries, a salmon poached in olive oil with sides of spring ramps and snap peas, and a classic stracciatella with farm egg, Parmesan, and peas.

Ippudo, 65 Fourth Ave., btw. E. 10th and E. 11th Sts.; (212) 388-0088; ippudony.com; Subway: 6 to Astor Place; Ramen Shop.; $. Don't expect to slink into this place incognito—just about everyone who enters the dining room gets a rousing welcome of "irasshaimasse!" from ramen chefs and serving staff. If that doesn't fire up your synapses, the high-decibel soundtrack should do the trick, where Jimi Hendrix's "Manic Depression" segues into deep disco or Japanese pop. It kicks in a state of heightened awareness, made even more acute by the fact that you're hungry, having waited in line in the cold for a seat at one of the city's most popular ramen restaurants (no reservations). This is the first of the Japanese chain's two NYC locations (the second is in Midtown at 321 W. 51st St., btw. Eighth and Ninth Aves.; 212-974-2500), and it's stylish and earthy, with witty touches like bamboo splayed like a spreading tree and neatly arranged dried ramen noodles under glass for a bar top. You are not here necessarily for the decor, however; you come for the comfort of a steaming bowl of ramen noodles in Ippudo's signature pork-bone broth—or the miso ramen, or the vegetable-based noodle soup. Ippudo does many things well, including some of the city's best pork buns and fantastic shishito peppers dusted with yuzu salt powder.

Mighty Quinns BBQ, 103 Second Ave., at 7th St.; (212) 677-3733; mightyquinnsbbq.com; Subway: 6 to Astor Place; Barbecue; $. The darling of the weekend Brooklyn Flea/Smorgasburg markets gets a lot of love (and a lotta long lines) for its slow-cooked barbecue, but will its luster dim in its new brick-and-mortar incarnation, open 7 days a week? The space is monochromatic and spare, with an Edison bulb here and stacked firewood there for a shot of Steampunk. The menu is short and to the point, deferring, one imagines, to the power of MQ 'cue to deliver the wow factor. It's easy to get distracted by sides like "burnt-end" baked beans (made with just about every meat on the menu), grilled ratatouille, and killer sweet potato casserole with maple and pecans, or quenchable drinks like house-made iced tea (with three different kinds of sugary syrup) and cold artisanal beer. But you've come for the slow-cooked meats (brisket, pulled pork, spare ribs, sausage, chicken, and wings), right? We hear tell that the brisket is where it's at.

Mission Chinese, 154 Orchard St., btw. Rivington and Stanton Sts.; (212) 529-8800; missionchinesefood.com; Subway: F to Delancey St. or J, M, Z to Essex St.; Chinese; $. Enter the mundane basement storefront and thread your way down a dark hallway; signs warn you to watch your step as you proceed past a narrow kitchen where woks are steaming like something out of Dante's circles of hell. Suddenly, darkness turns to light, and the narrow hallway opens onto a tented space that feels like someone's private backyard party. That such a bright, happy place lies at the end of a gloomy tunnel is one thing, but the inspired "Americanized Oriental" mashups of Chef

Danny Bowien make it even giddier. How about kung pao pastrami? Or a chicken fried rice with chicken liver and a dash of old-fashioned schmaltz? A Szechuan catfish gets the Deep South treatment with Tennessee bacon and mustard greens. It would all be too cute by half if the food didn't work, but it does—it's delicious—and the prices are ridiculously recession-friendly. It isn't every day that a high-profile chef—who also happens to be the 2013 James Beard Rising Star Chef award-winner—operates this way, but hallejulah for Mission Chinese.

Momofuku Ssäm Bar, 207 Second Ave., at 13th St.; (212) 254-3500; momofuku.com; Subway: L to 14th St./Third Ave.; Korean/Fusion; $$–$$$. The ever-inventive menus at Chef David Chang's Momofuku franchises hit the heights at Ssäm. It's not easy to categorize the award-winning cuisine, but isn't that the point? Chilled pea soup comes with snails and pork jowl, and a duck bologna sandwich is topped with caramelized onions and provolone. Whole rotisserie duck *ssäm* is the restaurant's large-format version of Peking duck—but here the Long Island–sourced bird is stuffed with duck and pork sausage under the skin before it's rotisserie-cooked. Pork is a Chang meme, and American country ham holds a vaunted spot in the Ssäm universe, and Benton's (of Kentucky) and Edwards (of Virginia) are represented here. Oh, and don't pass up the pickles, a Ssäm delicacy that food writer Ruth Reichl called "amazing."

Motorino, 349 E. 12th St., near First Ave.; (212) 777-2644; motorinopizza.com; Subway: L to 14th St./First Ave.; Pizza; $. In the ongoing pizza wars, many say that this East Village pizzeria makes the best Neapolitan-style pizza in Manhattan. Motorino's homespun, wood-fired pie certainly has the look: It's a thing of beauty, the flat midsection of red sauce dotted with dollops of charred basil and creamy mozzarella, the bubbly outer crust revealing a crispy, blistery pop on the outside and a chewy softness on the inside. Naples-inspired pies crafted with extra-virgin olive oil and artisanal ingredients and fired in vintage ovens are now found all over town, from Roberta's (which shows up at seasonal markets in Manhattan) to Forcella's to Farinella's. But to pizza aficionados, Motorino's remains tops.

The Redhead, 349 E. 13th St., at First Ave.; (212) 533-6212; theredheadnyc.com; Subway: L to 14th St./First Ave. New American; $$–$$$. Some places come with the kind of homey, honey-hued feng shui that makes you want to linger. The Redhead may not look like much (wood floors, low faux tin ceiling, modest furniture), and it's set on a nondescript sweep of 13th Street straddling the East Village and Stuy Town. But the Redhead is a little beacon of light and bonhomie. It's even become a restaurant industry hang, the kind of spot where you may stumble upon an informal after-hours kitchen-industry club regaling the bar up front with the night's misadventures. But ambience doesn't do it alone. The Redhead has a sure hand in the kitchen and a winning menu of reverently revitalized American standards that makes dining here a pleasure. It's got one of the city's top hamburgers and an addictive and Elvis-cized variation on a Southern staple: bacon peanut brittle.

Saro, 102 Norfolk St., near Delancey St.; (212) 505-7276; sarobistro .com; Subway: F, J, M, Z to Essex St./Delancey St.; Bosnian; $$. Where else but on the Lower East Side can you find a hot young chef in an old kosher bakery serving stylish interpretations of his Bosnian grandmother's recipes on antique dishes from Hyde Park flea markets? (With alt-rock blasting in the background?) This beguiling 3-year-old bistro on a side street off Delancey is a real find, and lo, it hasn't been appropriated by trendsters, at least not the louche types who hang out at the three bars lined up next door. The old-fashioned tea-room decor (floral wallpaper, vintage china, century-old tile floors) is so retro it's hip, and the food is never dull and often thrilling. Saro, named for Chef Eran Elhalal's grandmother, took over the space that had long been Ratner's bakery, and Elhalal is clearly passionate about the cuisine of his Austro-Hungarian forebears. He makes a daily savory pie, perhaps a *gibanica,* with Bulgarian sheep's milk and ricotta, and his chicken soup is bubbling over with homemade noodles and carrots. Entrees might include rabbit cooked with braised red cabbage or a terrific pork-shank osso buco with fresh braising greens, perhaps baby broccoli rabe with slivers of garlic and a shaving of lemon zest. Elhalal cooks with style and seasonality; don't miss the Saro Slaw, piquant and nutty with toasted sesame seeds and sauerkraut. The wine list spans the region, with some tasty award-winning Sauvignon Blanc from Slovenia (Pulles) and terrific beer from the Slovak Republic (Golden Pheasant).

Spur Tree, 76 Orchard St., btw. Broome and Grand Sts.; (212) 477-9977; spurtreelounge.com; Subway: F, J, M, Z to Essex St./ Delancey St. or B, D to Grand St.; Jamaican; $$. With reggae blasting and voluptuous lilies perfuming the room, Jamaica is coolly approximated in this slender Orchard Street spot. Sit at the half-moon bar and sip a frosty mojito or grab a table along the wall—you'll be sharing space with a good-looking crowd. Not to mention expertly prepared Jamaican specialties, like the marinated jerk chicken, the heat balanced by cool pineapple salsa, or the seafood curry roti, plump with shrimp, scallops, and salmon. Even something as seemingly pedestrian as rice and peas here becomes an addiction. With DJ music pumped loud on weekend nights and a kitchen that's open till 2 a.m., this is a date-night home run.

Katz's, 205 E. Houston St., at Ludlow St.; (212) 254-2246; katzsdeli catessen.com; Subway: F to Second Ave.; Deli; $–$$. Every day, the lines snake outside the door. Every day, the place swarms with diners, tourists, pastrami lovers, and cinema fans making a pilgrimage to the spot where Meg Ryan faked an orgasm in *When Harry Met Sally*. Every day, it seems, this classic New York deli, at this location since 1888, bustles with the business of serving food. The decor has changed little over the years; even a World War II sign reading "Send a salami to your boy in the Army" still hangs. You'll practically need a note from your doctor to order the pastrami on rye (it's stuffed with nearly a pound of meat), but as Woody Allen famously said, the heart wants what it wants. Ask for the pastrami, or the tender brisket sandwich, or the corned beef on rye. It may not make you pound your fists on the table, à la Meg Ryan, but then again, it just might.

Black Hound, 170 Second Ave., near E. 11th St.; (212) 979-9505; blackhoundny.com; Subway: L to 14th St./Third Ave. or 4, 5, 6, N, R to Union Square/14th St.; Dessert. Out of a Brooklyn kitchen comes these exquisite sweet treats, from elegant cakes to velvety chocolate truffles to delicate butter cookies, all beautifully made. Black Hound confections make fine gifts.

Doughnut Plant, 379 Grand St., btw. Essex and Clinton Sts.; (212) 505-3700; doughnutplant.com; Subway: F, J, M, Z to Delancey St./Essex St.; Doughnuts. There are doughnuts, and then there are

Good Cheap Eats

Food is expensive in Manhattan, no question, but there are gems out there that don't cost an arm and a leg. Here are a few of our favorite cheap eats.

Pork-and-chive dumplings, Prosperity Dumpling (Chinatown/Lower East Side, 46 Eldridge St., #1; 212-343-0683; prosperitydumpling.com) or Tasty Dumpling (Chinatown/Lower East Side; 54 Mulberry St.; 212- 349-0070)

Hot dog, Gray's Papaya (Upper West Side, 2090 Broadway; 212-799-0243; and other locations)

Mujudarra platter, Kalustyan's (Murray Hill, 123 Lexington Ave.; 212-685-3451; kalustyans.com)

Fried chicken, Blue Ribbon Fried Chicken (East Village, 28 E. 1st St.; 212-228-0404; blueribbonfriedchicken.com)

Milk shake, Shake Shack (multiple locations, shakeshack .com/)

French fries, Burger Joint (Midtown West, Le Parker Meridien, 119 W. 56th St.; 212-708-7414; and Greenwich Village, 33 W. 8th St.; 212-432-1400; burgerjointny.com)

Bagel and schmear of herbed cream cheese, Absolute Bagels (Upper West Side; 2788 Broadway; 212-932-2052; absolutebagels.com).

doughnuts. (And yes, there are cronuts.) Before Krispy Kreme was even a gleam in its founder's eye, Herman Isreal was cooking eggless yeast doughnuts in a bakery in North Carolina. Today Doughnut Plant proprietor Mark Isreal uses his grandfather's original doughnut recipe as a grand jumping-off point for an astonishing array of artisanal doughnuts, made, fittingly, here on the Lower East Side, once the domain of immigrant Jews. We defy you to find better-tasting doughnuts anywhere. Doughnut Plant doughnuts come with glazes of seasonal fruit or roasted nuts. They come filled with house-made jams and jellies. They come as cake doughnuts, as square doughnuts, as "doughseeds" (mini round doughnuts) with fillings like peanut butter, pistachio, wild blueberry, and cream.

Economy Candy, 108 Rivington St., btw. Ludlow and Essex Sts.; (212) 254-1531; economycandy.com; Subway: F, J, M, Z to Delancey St./Essex St.; Candy. That this temple to dime-store treats and factory-made candy has survived intact since the 1930s is one thing. That it's not only survived, but thrived, in an area quivering with artisanal zeal is quite another. Look for all your favorites—Jelly Belly, Pez, lollipops, Hershey everything—not to mention classics (candy cigarettes, bubble-gum cigars, wax fangs) teeth-achingly stacked to the (faux) tin ceiling.

Essex Street Market, 120 Essex St., at Delancey St.; essex streetmarket.com; Subway: F, J, M, Z to Delancey St./Essex St.; Food Market. Built in 1940 in Art Moderne style, the Essex Street Market is one of the city's culinary treasures. Inside a truly nondescript brick block on Essex Street is this small-scale warren of grocery vendors and impassioned food purveyors. The **Heritage Meat Shop** (heritagemeat shop.com) is the city's only retail space for Heritage Foods USA, the company that sells artisanal, humanely raised and slaughtered meat from heritage and rare breeds to more than 200 New York restaurants. Here you can buy meat from breeds like the Colombian Wyandotte chicken, which dates back to the 1870s, and Old Spot heritage black-and-white pigs. If you're a Southerner homesick for seriously good country ham, don't leave without sampling a few slices of Nancy Newsom's velvety, buttery dry-cured ham—so good it's the only Ameri-can ham to be showcased in the Jamon Museum in Spain. Also at the market are: **New Star Fishmarket** (212-475-8365; no website), which sells all manner of fresh seafood; the delicious handmade chocolates of **Roni-Sue's Chocolates** (roni-sue.com); the acclaimed artisanal breads of **Pain D'Avignon** (paindavignon-nyc.com); several small produce and grocery stores; and **Shopsin's General Store** (shopsins.com), the legendary domain of Chef Kenny Shopsin and family, who make hundreds, nay thousands, of dishes in their cramped, colorful eatery—check out the exhaustive menu at shopsins.com.

Hester St. Fair, corner of Hester and Essex Sts.; (917) 267-9496; hesterstreetfair.com; Subway: F, J, M, Z to Delancey St./Essex St.; Outdoor Market. This outdoor artisanal-food and crafts market is held on Saturday from late April to late October in a historic space once occupied by a Victorian-era pushcart market. It's a small but serendipitous place when you're casting about for vittles on a somewhat desultory stretch of Essex Street. Among the vendors who have worked the Hester St. Fair, look for the buttery lobster and shrimp rolls of Luke's Lobster; the New Orleans–style sno-balls of Imperial Woodpecker; the teriyaki balls of Mimi and Coco NY; and the sustainable ice-cream sandwiches from Melt Bakery.

Il Laboratorio del Gelato, 95 Orchard St., btw. Broome and Delancey Sts.; (212) 343-9922; laboratoriodel gelato.com; Subway: F, J, M, Z to Delancey St./Essex St.; Gelato. Il Laboratorio takes its ice cream seriously, and good thing—it's heavenly, with a long list of wildly imaginative gelato and sorbet flavors like chestnut honey, lemon verbena, and prune Armagnac. The Orchard Street location is the company "lab" and site of the first Il Laboratorio retail cafe.

Kossar's Bialys, 367 Grand St., just east of Essex St.; (212) 253-2138; Subway: F, J, M, Z to Delancey St./Essex St.; Bialys/Bagels. Another local institution, Kossar's Bialys opened for business in 1936 on Clinton Street. Flatter than a bagel and made with high-gluten flour, brewers' yeast, salt, onions, and good old New York tap water, bialys first originated in Bialystok, Poland. Today they're still baked fresh here on the premises (along with fresh bagels) and sold for about $12 a dozen.

Russ & Daughters, 179 E. Houston St., btw. Orchard and Ludlow Sts.; (212) 475-4880; russanddaughters.com; Subway: F to Second Ave.; Deli/Market. What began as a family-owned pushcart in 1911 is still chugging along as one of the city's vintage treasures, still operated by the same family, whose patriarch, Joel Russ, named the business for his three daughters in 1933. Inside the store are creamy white dairy cases filled with a deli man's dream assortment of smoked or cured lox and nova, sable, whitefish, herring, and chopped liver. Order up a pound of the hand-sliced Gaspé (Eastern) nova, some bagels and cream cheese, a quart of fresh orange juice, and a whitefish chub or two and have yourself a real Manhattan breakfast.

Greenwich Village, the Meat-Packing District & Chelsea

Much of leafy, sun-dappled **Greenwich Village** predates the city's orderly 1811 design plan, meaning that streets often meander right off the grid. The small-scale neighborhood that long nurtured a culture of artists and rabblerousers is now a picturesque high-rent district. Historic preservationists have been instrumental in protecting the Village's centuries-old architecture, however, even if NYU seems hellbent on gobbling up mighty pieces and parcels of space. For food lovers, the Village specializes in those singularly serendipitous spots one might find on an evening ramble, little cafes where candles flicker enticingly and the hearth beckons with a golden glow. Next door, the **Meat-Packing District** is where fashionistas and upscale clubbers strut the cobblestoned plaza, once the chaotic realm of the city's whole-sale meatpacking industry. These days a different kind of meat is on display, as models in stilettos catwalk the cobblestones on near-daily photo shoots. The High Line has made the Meat-Packing District one of the city's most popular neighborhoods, and there are plenty of stylish spots to dine around the restored elevated tracks. The Meat-Packing District shares the High Line with its appealing low-rise neighbor to the north and east, **Chelsea,** long a traditional neighborhood for urban gays. Chelsea is littered with art galleries at its westernmost edges, now dubbed the Chelsea Art District. These neighborhoods have their share of big statement restaurants from big-time chefs, but if you really want to probe the area's dining DNA, find one of those intimate, flavorful spots with candles flickering and hearth beckoning. They channel the soul of the Village and its brethren to the north.

Foodie Faves

Babbo, 110 Waverly Place, btw. MacDougal St. and Sixth Ave.; (212) 777-0303; babbonyc.com; Subway: A, C, E, F, B, D to W. 4th St.; Italian; $$$$. For many New Yorkers, this is the crown jewel in Mario Batali's considerable empire of Manhattan restaurants. It certainly has staying power. Even some 15 years after Batali and partner Joe Bastianich opened the restaurant to near-universal acclaim (and a three-star review from *New York Times* food critic Ruth Reichl), Babbo remains a tough table to snag. Maybe it's the location in the beloved Coach House, which had served the Village good grub in a historic, 19th-century location for some 44 years (in fact, the old Coach House façade has been barely altered). Maybe it's the glowing interior, with a buttery luster and extravagant sprays of flowers. It sure ain't the low, low prices (alas, this is one expensive joint). No, Babbo would never have lasted this long if the food weren't honest, soulful, and often sublime. It's refined Italian *enoteca* fare, impeccably crafted with quality ingredients that change with the seasons. We love the pasta tasting menu, the pastas silky and flavorful, perhaps a Chianti-stained pappardelle with a wild boar *ragù* or a goose-liver ravioli. *Secondi* might be a braised beef with porcini mushrooms and a grilled pork chop with cherry peppers and sweet cipollini onions. Even today, whenever we stroll by Babbo, we put our noses to the window longingly; with candles flickering, fresh flowers preening, and happy people chattering, this is still the place to be.

Barbuto, 775 Washington St., at 12th St.; (212) 924-9700; barbuto nyc.com; Subway: L to Eighth Ave./14th St. or A, C, E, 1, 2, 3 to 14th St.; Italian/New American; $$$. The Berkeley native who helped bring California-influenced dining to New York, *Top Chef* Master Jonathan Waxman is the head toque at this casual indoor-outdoor bistro in the Meatpacking District, where big garage doors open up in the warm seasons onto sunny Washington Street. The grill is an essential element in the cooking at Barbuto, not to mention the holy trinity of fresh, seasonal, and sustainable. Waxman and company give Italian classics a light, Greenmarket touch: Fresh gnocchi comes with baby carrots and sugar snaps, and soft-shell crab is lightly fried and comes with avocado and peas. Barbuto turns out crisply roasted meat and fish dishes, including Waxman's signature roast chicken, topped with salsa verde, but you might be happy as a clam with a simple but perfectly seasoned risotto alla primavera or the kale salad, here made Sicilian-style with anchovies and breadcrumbs.

Blue Hill, Washington Place, btw. Sixth Ave. and MacDougal St.; (212) 539-1776; bluehillfarm.com; Subway: A, B, C, D, E, F to W. 4th St.; New American; $$$$. First Couple Barry and Michelle chose this Village spot as their first NYC date-night destination shortly after the 2008 inauguration, and it's easy to see why: It's got a culinary artist in Chef Dan Barber, exemplary farm-to-table food, and a silky, understated Barack-cool atmosphere. The only hint that this below-street-level spot was once a notorious speakeasy is the dim lighting—good thing they give out little blue lights to read the menu. In spite of the nightly packed house and an undercurrent of electric anticipation, the place has an almost elegant serenity. Yes, the conversation hums and the service is smoothly efficient, but the real party is on the plate. Blue Hill sources much of its food from its affiliated farm upstate, Stone Barns, on the site of the Rockefeller family's old Pocantico estate, now pastureland and home to heritage and rare livestock breeds. An evening menu might feature Stone Barns pastured chicken with morel mushrooms and swiss chard; roast pork served with Stone Barns flint corn; or a Stone Barns blood sausage. We are still talking about the roasted brussels sprouts, almost a menu cliché these days, but in Barber's hands the Vermeer of vegetables.

Blue Ribbon Bakery, 35 Downing St., at Bedford St.; (212) 337-0404; blueribbonrestaurants .com; Subway: A, B, C, D, E, F to W. 4th St.; New American; $$–$$$. You can rely on this neighborhood favorite, an early promoter of farm-to-table dining, for flavorful American-bistro food. Blue Ribbon Bakery is part of the Blue Ribbon franchise; Blue Ribbon Brasserie, Blue Ribbon Sushi, and the Blue Ribbon Market are nearby. A Blue Ribbon Beer Garden has opened up on Allen Street, and a Blue Ribbon fried chicken joint is over in the East Village. All are admirable, but this casual, candlelit space is the flagship, opened in 1992, and it's still a tough place to get a table on a weekend night (it takes no reservations for parties of five people or fewer). The menu features both grownup food (rack of lamb, duck confit, New Orleans–style barbecue shrimp) and kid pleasers like burgers and Blue Ribbon's storied fried chicken. You could make a dinner out of the extensive selection of small plates, and the excellent wine list contains a pretty dense selection for a casual neighborhood joint. If you have a large group, ask for one of the rooms downstairs, an atmospheric enclave enveloped in 19th-century brick walls. The 135-year-old basement brick oven was discovered in 1995 and has been handsomely restored—the restaurant was more or less built around it. The oven still cranks out homemade breads, crostini, and other baked delicacies.

Buvette, 42 Grove St., btw. Bleecker and Bedford Sts.; (212) 255-3590; ilovebuvette.com; Subway: 1 to Christopher St.; Modern French; $$–$$$. Open from breakfast into the late night, 8 a.m. to 2 a.m., this self-described "gastroteque" is a delight, with a Paris-meets-Steampunk charm offensive that feels vintage and smart and buzzing all at once. It's got one of the city's best breakfasts, where you may share a communal table in back with a gaggle of theater types or hungover club-goers—the La Columbe coffee, walnut-cranberry tartines, and rich nutella crepes are morning balm to all. At dinner the place takes on an amber glow; you might start a meal with a pesto and prosciutto tartinette and then move on to classic coq au vin or cassoulet, with a miniature pot of green lentils stewed with kale on the side. Or you can find a perch at the marble bar or by the wood-frame windows and watch the snow fall on the brownstones of the Village.

Co., 230 Ninth Ave., at 24th St.; (212) 243-1105; co-pane.com; Subway: C, E, to 23rd St.; Pizza/Bakery; $–$$. Some of the city's most flavorful and innovative pizzas are served in this casual pizzeria, the domain of Jim Lahey, the bread wunderkind who created the much-loved Sullivan Street Bakery and is well-known among home bakers for his famous no-knead bread recipe. There you could get a taste of Lahey's pizza to come, with wonderful square slices of zucchini-and-Parmesan or potato-and-onion pizzas and a bubbly, otherworldly *pizza bianca* built with quality ingredients (olive oil, sea salt, rosemary) and so much flavor it's hard to put down. Lahey opened this smart, uncluttered, sit-down pizzeria in 2009, and his repertoire now includes pizza classics such as *boscaiola,* a sausage-and-mushroom pizza, and a triple-cheese flambé pizza (béchamel, Parmesan, mozzarella) topped with caramelized onions and lardons. You can get that wonderful *pizza bianca* here as well, not to mention artisansal soups, salads, and meatballs and craft beers to wash it all down.

Cookshop, 156 Tenth Ave., at 20th St.; (212) 924-4440; cookshopny.com; Subway: C, E to 23rd St.; New American; $$$. Things are cooking at Cookshop, and not because of any latest/ greatest sizzle. No, this relative old-timer has kept the heat on since it opened in 2005—and it's still one of those places where diners at nearby tables swivel in their seats to see what others are having. Cookshop has plenty going for it, not least of which is location: This is the ideal lunch or dinner spot to build into a High Line or Chelsea art gallery crawl. (In warm weather, you can dine at an outside table facing Tenth Avenue.) It's got a chef with an impressive pedigree (the Odeon, An American Place, Five Points) and a kitchen that's an unofficial incubator for some of the city's hottest chefs. The dining room is big and sunny, with earthy granite floors and a wood-slat ceiling and a steady bustle and hum. But mostly it has good, honest, locavore food, much of it alchemized in the blazing wood-burning oven: spit-roasted farm chicken, roast Berkshire *porchetta,* nicely charred brook trout. We were dazzled by the state-of-the-art minestrone, shellfish *brodetto* in saffron-clam broth, and a simple but satisfying, garlicky pasta with broccoli. Deviled eggs come topped with a piquant onion relish, and the chicken kale salad, says our friend Amanda, is "autumn on a plate." Cookshop is a happy buzz at lunch and brunch; at night, settle in for leisurely fine dining.

Da Umberto, 107 West 17th St., at 7th Ave.; (212) 989-0303; daumbertonyc.com; Subway: 1, 2, 3 to 14th St.; Italian; $$$. If you're planning a discreet assignation with a similarly minded foodie, this sexy, assured Northern Italian might fit the bill. In business for 25 years, da Umberto does so many things well, from the effusive greeting to the easy, unintrusive service. With a sleek, flower-filled decor, it *feels* like a special-occasion place, but it also has the soul of an Italian mama. You will feel very pampered here. Have your waiter assemble a platter of assorted vegetable antipasti, or order up the crispy *carciofi* or baby squid grilled in lemon oil. Pastas are simple and elegant, from a finely wrought linguine *vongole* to rich truffled mushroom ravioli. A roast *porchetta* is truly succulent, as is the mixed grill of perfectly cooked seafood. Da Umberto may wear a sophisticated sheen, but this is one beautifully oiled machine, humming along in leisurely, old-world fashion.

Gotham Bar & Grill, 12 E. 12th St., btw. University Place and Fifth Ave.; (212) 620-4020; gothambarandgrill.com; Subway: N, R, 4, 5, 6, L to Union Square/14th St.; New American; $$$$. Alfred Portale has been the pioneering chef of this sumptuous 12th Street space since it opened in 1984. It's hard to believe that this oasis of calm was once on the cutting edge of Manhattan cuisine, a place that helped bring haute-casual dining and ingredients-based seasonality onto the dining scene. The lofty space still has a sunny grandeur; you really only appreciate the sheer luxury of space when you sit down to dine. The restaurant is just two blocks from Union Square Greenmarket, and the menu is a farm-to-table primer. Roasted free-range chicken is ringed by a constellation of blue-foot chanterelle mushrooms, Thumbelina carrots, and onions. Gold tomato gazpacho comes with peekytoe crab, *haricots verts,* and mango. Swiss chard, roasted cipollini onions, and potato puree are the farmers' market accompaniment to rack of lamb. Is everyone and his brother doing this kind of food now? Perhaps, but few do it better, and this room still has the power to make one swoon.

The Green Table, The Cleaver Company, Chelsea Market, 75 Ninth Ave., btw. 15th and 16th Sts.; (212) 741-6623; cleaverco.com; Subway: A, C, E, L to 14th St./Eighth Ave.; New American; $$. Doing farm-to-chef slow food before it was cool—and doing it deliciously—the Cleaver Company is one of the city's most respected catering companies, begun by Chef Mary Cleaver. It has had a presence in Chelsea Market from the market's inception in 1997, for many years a little storefront selling handmade pot pies and homey small-batch lunches (turkey meat loaf, for example) that tasted like Mom's—if Mom were a serious chef who was also among the first food professionals in the city to embrace the locavore sensibility. Today the Cleaver Company remains committed to producing food from sustainably and humanely sourced organic ingredients. The Green Table & Wine Bar, opened in 2003, embodies that philosophy. Diners eat at candlelit farm tables on fresh market foods: squash carpaccio; Thai market curry with summer vegetables; a mac 'n' cheese made with goat cheese, Colby, cheddar, and Parmesan; or the Green Table burger; fashioned with Wrighteous Organic beef and topped with house-made kimchee, tomato relish, and bacon. It's a sweetly rustic spot for lunch and dinner, with a good selection of wines and beer to go with the delicious artisanal food.

Kin Shop, 469 Sixth Ave., btw. 11th and 12th Sts.; (212) 675-4638; kinshopnyc.com; Subway: 1, 2, 3, to 14th St; Thai; $$–$$$. *Top Chef* contestants litter the Manhattan foodscape, opening both splashy, high-profile endeavors (Hung Huynh, The General and Catch) and not-so-big (but somewhat splashy) spots (Leah Cohen, Pig and Khao). First-season winner Harold Dieterle leans toward the latter, and his three Manhattan locations (Perilla, the Marrow, and Kin Shop) appear to be in it for the long haul. In Kin Shop, Chef Dieterle proves he has the chops to finesse traditional Thai dishes. But the thrill is to see how he fuses a boldly flavorful menu all his own from the cuisine's classic ingredients. As one writer said of Dieterle's efforts, "Imagine Mozart at the volume of Metallica." If you're still not convinced, consider that Kin Shop is a favorite stop for other big-time chefs, perhaps the ultimate tribute to a cooking chef. Start with a stir-fry of "aquatic" vegetables (water spinach, water chestnuts, watercress) or the fried pork belly and crispy oyster salad in a sassy chile-lime vinaigrette. Noodle and curry dishes comprise the entrees—like the duck-fat-poached arctic char or curry noodles with braised brisket—and stars denote the level of heat. Suggestion: Go prix-fixe to sample the range of Chef Dieterle's repertoire.

Knickerbocker Bar & Grill, 33 University Place, at 9th St.; (212) 228-8490; knickerbockerbarandgrill.com; Subway: N, R to 8th St./NYU or 6 to Astor Place; Steak House/New American; $$$. With a whiff of old-school glamour, curvy leather banquettes, and Saul Steinberg prints, this neighborhood favorite has an unapologetically throwback feel. A big piano is on hand for jazzy, boozy weekend performances, and if you haven't noticed from the smoky scent of charred meat that's practically pumped out the back door, Knickerbocker serves one heck of a porterhouse steak (and a righteous Angus burger). But this is that jazzy throwback steak house with a modern sensibility, which means that you don't have to be a carnivore to have a fine meal—look for interesting seafood pastas, excellent grilled fish, and a plethora of salads, including our favorite Caesar, just right. We also have it on good faith that the bartender serves one of the most precise old-fashioneds in the city. Be sure to come at Halloween, when Knickerbocker's is a set designer's spooky banquet. (See Chef Derrick Van Duzer's recipe for **Pumpkin Cheese Custard** Stuffing on p. 230.)

L'Artusi, 228 10th St., btw. Hudson and Bleecker Sts.; (212) 255-5757; lartusi.com; Subway: 1 to Christopher St. or A, B, C, D, E, F, V to W. 4th St.; Italian; $$$. Sister restaurant to the little West Village dynamo dell'anima, the two-story L'Artusi is bigger and brighter but no less sizzling, with scenesters swarming the long marble bar downstairs and keeping the kitchen in high gear all night long. Don't let the ruckus keep you away. The Northern Italian cuisine at L'Artusi is quite good and often sublime. In a soothing space with slate-gray floors and

TOURIST TRAPS WE SECRETLY LOVE: SPICE MARKET

Chef Jean-Georges's transporting hymn to Southeast Asian street food delivers a cinematic punch with artifacts plucked from Bombay palaces and Burmese temples. While the sultry colonial/Oriental mashup of a former meatpacking warehouse dials the wow factor to 11, the menu roams confidently all over the Asian culinary spectrum. Dishes, served family style, include peekytoe crab dumplings with fresh sugar snap peas, a steamed red snapper with a tomato lemongrass dashi, and chile-garlic egg noodles sauteed with seared shrimp and star anise. Yes, Spice Market can get a lot of tourist business in a too-trendy neighborhood, but the ambience is a real trip, and the food is flavorful and often transcendent (403 W. 13th St., at Ninth Ave.; 212-675-2322; spicemarketnewyork.com; Subway: A, C, E, 1, 2, 3 to 14th St.; Southeast Asian; $$$).

white chairs, diners swill specialty cocktails or wine drawn from a list of Italian varietals that stretches from Italy's boot (the Calabrian Ciro Bianco is a great buy) to its northern tip. Of the briny *crudos* to start, the hamachi tartare comes with white gazpacho, and day-boat scallops are dressed in olive oil, sea salt, a spritz of lemon, and a dash of spicy *espelette* (chili pepper). Look for rich pastas like *pici nero* with peekytoe crab and Parmesan or garganelli with mushroom *ragù* and ricotta and good grilled fish and meats. Whatever you eat, the mood at L'Artusi is celebratory—so if it's a fizzy special-occasion spot you're after, this has it going on in spades.

The Little Owl, 90 Bedford St., at Grove St.; (212) 741-4695; thelittleowlnyc.com; Subway: 1 to Christopher St. or A, B, C, D, E, F, V to W. 4th St.; Mediterranean; $$$. The ultimate Village boîte doesn't let its sweet amber glow get in the way of some searingly tasty cooking. The Little Owl is famous for its gravy meatball sliders, on the menu at both lunch and dinner, but you can't go wrong with just about anything you order, including a classic bacon cheeseburger served with spiced fries. The menu changes seasonally, and may showcase a nice sunflower and beet salad or flavorful Sicilian tuna toast. Succulent lamb chops are roasted to a salty crisp and a branzino grill comes with a Provençal sauté of summer squash. Keep in mind that the Little Owl is truly little, with just 28 seats, but high ceilings and big picture windows give it more expansive feel. Still, with so few seats it takes some finessing to snag a table; reserve as early as possible.

Morandi, 211 Waverly Place, at Charles St.; (212) 627-7575; morandiny.com; Subway: 1, 2, 3 to 14th St., 1 to Christopher St. or A, B, C, D, E, F, V to W. 4th St.; Italian; $$–$$$. Restaurateur Keith McNally's 2007 ode to the rustic Italian trattoria is a happy spot, where a Roman sunniness prevails at the alfresco tables out front. At lunchtime and weekend brunch, the place is packed with families, pretty young things, and neighborhood locals (with their dogs in tow) digging into the Italian breakfasts (foccacia with smoked fish; bruschetta con ricotta; crepes and Nutella), panini (portobello mushrooms and smoked cheese on rosemary foccacia; grilled *piadina* [flatbread] with speck, cheese, and zucchini), and pasta (Genovese-style pesto pasta with green beans and potatoes). At night, Morandi becomes the buzzing domain of those pretty young things (and pretty older things), who appreciate the sexy trattoria stage set and nibbling around a deftly curated menu that includes fresh *insalate* (salads) and soups, bruschetta, *fritti* like excellent fried artichokes, and simple grilled steak, chicken, or fish.

Num Pang, 21 E. 12th St., btw. University Place and Fifth Ave.; (212) 255-3271; numpangnyc.com; Subway: L, N, R, 4, 5, 6 to Union Square/14th St.; Cambodian Sandwiches; $. You can find our friend

Steven among the daily devoted waiting in the long line outside this little storefront shop off University Place. Steven is just one of the many addicted to Num Pang's mind-blowing Cambodian-style sandwiches made to order on fresh-baked semolina baguettes. For the coconut Tiger shrimp sandwich, shrimp marinated in coconut milk are topped with pickled carrots, cucumber slices, and toasted coconut chips; the baguette is smeared with chile mayo. For a sweet and spicy flavor sensation, try the sandwich with hoisin meatballs or the five-spice-glazed pork belly. Num Pang has been such a success that it now has three more Manhattan locations, including one in Chelsea Market.

Perla, **24 Minetta Ln., btw. Bleecker and West 3rd Sts.; (212) 933-1824; perlanyc.com; Subway: A, B, C, D, E, F, V to W. 4th St.; Italian; $$$.** Anywhere else, this little jewel of a Village bistro would be a respite of peaceful quietude. But being a hot ticket in a hot restaurant town means operating on a whole other level, and for now this high-decibel high-wire act is the very model of brutal efficiency, with a smiling waitstaff that's almost maniacally helpful. In spite of it all, youngsters commandeering red leather banquettes and clinking house cocktails seem to be having a fine time (Perla, one writer said, "feels like '21' for people under 40"). Underscoring the sexy speakeasy decor are wooden booths, wood floors, antique mirrors, tin lamps, and flickering candles; globes of all ilk are a design motif. It's a bit cramped anywhere you sit, but tables near the back (and away from the centrally located bar) put you close to the burning heart of the kitchen (aka the wood-burning brick oven). Here Chef Michael Toscano rises above the dining-room frenzy with sensational takes on Italian food. That flaming oven gets a lot of action, cooking pizzas by day and roasting branzino, steak, even a veal head by night. Look for fresh, intuitive takes on traditional pasta dishes, like pappardelle with duck *ragù* (here with foie gras) and linguine with

Manila clams (given a springtime jolt with fresh ramps). The roasted meats and grilled fish are exemplary, and the Greenmarket shows up on your plate with satisfying regularity (leg of lamb with radicchio and shishito peppers; quail with farro and swiss chard; tilefish with fresh peas). This chef is cooking, and so is Perla.

Recette, 328 W. 12th St., at Greenwich St.; (212) 414-3000; recettenyc.com; Subway: A, C, E, 1, 2, 3 to 14th St.; Urban American; $$$–$$$$. From the outside, Recette has the quaint looks of a French country bistro. Inside is culinary mayhem, of the very good kind, where kitchen wunderkind Chef Jesse Schenker is a 21st-century alchemist with a razor-sharp palate. The menu is designed around small plates and snacks, and here one of the tasting menus is definitely the way to go. You might start with snacks of salt-cod fritters or bone marrow toast topped with onion marmalade. Plates range from Schenker's much-lauded Berkshire pork belly with rock shrimp, turnips, romesco, and sherry caramel to charred *pulpo* with a "pork and bean puree." Christina Lee's desserts are ethereally inventive: Sample a rhubarb creamsicle or the neatly inverted s'mores, here with graham cracker ice cream and "hot" chocolate ganache. It's food to chew on, so to speak, so take a seat and put yourself in Chef Schenker's capable hands.

RedFarm, 529 Hudson St., at Charles St.; (212) 792-9700; redfarmnyc.com; Subway: 1 to Christopher St.; Pan-Asian; $$. Joe Ng was the chef behind the wonderful dumplings at the old Chinatown Brasserie, and now he's overseeing a pan-Asian fusion menu on a much less operatic stage. The space may be modest—it's on the upstairs level of a Village town house, with rustic farmhouse beams and wooden tables—but it's light and airy and always packed with diners having their way with the still-excellent dumplings, from Ng's classic shrimp and snow pea leaf to panfried lamb to on-trend dim sum like pastrami egg roll and a shumai shooter in a carrot ginger bisque. The entrees are fresh and tasty, with a Greenmarket bent. Sample okra and Thai eggplant yellow curry, three-chile chicken, or Dungeness and rock crab long-life noodles. You may have a wait to get a table, and reservations are taken only for large parties, but we think RedFarm is worth the wait.

Ribalta, 48 E. 12th St., btw. University Place and Broadway; (212) 777-7781; ribaltapizzarestaurant.com; Subway: N, R, 4, 5, 6, L to Union Square/14th St.; Pizza/Trattoria; $$. With an effusive Roman welcome, black-and-white Fellini movies playing silently on the wall, and an ambitious menu that includes inventive salads, small plates, and pastas, Ribalta is so much more than a mere pizzeria. Still, the made-to-order pizza is killer, particularly the house specialty, pizza in *pala,* with twice-cooked dough for a fat, crispy exterior and a chewy interior. Whatever toppings you include, don't pass up the flavorful San Marzano cherry tomatoes. You might start with brussels sprouts baked with pancetta and pecorino romano in a terra-cotta *cocotte* or the light and flavorful zucchini *scapece,* sauteed with vinegar, mint, and garlic. Pastas include ziti alla Genovese, in a veal and onion *ragù,* or *paccheri* with cod, cherry tomatoes, olives, and capers—a variation on puttanesca. But make sure someone at your table orders a pizza in *pala* or the house pizza Napoletana, baked by a master pizzamaker in Ribalta's flaming brick ovens—it's *la dolce vita* in a pie.

The Spotted Pig, 314 W. 11th St., at Greenwich St.; (212) 620-0393; thespottedpig.com; Subway: 1 to Christopher St. or A, C, E to 14th St.; British/Italian; $$–$$$. You'd have to be pretty hard-hearted not to fall for this Village charmer. Enveloped in flowering vines and plants, the Spotted Pig has the soul of a British pub downstairs and the drawing-room graciousness of a British grandmum up, where rooms have fluttering curtains, vintage tea cups, and brocaded banquettes. Celebrated chef (and English expat) April Bloomfield calls her gastropub food "seasonal British and Italian" with an emphasis on fresh ingredients. Bloomfield is notoriously masterful with meat, entrails, pig's ears, and the like—the Spotted Pig chargrilled burger is a wonder and the skirt steak with horseradish cream is meltingly good—but the shocker is that few chefs are as deft as Bloomfield is at cooking vegetables. Whatever you order, do not pass up a side of her veggies—whatever's on the menu, whether broccoli rabe, beets and greens, or roasted carrots with thyme. In the gastropub tradition, a good selection of draft and craft beers is served.

Tertulia, 359 Sixth Ave., at Washington Place; (646) 559-9909; tertulianyc.com; Subway: A, B, C, D, E, F, V to W. 4th St.; Tapas/ Spanish; $$–$$$. Seamus Mullen is the brains (and heart) behind this wonderful Spanish gastropub/tapas bar, which opened on a nondescript stretch of Sixth Avenue in 2011. Even when it was new and sizzling, Tertulia displayed a confidence and capability beyond its years, with a kitchen fully in command of its menu and its audience. Mullen was instrumental in making the tapas bar Boqueria a local favorite, but Tertulia is all his—and it's here that Mullen continues his love affair with cured *jamon*. The inviting two-room space has exposed red-brick walls, varnished wood tables, and a big golden glow coming from the open grill in back. Tertulia's warm, embracing rusticity—the cozy cider houses of Spain's Basque country were said to be a big inspiration—makes it the kind of place you want to tuck into on a cold winter night. Start with the blister-fried shishito peppers swathed in sea salt or the crushed egg with potato and Ibérico ham—Mullen pulls big flavors out of even the most mundane ingredients. Don't pass up the brussels sprouts with pork belly or the *pulpo a la brasa* (grilled octopus with beans, almonds, and a kale pistou). The menu is seasonal, but there is usually a big platter of paella to share, and the extensive wine list is packed with good-value Spanish varietals.

Tía Pol, 205 Tenth Ave., btw. 22nd and 23rd Sts.; (212) 675-8805; tiapol.com; Subway: C, E to 23rd St.; Tapas/Spanish; $$. You can tell a lot about a place by the food it serves its staff. On a pre-dinner summer night, a lush, homey staff spread was laid out on a back table of this nine-year-old tapas restaurant. The main dish was some kind of soulfully scented layered casserole, several inches thick, that billowed perfumed steam as it was spooned onto plates. If it had been on the menu, I would have ordered it on the spot. The long, narrow industrial space feels raw and unfinished, but that's just because it needs every inch of space to cram in the tapas fans who pack the place nightly. They come for delicious Spanish tapas, like mushroom croquettes, crisp on the outside and creamy and earthy inside. Garlicky *gambas* (shrimp) comes in a small baking dish with olive oil and chile. Anything with Serrano ham is recommended, and we were popping the salt-blistered green peppers (*pimientos*) like candy. It's a party here every night. The evening we stopped in, the bartender was seating people, and the waitress was doubling as the bartender, and it all felt like a genuine labor of love, right down to the perfumed banquet laid out for staff on that little table in back.

Wallsé, 334 W. 11th St., at Washington St.; (212) 352-2300; kg-ny.com/wallse; Subway: 1 to Christopher St. or A, C, E to 14th St.; Viennese; $$$–$$$$. In a serenely monochromatic space in a West Village townhouse, Chef Kurt Gutenbrunner fashions elegant versions of classic Viennese dishes. It's a handsome space, with the contrast of crisp white table linens against ebony floors. Tall windows and splashy paintings bring in pops of color and light. The menu is full of color as well: Chef Gutenbrunner is a big proponent of seasonality and fresh ingredients. A spring menu might include green asparagus with purple marble potatoes and speck, or lobster ravioli with chanterelle mushrooms and

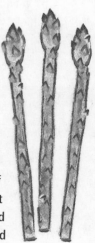

fava beans. Austrian classics like goulash and wiener schnitzel with ling-onberries are here state of the art, but Gutenbrunner is also a master with fish: the wild striped bass is an ode to springtime, with a flavorful jumble of peas, artichokes, chanterelles, and sherry sauce. The Viennese desserts should not be missed; how can you resist the "Mozart" strudel: a chocolate, pistachio and nougat parfait?

Landmarks & Old-School Faves

John's Pizzeria, 278 Bleecker St., btw. Seventh Ave. and Morton St.; (212) 243-1680; johnsbrickovenpizza.com; Subway: 1, 9 to Christopher St.; Pizza; $. Little has changed in this longtime Bleecker Street favorite, founded in 1929, where customers cram into hard wooden booths, and an Olde Italy mural covers the wall. The brick ovens still blaze in back. You can't buy pizza by the slice here, they don't take reservations, and you pay with cash only. Oh, and you may have to wait for a table. But the thin-crust pizza pies arrive at the table with a bubbly char and a satisfying chewiness—you know when you're eating a John's pizza. It's delicious.

Specialty Stores, Markets & Producers

Blue Ribbon Market, 14 Bedford St., near Downing St.; (212) 647-0408; blueribbonrestaurants.com; Subway: 1, 9 to Houston St.; Country Market. This small "country" market showcases a select group of foods and staples often served in the Blue Ribbon restaurants, with an emphasis on breads. It's got a handful of good grain-based

Cornelia Street:
Foodie Heaven in a Village Alley

This short, historic block in the heart of the Village has an embarrassment of really fine places to dine, of the cozy, seductive, and candlelit variety. The range of cuisines on this little stretch of real estate is remarkable. The newest spot is **Wong** (7 Cornelia St.; wongnewyork.com), where Chef Simpson Wong prepares his fresh, seasonal, and highly personal take on traditional Asian cuisine. **Le Gigot** (18 Cornelia St.; legigot restaurant.com), a dreamy little Provençal boîte in the West Village, serves French classics like boeuf bourguignon and bouillabaisse. Just next door at **Pearl Oyster Bar** (18 Cornelia St.; pearloysterbar.com), Rebecca Charles prepares delicious straight-up versions of New England seafood classics, such as a state-of-the-art lobster roll. Just south is **Home** (20 Cornelia St.; home restaurantnyc.com), which has been serving farm-to-table food in warm, homey environs since 1993. Sit in the flower-filled garden in back or admire the rustic Italian farmhouse decor inside as you savor organic Italian specialties at lovely **Palma** (28 Cornelia St.; palmanyc.com). On the west side of the street, charming and cozy **Pó** (31 Cornelia St.; porestaurant .com) serves the same high-quality Italian dishes it did when Mario Batali was its first chef. At **Cornelia Street Cafe** (29 Cornelia St.; corneliastreetcafe.com), you can dine at candlelit streetside tables on a wide-ranging bistro menu; cabaret entertainment is ongoing downstairs.

salads, such as quinoa with cranberries and slivered almonds or pesto couscous, as well as savories like bacon-tomato-spinach quiche and watercress soup. The market also sells artisanal meats and cheeses and homemade lemonades and sweet iced teas.

Broadway Panhandler, 65 E. 8th St., near Mercer St.; (866) 266-5927; broad waypanhandler.com; Subway: N, R to 8th St./NYU or 6 to Astor Place.; **Cookware Store.** This sprawling store is filled top to bottom with fine cookware, bakeware, ovenware, utensils, glasses, coffeemakers and blenders, baking accoutrements, aprons and just about every gadget or object of culinary desire the home cook and professional chef might need. Brands include Cuisinart, All-Clad, and Le Creuset.

Chelsea Market, 75 Ninth Ave., btw. 15th and 16th Sts.; chelsea market.com; Subway: A, C, E, L to 14th St./Eighth Ave.; **Food Arcade.** This vintage Nabisco factory reborn as a bustling food arcade is a must-do on any food tour of Manhattan. Not only is it packed with some of the finest food shops in the city, but it's a brilliant retrofitting of a Victorian-era biscuit factory. The charm is that many of the factory's industrial components have been utilized as functional design elements, like a water "fountain" that's actually a ripped-open water main gushing into a crumbling brick cavity in the floor. Cast-iron light poles have been turned upside down and transformed into electric "torches." Among fish stores, bakeries, and produce stalls, you'll find top-quality take-out eateries like **Hale and Hearty Soups** (haleandhearty.com), **Dickson's Farmstand Meats** (dicksonsfarmstand.com), **Amy's Bread** (amysbread.com), **Buon Italia** (buonitalia.com), **Ronnybrook Dairy Farm** (ronnybrook.com), **Sarabeth's Bakery** (sarabeth.com), **Fat Witch Bakery** (fatwitch.com), **Num Pang** sandwich shop (numpangnyc.com), and the **Lobster Place** (lobsterplace.com), all with cafe tables nearby. The caterer **Cleaver Company** (cleaverco.com) has a terrific sustainable-foods restaurant, the **Green Table,** and the Lobster Place has a full-service oyster bar, **Cull & Pistol** (cullandpistol.com). **Chelsea Thai** (212-924-2999) is easily one of our favorite Thai takeout restaurants.

Chelsea Market is just off the High Line, and when the weather's nice, you can grab picnic fixings from the market and dine on the High Line to Hudson River views.

Faicco's Pork Shop, 260 Bleecker St., near Leroy St.; (212) 243-1974; Subway: A, B, C, D, E, F, V to W. 4th St.; Butcher/Market. A century-old Italian meat shop run by the same family since 1898, Faicco's has an impressive Italian sausage selection, but the store is more than just pork. It sells a wide range of trimmed meats, good meatballs and ready-made lasagna, appetizers, sauces, pastas, cheeses, olives, oils, and vinegars—at surprisingly reasonable prices for the neighborhood.

Florence Prime Meat Market, 5 Jones St., at Bleecker St.; (212) 242-6531; Subway: 1, 9 to Christopher St. or A, B, C, D, E, F, V to W. Fourth St.; Butcher. This classic butcher shop in the heart of the Village has sawdust on the floor, a scalloped green awning, and a screen door that keeps flies at bay. It's a little piece of old New York and still plenty appreciated for its hand-cut steaks, fresh ground meat, and personal service.

Murray's Cheese Shop, 254 Bleecker St., btw. Sixth and Seventh Aves.; (212) 243-3289; murrayscheese.com; Subway: 1 to Christopher St. or A, C, E, F, V, B, D to W. 4th St.; Cheese Shop. A regular on organized food tours, this newly expanded, smart-looking Village old-timer looks great for its age (70+). It's a cheese blitzkreig: Honestly, I don't know what cheese you *won't* find here. But Murray's is more than just cheese these days. It also has an excellent selection of *salumi,* olives, nuts, pastas, and crackers and even artisanal beers. Sandwiches and soups are made daily at the front of the store, and if they whet your appetite for more, Murray's now has a next-door restaurant, **Murray's Cheese Bar** (264 Bleecker St.; 646-476-8882), serving up cheesy standards like mac 'n' cheese, spaghetti *cacio e pepe,* cheese melts, and cheeseburgers. Say cheese!

Peanut Butter & Co., 240 Sullivan St., btw. Bleecker and W. 3rd Sts.; (212) 677-3995; ilovepeanutbutter.com; Subway: A, B, C, D, E, F, V to W. 4th St.; **Peanut Butter.** If you love peanut butter, this is the place for you, a sandwich shop and storefront selling all manner of house-made peanut butter products. The house brand is freshly ground from top-quality peanuts, and it's state of the art. Inside the golden-hued little cafe/shop you can take yours to go or dine in on dishes like Ants on a Log (celery stalk coated with peanut butter and raisins) or the Elvis (grilled peanut butter sandwich with bananas, honey, and bacon). Peanut butter sundaes, parfaits, brownies, cookies, pies: All are sold here for the peanut lover in you.

Raffetto's, 144 W. Houston St., at MacDougal St.; (212) 777-1261; raffettospasta.com; Subway: 1 to Houston St.; **Ravioli/Pasta Shop.** Straddling SoHo and the Village, this old-school ravioli shop is one of the last of the city's custom-made pasta shops. In business since 1906, Raffetto's is still run by the Raffetto family, but the store's original repertoire of ravioli and egg noodles has been greatly expanded to include some 50 kinds of pastas. Raviolis once relegated to mere meat and cheese stuffings are now offered in such flavors as eggplant *pomodoro,* seafood in black squid, and Gorgonzola and walnut.

Rocco's, 243 Bleecker St., btw. Carmine and Leroy Sts.; (212) 242-6031; pasticceriarocco.com; Subway: A, B, C, D, E, F, V to W. 4th St.; **Italian Pastries.** This is the last of the old-fashioned Italian *pasticceria* (pastry shops) on the traditional Italian strip of Bleecker Street between Sixth and Seventh Avenues. This is the place to buy pound boxes of assorted fancy Italian cookies and biscotti; or pastries like chocolate éclairs or babas au rhum; or classic Italian desserts: housemade tiramisu, banana cream pie, gelato. Don't leave without sampling Rocco's cannoli, a made-to-order treat and the creation of pastry chef Rocco Generoso, whose family has owned the pastry shop since 1974.

Stumptown Coffee, 30 W. 8th St., at MacDougal St.; (347) 414-7802; stumptowncoffee.com; Subway: A, B, C, D, E, F, M to W. 4th St.; **Coffee Shop.** This Portland, Oregon, transplant has slowly entered the New York market, and this is its first large-scale stand-alone shop. It's got a handsome Steampunk rusticity, and employees wear old-fashioned vests, bow ties, and newsboy caps. The coffee is terrific, and the welcome is warm—how's that for a Manhattan morning?

Sweet Corner Bakeshop, 535 Hudson St., at Charles St.; (212) 206-8500; sweetcorner.com; Subway: 1 to Christopher St.; **Bakery.** Delicate wedding and special-occasion cakes may be this bakery's bread and butter, but it's the sea-salt chocolate chip cookies baked on premises that keep us coming back.

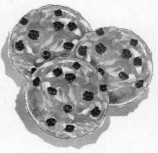

Union Square, Gramercy Park, Flatiron & NoMad

The heart, it seems, of modern-day New York, is Union Square. This 2.6-acre rectangular park stretching between 14th Street and 17th Street is more raucous and bustling (it's a major subway hub and a traditional rallying point for protesters and rabble-rousers) than quiet and contemplative. In the park's shady center, colorful metal chairs are set out beneath old-growth trees, where birds flit among flowering gardens. Occupying the park's north and west flanks is the city's biggest Greenmarket. Here farmers and food purveyors from Long Island, New Jersey, and Pennsylvania farms show up at the crack of dawn 4 days a week bearing fresh produce, eggs, meat, seafood, bread—you name it. On market days in summer, when Jersey tomatoes are fat and ripe and cornsilk is dotted with dew, the market practically shimmers with life. Union Square's refined neighbor to the northeast, Gramercy Park, has a jewel of a park shadowed by elegant low-rise apartment buildings and some very fine restaurants. Just north of Union Square, the Flatiron District is so named for the landmark building with the remarkable wedge shape; it's the unofficial greeter for lower Fifth Avenue. The Flatiron District neatly marries business with pleasure, with big-brand stores and boutique shops limning Fifth and Sixth Avenues and lots of interesting cafes and food shops in between. Finally, the newly designated NoMad refers roughly to the neighborhood surrounding Madison Park on the north side of 23rd Street. It's an emerging area but one with some of the most buzzed-about restaurants in town, including the original Shake Shack, Eleven Madison Park, NoMad, and the Ace Hotel's smokin' double bill: the Breslin and John Dory.

Foodie Faves

ABC Cocina, ABC Carpet & Home, 38 E. 19th St., at Broadway; (212) 677-2233; abccocinanyc.com; Subway: L, N, R, 4, 5, 6 to Union Square/14th St.; Mexican; $$. Jean-Georges's take on tapas and the modern Latino oeuvre has been an instant winner since it opened in mid-2013. The menu echos that of ABC Kitchen, here run through the Nuevo Latino spin cycle. So you have salmon cured with mezcal, crunchy calamari in an ancho chile glaze, and "burnt ends" beef tenderloin with a chimichurri sauce. Expect terrific tacos and empanadas (spring pea empanadas, glazed short-rib tacos, mushroom tacos with mole, kale, and lime) and classic rice dishes like *arroz con pollo*. Even the *New York Times* jumped on the pea guacamole recipe—it's a real winner, with mashed-up spring peas and crispy tortillas to dip.

ABC Kitchen, ABC Carpet & Home, 35 E. 18th St., at Broadway; (212) 475-5829; abckitchennyc.net; Subway: L, N, R, 4, 5, 6 to Union Square/14th St.; New American; $$$. Farm to table hits the heights at this Michelin-starred restaurant overseen by superstar chef Jean-Georges Vongerichten inside the wondrous confines of the ABC Carpet & Home store. The mood is sunny and buoyant, with a colorful locavore menu that dovetails beautifully with the golden California vibe and soothing egg-white palette. If you're passionate about eating local, organic, seasonal and sustainably raised food, you'll be in your element. If you're equally passionate about flavor, you'll be over the moon. (And if you're passionate about the decor, it's pretty much all for sale right there in ABC Carpet.) You can start with the sweet pea soup or the pretzel-dusted calamari. Crab toast comes with lemon aioli, and roasted Greenmarket beets come topped with a dollop of house-made yogurt. If it's spring you might choose spaghetti with a pistachio pesto and sugar snap peas. Entrees include light and tasty fish dishes such as black sea bass cooked with chiles and herbs or hearty rib-stickers like roast suckling pig with braised turnips and a smoked bacon marmalade. ABC Kitchen makes a great whole-wheat pizza, whether mushroom and Parmesan or the asparagus, bacon, ricotta, and Parmesan.

The Breslin, the Ace Hotel, 16 W. 29th St., at Broadway; (212) 679-1939; thebreslin.com; Subway: N, R to 28th St.; British; $$–$$$. A Gothic reverie of dark wood, beveled glass, and intimate niches, this gastropub in the Ace Hotel seems plucked right out of an English woodcut. You can dine in wooden booths or belly up to the bar, where boiled peanuts and caramel popcorn are typical bar snacks. Despite Chef April Bloomfield's acclaimed facility with meat (the juicy lamb burger comes with feta and cumin mayo), seasonal is king here, and a recent spring menu popped with the fresh snap of young vegetables. A spring vegetable soup came to the table brimming with asparagus, artichoke hearts, and flageolet beans, and a roasted lamb chop was pillowed on a bed of fava beans, chickpeas, and Gaeta olives. So, despite the prevalence of flashy meat dishes (that juicy lamb burger; pig's foot for two; blood sausage with fried duck egg), vegetarians will have a field day, pardon the pun, with the sampling of veggie-centric sides: peas, favas, and snaps with gremolata; tomato-braised string beans; slow-cooked

SERENDIPITOUS FINDS

Cafe Medina (9 E. 17th St., btw. Fifth Ave. and Broadway; 212-242-2777; cafemedina.com; Soup, $). Back in the soup craze days, fed by the unforgettable *Seinfeld* "Soup Nazi" episode and the real Soup Nazi who ruled the soup trade from his little storefont on 55th St., the city was filled with soupmasters (remember Soup Nutsy? Daily Soup?). These days, only the excellent local chain Hale and Hearty remains. Oh, and this little spot off Union Square, which offers around eight delicious house-made soups daily, from fava bean and spinach to a Mexican chicken tomatillo. Vegans will appreciate the many vegan offerings—but the bottom line is, all of the Cafe Medina soups are hearty and delicious, almost like your mama makes.

squash with basil. Just off the hopping Ace Hotel lobby, the Breslin is no cliché of a hotel restaurant. It's a more than fine stand-alone spot.

The City Bakery, 3 W. 18th St.; btw. Fifth and Sixth Aves.; (212) 366-1414; thecitybakery.com; Subway: L, N, R, 4, 5, 6 to Union Square/14th St.; Bakery/Salad Bar; $–$$. It's not easy to describe the much-loved City Bakery. Is it a healthy-eating Greenmarket joint? Does it serve comfort food from environmentally sustainable and seasonally sourced ingredients? Is it a restaurant or just some glorified salad bar, albeit with seating (upstairs and down)? Is it even a bakery? Well, the City Bakery is all of those things, and more. It's the salad bar of your dreams, a collection of house-made dishes that changes daily and ranges from vegan grains and sauteed veggies to ultra-cheesy mac 'n' cheese and soul-warming chicken noodle soup. It's a bakery, all right, making cookies as big as the Ritz, pretzel croissants, and maple bacon biscuits. It's a true neighborhood magnet and has been ever since Maury Rubin opened the City Bakery in a space a block away in 1990.

Everything has a fresh-made deliciousness, from the cornmeal-crusted catfish to the broccoli rabe pesto pasta. This big, airy spot is always percolating—if you visit in winter, be sure to warm up with a cup of deeply rich City Bakery hot chocolate.

Eleven Madison Park, 11 Madison Ave., at 24th St.; (212) 889-0905; elevenmadisonpark.com; Subway: N, R, 6 to 23rd St.; New American/French; $$$$. For many, this Art Deco stunner is a must-do on any Manhattan food tour. It's the swanky restaurant in your favorite 1930s screwball comedy, the one where the movie heroine swans about in floor-length satins and tables are topped with gleaming Champagne buckets. Eleven Madison Park has in fact been the movie-set tableau for plenty of modern-day movies (it's where Mr. Big broke the news of his engagement to another woman to Carrie Bradshaw in *Sex and the City*), but the real magic is on the plate. James Beard Award–winning chef Daniel Humm is at the helm of Eleven Madison Park in both front and back rooms, and the whole joint purrs. It's a tasting menu only, and pricey at that, with an innovative and often witty procession of courses.

15 East, 15 E. 15th St., near Fifth Ave.; (212) 647-0015; 15east restaurant.com; Subway: L, N, R, 4, 5, 6 to Union Square/14th St.; Japanese/Sushi; $$$$. The team behind Toqueville opened this Michelin-starred Japanese restaurant in the narrow, serene space long occupied by Toqueville. Just off Union Square, 15 East is a simple, gracious, special-occasion spot that serves exemplary no-frills sushi. Freshness is key here; the seasonal fish that shows up on your plate underscores the restaurant's sea-to-table commitment. Greenmarket complements deepen the locavore cred, and handmade soba noodles and tofu show off the house's artisanal skills. We recommend that you put yourself in the kitchen's capable hands with the six-course tasting menu or the sushi *omakase* ("from the heart").

Gramercy Tavern, 42 E. 20th St., btw. Broadway and Park Ave.; (212) 477-0777; gramercytavern.com; Subway: L, N, R, 4, 5, 6 to Union Square/14th St.; New American; $$$$. This Michelin-starred temple to casual fine dining just keeps humming along, offering one of the most satisfying dining experiences in Manhattan, whether you break bread in the elegant main dining room or in the buzzing tavern. It feels so vibrant, in fact, that it's hard to believe the restaurant is hitting 20 years old. Venerated restaurateur Danny Meyer takes hospitality to an exalted level here, and Executive Chef Michael Anthony hits the high notes with a thoughtful American menu that emphasizes Greenmarket freshness and seasonality. The decor is early American meets expansive Frank Lloyd Wright Prairie, with muscular glass windows in the tavern and grace notes of copper and gleaming wood. The spring offerings of a recent farm-to-sea seasonal tasting menu included dishes like warm lobster salad with fingerling potatoes and purslane; a sweet pea salad; and ricotta tortellini with shiitake mushrooms and fava beans. The more casual (and less expensive) tavern is ever popular, but it operates on a first-come, first-served basis (no reservations)—but sipping an artisanal cocktail at the burnished Gramercy Tavern bar is one fine way to wait your turn to dine.

Hill Country, 30 W. 26th St., btw. Broadway and Sixth Ave.; (212) 255-4444; hillcountryny.com; Subway: N, R, 6 to 28th St.; Barbecue; $$. Barbecue is the flaming star in the Hill Country solar system, but savory cornbread wedges and house sides (campfire baked beans, corn pudding, braised collards, Texas black-eyed "caviar") provide plenty of sparks. This big, multilevel spot has a Texas roadhouse decor, with nouveau honky-tonk rhythms (an array of live American "roots music" bands) kicking up the imaginary sawdust in the Boots Bar downstairs. But it's the Texas slow-smoked, dry-rub barbecue, cooked on premises every day, that draws the hordes. Sample meltingly tender brisket, beef or pork ribs, smoked chicken or sausage—even a beer-can guinea hen. Sip a longneck soda or sweet tea and bathe in the good-time aura of the Lone Star State via West 26th Street.

Incognito Bistro, 30 W. 18th St., btw. Fifth and Sixth Aves.; (212) 414-1231; incognitobistro.com; Subway: 1 to 18th St.; Italian; $$–$$$. This affable Italian was opened by a former executive chef at da Umberto. It's a percolating neighborhood spot that's a little more casual and a little less pricey than da Umberto, and the food is quite good, including hearty pastas and a wide range of smart salads. But the homemade pizzas are truly sublime, tasting like no others in the city, with crisply charred crusts and savory tomato sauce. Order one topped with sausage and broccoli rabe and devour it at the bar as you watch local families and friends come and go.

Maialino, 2 Lexington Ave., at 21st St.; (212) 777-2410; maialino nyc.com; Subway: 6 to 23rd St.; Italian Trattoria; $$$. With farmhouse tables and broad picture windows capturing the glistening green of Gramercy Park just across 21st Street, Maialino is both a sunny neighborhood hang and a worthy destination restaurant. It's a Manhattan version of a Roman trattoria, with creamy walls, checked tablecloths, and handsome tile floors, another impeccably realized dining room in the Danny Meyer universe. Maialino has become a power breakfast and family brunch spot, where you can dine on Roman specialties like *cacio e pepe* (soft scrambled eggs with pecorino and pepper) or a nice *frittata bianca,* with spring onion, squash, and Parmesan cheese. It's a Roman holiday at night, when you might start your meal with fried artichokes (here with anchovy sauce) or an heirloom squash *fritto misto* and then move on to one of the finely rendered pastas (pappardelle with a pork *ragù* or a malfatti with braised suckling pig and arugula). Among the Roman-style *secondi,* the *baccalà* (poached cod) comes with seasonal vegetables, and the *abbachio al forno* (lamb shoulder) is prepared with braised artichokes and potatoes. The neighborhood is in the house for the Sunday-night pasta tasting menu, a convivial repast especially in winter, when Gramercy Park shimmers in the icy blue of night.

NoMad, 1170 Broadway, at 28th St.; (212) 796-1500; thenomad hotel.com; Subway: C, E to 23rd St.; New American; $$$–$$$$. It's a sumptuous stage set, the kind of place the Addams Family would call home if they had good taste and plenty of dough. But with truly accomplished "refined yet approachable" food coming out of a busy kitchen, this is serious eating as well. Composed of several large, unique spaces, the restaurant is an eye-popping mashup of design concepts—the overall feel is one of strolling through the great rooms of an English country estate. The Atrium courtyard has a glass roof that fills the big room with tinny light. The sumptuous Victorian Parlour has a claret bordello palette. The Library looks like every old moneyed library should: lots of burnished wood and tufted sofas. You can swan all over the place if you like, but if you want to sit and dine, you'll need to book well in advance; this is one hot ticket. The American/European menu is overseen by the 2012 winner of the James Beard Outstanding Chef award, Daniel Humm (of Eleven Madison Park). It's seasonal fare, like a springtime hake slow-cooked with English peas, ramps, and hen of the woods mushrooms, or a hearty late-summer suckling pig confit with cherries, arugula, and bacon marmalade. Preparation is meticulous; the food looks beautiful on the plate. Bottom line: Come for the theater; the happy surprise is the food.

Novita, 102 E. 22nd St., btw. Park Ave. South and Lexington Ave.; (212) 677-2222; novitanyc.com; Subway: 6 to 23rd St.; Italian; $$$. You could do a lot worse for a romantic assignation than this casual-elegant Italian trattoria tucked off boisterous Park Avenue and suffused in amber light. The below-street-level space is small but urbane, with crisp white linens, glistening glassware, and butter-yellow walls. It would be just one more in the city's long lineup of stylish and genteel Italian restaurants if not for the sure hand of the kitchen, where unfussy seasonal Italian classics are thoughtfully prepared. The flavorful pastas include *tagliolini all'aragosta* (a creamy lobster *ragù* with asparagus and tomato), homemade *strozzapreti* with pesto, pappardelle with lamb *ragù*, and *rigatoni al tonno* (with seared yellowfin tuna, olives, and tomato). Both seafood (pan-roasted sea bass with artichokes; pan-sautéed diver scallops and shrimp with broccoli rabe) and meat (slow-braised Jamison Farm lamb shank with sautéed baby spinach; a classic *vitello Milanese*) are deftly executed. In the warm weather, cafe tables are set up outside, a steamy Gotham street scene but for the ethereal flavors of Italy on your plate.

Pure Food & Wine, 54 Irving Place, at 17th St.; (212) 477-1010; oneluckyduck.com; Subway: L, N, R, 4, 5, 6 to Union Square/14th St.; Raw Foods; $$. The delicious food is a revelation at the standard-bearer of the Raw Food movement, where nothing is cooked above 118°F (48°C)—thus preserving, say the raw foodies, the food's essential vitamins, minerals, and enzymes. This refined raw vegan cuisine at Pure Food & Wine is served in a warm candlelit dining room on a sweet stretch of little Irving Place. The menu is inventive and cheeky, even; here a "Philly roll" is composed of avocado, kimchee, and "cream" (cashew) cheese. No dairy is served here (and little gluten), so a "Caesar" salad comes not with Parmesan cheese but a pumpkin-seed/macadamia "Parmesan." A portabello mushroom and hemp-seed burger comes with tea-smoked cashew cheese. The Pure Food & Wine lasagna is fashioned of zucchini, heirloom tomatoes, basil pistachio pesto, sun-dried tomato marinara, and a macadamia-pumpkinseed ricotta. The wine menu offers only biodynamic, organic, or sustainable wines.

sweetgreen, 1164 Broadway, btw. 27th and 28th Sts.; (646) 449-8884; sweetgreen.com; Subway: 6 to 28th St.; Organic Salads; $. This farm-to-table salad shop opened it first location in the NoMad hotel in mid-2013. It's the kind of head-thumping, why-didn't-I-think-of-that concept guaranteed to hit the hot buttons of city locavores and slow foodies. This DC–based cult chain takes the made-to-order-salad concept to new heights, offering a range of salads and healthy grain bowls (farro, quinoa) made with locally sourced ingredients, many from organic farms—check out the chalkboard of local purveyors represented, updated daily. The signature salads include Guacamole Greens and a Spicy Sabzi and Earth Bowl, and soups are offered year-round.

Union Square Cafe, 21 E. 16th St., btw. Fifth Ave. and Broadway; (212) 243-4020; unionsquarecafe.com; Subway: L, N, R, 4, 5, 6 to Union Square/14th St.; New American; $$$–$$$$. Restaurateur Danny Meyer's experiment in casual fine dining began here some 30 years ago. This groundbreaking, award-winning restaurant (Meyer's first) is still at the top of its game, an exemplar of easy sophistication and seamless hospitality. The Union Square Cafe was one of the first eateries to espouse the farm-to-table philosophy, with the Union Square Greenmarket next door practically its own personal culinary laboratory. It was also one of the first to show that you could ditch fussy formality and still provide a first-class fine-dining experience. Of course, good food has a lot to do with that. The seasonal American menu at Union Square Cafe borrows from the elegant simplicity of the Italian school—dishes are uncomplicated but always flavorful. A recent dinner menu included pastas such as frascatelli with chanterelle mushrooms in a peppery cream sauce and a Naples-influenced spaghettini with flaky halibut and rapini with chile and breadcrumbs. Pan-roasted chicken is an old reliable here, and you can slurp down briny oysters on the half shell—and the veggie sides are delicious all on their own. Service is smooth as silk, and big sprays of flowers still make this feel like a celebration. Don't miss it.

Landmarks & Old-School Faves

Eisenberg's, 174 Fifth Ave., near 22nd St.; (212) 675-5096; eisenbergs nyc.com; **Subway: N, R, 6 to 23rd St.; Deli; $.** Once upon a time, kiddies, Manhattan used to be lousy with atmospheric little delis like Eisenberg's. Walking into this long, narrow lunch counter/sandwich shop is like time-traveling into a faded old photo from your great-grandma's childhood. Eisenberg's still cranks out classic egg creams and pastrami platters, and its counter guys still wear crisp white soda-jerk hats. But this is no museum. Eisenberg's bustles with the business of feeding folks all day long. In the shadow of the Flatiron building since 1929, Eisenberg's has managed to stay in the black by changing little over the course of 80 years, sure death for many of Manhattan's current crop of hot spots and pop-up installations. Take a seat on one of the red-leather counter stools and order a lime rickey and Eisenberg's killer tunafish (yes, you can order it on whole-wheat) and admire an old-timer at work.

Specialty Stores, Markets & Producers

Eataly, 200 Fifth Ave, btw. 23rd and 24th Sts.; (212) 229-2560; eatalyny.com; **Subway: N, R to 23rd St.; Italian Food Marketplace.** This big, bright, 32,000-square-foot Italian-food marketplace has been the toast of the town since it opened in 2010 in the old Toy Building on Lower Fifth Avenue, the joint effort of three of the city's most influential food figures, Mario Batali, Joe Bastianich, and Lidia Bastianich. With lofty ceilings and classic tile floors, this sprawling Italian market/emporium/dining destination is a dream of a food market. You move from one elegant little eating area to another, each one filled with chattering customers standing at marble bars or sitting at tables dining on delicacies like roast meats, fresh *crudo,* and house-made gelato. Eataly has seven sit-down restaurants with tables and bar stools. The rooftop Birreria is also a brewery, where you can sample house-brewed ales and even dine on a wide-ranging menu of salads, cheeses, *salumi,* and hearty meat entrees (*pollo cacciatore,* grilled lamp chops). You don't have to dine in at Eataly, however; you can buy your supper from the endless supply of artisanal Italian goodies, from pastas to pizza to cheese to bread to *salumi* to fresh produce to beer. If you love Italian food—if you love food, period—Eataly is *splendido.*

Kalustyan's, 123 Lexington Ave., btw. 27th and 28th Sts.; (212) 685-3451; kalustyans.com; Subway: F to Second Ave.; Middle Eastern Food Market. Downstairs in the Middle Eastern market, wooden barrels are filled with nuts, grains, and spices, and shelves have every kind of cooking oil, vinegar, and condiment you can imagine. But upstairs is the real find: a modest little cafe where trays are steaming with all manner of house-made Middle Eastern specialties. Order a sublime *mujadarra* (lentils and bulghur wheat cooked with caramelized onions) in pita or platter, fresh lentil soup, or other homemade specialties, and it's no wonder Kalustyan's has been here since 1944.

L.A. Burdick Handmade Chocolates, 5 E. 20th St., btw. Fifth Ave. and Broadway; (212) 796-0143; burdickchocolate.com; Subway: N, R, 6 to 23rd St.; Chocolate. Sample the delicious chocolates, pastries, and other confections at L.A. Burdick's first location in New York. The Flatiron location is both store and cafe, where you can warm up with a cup of the shop's single-source hot chocolate or buy a box of assorted specialty chocolates.

Union Square Greenmarket, Union Square, between 14th and 17th Sts.; grownyc.org/greenmarket; Farmers' Market. The big kahuna of the city's Greenmarkets, this farmers' market brings the farm to the city four days a week (Mon, Wed, Fri, and Sat). It's sprawling and colorful, and vendors are required to adhere to the city's strict Greenmarket regulations (they can only sell what they grow or make). In the height of the summer season, the great bounty of Long Island and Jersey soil spills over in scores of farm stalls: fresh corn, fat Jersey tomatoes, every vegetable you can imagine (and their baby components), and flowers. We are proud to say that when summer's end spells the end of corn season for our North Carolina relatives, our NYC Greenmarkets are still bringing in fresh, delicious corn on the cob—often into October. It's a year-round market, so even in the dead of winter a few stalwarts show up at the break of morning to sell artisanal meats, Long Island seafood, free-range eggs, dairy products, muffins and cookies, apples, root and greenhouse vegetables, and more. It's a fresh-food lollapalooza (Wed and Sat are Union Square's biggest markets) and, since 1976, a miracle for city folk and city chefs (in the early days they would arrive in the morning in their kitchen whites to plot out the evening meals). With 54 Greenmarkets operating somewhere in the city 7 days a week, these farmers' markets have become an essential element in the city's food web, and Union Square's is the big one. For specifics on where you can find a Greenmarket in the city, go to grownyc.org/greenmarket.

Midtown

Midtown West: The Garment District, Hell's Kitchen & Times Square

If you're looking to get away from it all, Manhattan's lively western mid-section may be the last place you want to be. Here the hustle and bustle of the city is ratcheted up to a roar. Times Square alone is a nonstop party, with theaters, restaurants, and shops tap-dancing 'round the clock to entertain the descending hordes. This is largely where Manhattan's handful of theme restaurants and big chain eateries (Olive Garden, Red Lobster) are congregated. Just south, the Garment District is a bustling office district stoking the rag trade, with Macy's as its unofficial flagship. Once a gang-ridden tenement slum of working-class Irish, Hell's Kitchen, to the west of Times Square, still has a rowdy feel, especially in the 40s and 50s along Ninth Avenue, with wall-to-wall bars, cafes, ethnic eater-ies, and food purveyors—but it also has quiet, leafy residential streets. Hell's Kitchen (aka Clinton) is well known for the Ninth Avenue Interna-tional Food Festival, celebrated annually in May.

Benoit, 60 W. 55th St., btw. Fifth and Sixth Aves.; (646) 943-7373; benoitny.com; Subway: N, R to 57th St.; French Bistro; $$$. All is right and fizzy in the world when you dine at Benoit. A ceiling painted in blue sky with wispy clouds oversees a main dining room of red-velvet banquettes, Parisian tile floors, and Art Nouveau lamps and mirrors. This is casual bistro dining, via celebrated French chef Alain Ducasse (who took over the original Benoit bistro in Paris in 2005). It's light, casual, and more gently priced than Ducasse's now-closed Adour, with a smart bistro menu calculated to hit the hot buttons of locals and the tourist trade alike. (Ignore the ugly bar up front.) The food veers toward light and savory, and the service manages to be both warm and impeccable. All diners are greeted with a platter of cheese gougères, mini choux-pastry puffs that are utterly addictive (see recipe on p. 213), as well as bread in a snappy cloth Benoit bag. A good nosh is the sampling of hors d'oeuvres (five for $16), which provides entry into the Ducasse brain trust. Again, light and flavorful are the guiding principles, with excellent ingredients needing only a nudge or creative pairing to delight. A *daurade tartare* glistens with sea salt, and the eggplant caviar has just the right mix of texture and flavor. French bistro classics like *moules marinières,* niçoise salad, hanger steak-frites, and roast chicken are exemplary.

Cafe Edison, Hotel Edison, 227 W. 47th St., btw. Broadway and Eighth Ave.; (212) 840-5000; edisonhotelnyc.com; Subway: N, R to 49th St. or 1, 2, 3, N, R to 42nd St./Times Square; Deli; $. This old-fashioned deli in a prime Times Square location has an anachronistic feel—they sure don't make 'em like this anymore. And what is "this" anyway? A hotel-lobby restaurant serving old-school deli food in a vintage Deco ballroom that feels like a grande dame slightly gone to seed. As for the Hotel Edison, this big, circa-1931 lodging has sometimes straddled the line between state of the art and seedy, but its mere stubborn longevity has confirmed it as a classic. The hotel ballroom began as a sexy Swing-era dance club, and in its 1970s incarnation was a theater showing the infamously racy (and infamously long-running) musical production *Oh Calcutta!*. So when you sample the Cafe Edison's exemplary pastrami on rye or matzoh ball soup, give a silent shout-out to the ghosts of those who prowled within these ballroom walls.

Daisy May's BBQ, 623 Eleventh Ave., at 46th St.; (212) 977-10017; daisymaysbbq.com; Subway: A, C, E, S to 42nd St./Eighth Ave.; Barbecue; $. The city has many worthy contenders to the barbecue throne, but for our money few come close to approximating genuine Carolina pulled-pork barbecue than Daisy May's. Daisy May's dispenses its barbecue sandwiches and mason jars of sweet tea from a handful of strategically positioned food trucks throughout the city, but its one brick-and-mortar location lies in the boonies of Manhattan's wild west. It may not be the boonies for long, with the megadevelopment Hudson Yards rising on the western horizon south of 44th Street. In any case, it's a must-stop for barbecue fans, offering a country-wide tasting tour, from Carolina pulled pork to Kansas City ribs to Texas sliced-beef brisket to Memphis dry-rub pork ribs. Order up a couple of sides (baked beans, creamed corn, bourbon peaches) and wash it all down with a mason jar of sweet tea.

Esca, 402 W. 43rd St., btw. Ninth and Tenth Aves.; (212) 564-7272; esca-nyc.com; Subway: A, C, E, S to 42nd St./Eighth Ave.; Italian Seafood; $$$. This lovely Italian-inflected seafood restaurant may not have the most ideal location (it's a block from Port Authority on the bottom floor of a residential tower lording over West 42nd Street). It's been around for nearly 15 years—the buzz of the new and the hot having

TOURIST TRAPS WE SECRETLY LOVE: CARMINE'S THEATER DISTRICT

Yes, it's branched out to Vegas and DC (the latter a 700-seat behemoth), and yes, the theme—an homage to the "big marquee restaurants" of New York's yesteryear—is just that, a theme. But the vast dining room manages to feel both warmly welcoming and celebratory, and the family-style portions of Southern Italian favorites are thoughtfully prepared and very often right on the money. With more than a nod to the family-style red-sauce restaurants still reeling 'em in in the Bronx's Little Italy, Carmine's feeds a whole lot of people daily with an admirable amount of grace and artistry. Brill Building old-timers have even found a nest at the happening bar. Order up big platters of chicken scarpariello, linguine with shrimp and marinara, and baked clams—and keep in mind that waits can be lengthy during the pre- and post-theater hours, so plan accordingly (200 W. 44th St., btw. Seventh and Eighth Aves.; 212-221-3800; carminesnyc.com; Subway: 1, 2, 3, 7, A, C, E, S to 42nd St./Times Square).

long receded. But on an early Thursday night at the end of a sweltering summer day, the place is thrumming with smart-looking city folk, as candles flicker and Buffalo Springfield pounds in the background. The cognoscenti make a pilgrimage here for sea-to-table ambrosia, served up in a series of rooms of butter-yellow walls, green slate floors, and elegant wood trim, a massive spray of greenery guarding the door. Unlike other, more hushed upscale fish houses, Esca crackles with energy and flirty bonhomie. It's part of the Mario Batali/Joe Bastianich culinary empire, with Chef David Pasternack overseeing a kitchen that is firing on all cylinders. In the dining room, the serving staff swarms tables and no water glass goes unfilled (but it never feels obsequious).

You can sample a *crudo* tasting menu, have one of the deftly prepared pastas (the summer menu featured an Amalfitana-style fettuccine with Gulf shrimp, crawfish, Sungold tomatoes, and cherry bomb peppers (see recipe on p. 228) or house-made *mafalde* with rock shrimp, bay scallops, chiles and fresh corn) or go full bore with a branzino cooked in sea salt, or a Sicilian-style *zuppa di pesce*. For our money, Esca is the best fish house in town.

Hangawi, 12 E. 32nd St., btw. Fifth and Madison Aves.; (212) 213-0077; hangawirestaurant.com; Subway: 6 to 33rd St.; Korean Vegetarian; $$–$$$. On the edges of the little neighborhood known as Koreatown, home to a bustling lineup of barbecue restaurants, kara-oke bars, and *mandoo* (dumpling) joints, is this blissed-out haven of Zen quietude and refined vegetarian dishes, Korean style. It's a lovely spot, done like a traditional Korean home, with lots of warm wood and soft amber light and tables low to the floor—where diners are seated, shoes removed. A fountain burbles as diners sample such delicacies as organic kale dumplings, kabocha pumpkin pancakes, sweet potato fritters, and dandelion and avocado salad. Stone bowls arrive at the table steaming with vegetable rice and noodle dishes. You can get classic bibimbap, hearty porridges, and tofu hot pots. It's a great spot to decompress in the middle of a hectic shopping expedition in the Macy's neighborhood—and a four-course prix-fixe lunch lets you graze the Hangawi landscape.

Le Bernardin, 55 W. 51st St., btw. Sixth and Seventh Aves.; (212) 489-1515; le-bernardin.com; Subway: N, R to 49th St. or 1 to 50th St.; Seafood/French; $$$$. Chef Eric Ripert is one of the giants on the NYC culinary scene and a culinary artist. Fish is his medium, with preparations informed by a background in classical French technique learned at places like La Tour d'Argent and Jamin in Paris. Ripert took the helm of the already acclaimed Le Bernardin in 1994, and he was only 29 years old when he garnered four stars from the *New York Times*.

Today the restaurant remains nearly perfect in every sense, one that continues to amass awards and stars and a steady clientele devoted to the understated elegance of its cooking and near-fanatical obeisance to fresh, local, sustainable, and seasonal. A dinner prix-fixe might begin with wild striped-bass tartare, a clam sashimi in a grape-lime *sauce vierge,* or a charred octopus *a la plancha* and then move on to "barely cooked" wild salmon in a Japanese maitake sauce or a whole red snapper baked in an *herbes de Provence* salt crust. It's all wonderful, from the cosseting service to the dining room environs, with its soaring sprays of flowers and sweeping photo-mural of frothy ocean spray.

Marea, 240 Central Park S., near Broadway; (212) 582-5100; marea-nyc.com; Subway: 1, A, B, C, D to 59th St./Columbus Circle; Seafood/Italian; $$$–$$$$. Whenever we mention Marea to locals, the response is inevitably rapturous. The restaurant may have opened 3 years ago but New Yorkers are still smitten with Chef Michael White's refined homage to the Italian coastline. The summer night we visited, a scrum of political protesters was making noise along 57th Street, but all was coolly elegant inside Marea. Cocktail music hummed against the clicking of Louboutins as a courtly, moneyed crowd dined in leather chairs at generously spaced round tables. The soothing interior combines gleaming cognac walls, creamy blinds, and a buttery marble bar—smart red lamps pop in a sea of linen white. This is the spot to sip Bellinis—here state of the art, made with fresh peach puree—and sample sparkling *crudo,* from Pacific langoustines dressed in pink salt to seared wahoo with wild mushroom and lobster roe. The menu changes seasonally, but a recent summer menu included *capesante* (seared sea scallops with grilled peaches, *puntarelle,* chanterelle mushrooms and a hint of *guanciale*) and a butter-poached lobster with crispy polenta, bacon, and heirloom tomatoes. Marea feels like a dream, or a version of upper-echelon Manhattan, via Hollywood—with exquisite food. It's fun to play mogul for a night.

Mercato, 352 W. 39th St., btw. Eighth and Ninth Aves.; (212) 643-2000; mercatonyc.com; Subway: A, C, E to 42nd St.; Sicilian; $$. This genuine slice of Italy is great value and a real find, considering that it's tucked away on a fairly desultory Hell's Kitchen street best known for its string of budget chain hotels. The narrow trattoria is broken into two main rooms, all high ceilings, rustic wood, exposed brick, and hanging lamps lit with Edison bulbs. It's the look du jour, but it works. Expect thoughtfully prepared appetizers like the Mercato salad, the house version of the French niçoise; a *frittura di pesce* (seafood fry); and a *polpette con crostini,* meatballs in a tomato sauce on garlic crostini. Pastas might be a homemade Sardinian cavatelli with a wild boar *ragù* or a nice Sicilican-style orecchiette with broccoli rabe, anchovies, bread crumbs, garlic, and olive oil. The savory entrees include cioppino with garlic *crostone* bread, *spezzatino di manzo al vino rosso* (beef stew braised in wine), or a finger-licking *porchetta* (pork belly) roasted with fresh herbs. Mercato has an interesting and well-priced wine list featuring varietals from all over the boot, and prices in general are gentle, making this a very smart off-the-beaten-path choice in the Times Square/Port Authority area.

The Modern, the Museum of Modern Art, 9 W. 53rd St., btw. Fifth and Sixth Aves.; (212) 333-1220; themodernnyc.com; Subway: E, V to Fifth Ave./53rd St.; New American/French; $$$. Crisply urbane, outfitted in soothing monochromes, the Modern has views you simply won't find anywhere else. Big glass windows overlook the outdoor sculpture garden of the Museum of Modern Art, a green oasis where Picasso's bronze goat grazes amid carpets of ivy. Inside, the views are pretty swell as well, where it's fun to watch the local tribe in action. The Modern has rung up accolades for its food and wine service, including a three-star review from the *New York Times* in 2013. The seasonal New American/French menu includes, to start, a beet-marinated arctic char dusted with foie gras powder or a John Dory gratinée with a beggar's-purse of bouchot mussels. The finely etched entrees include a chorizo-crusted cod and a quail baked *en terre glaise* (in clay) with an all-American macaroni gratin. As in all Danny Meyer restaurants, the "hospitality quotient"—that would be service—is dialed to 11. You can also have a fine meal of large and small plates in the more casual bar room, which thrums with energy, the Manhattan tribe in its element.

Szechuan Gourmet, 21 W. 39th St., btw. Fifth and Sixth Aves.; (212) 921-0233; szechuan-gourmet.com; Subway: B, D, F to 42nd St./ Bryant Park; Szechuan; $–$$. In a borough where it's no longer easy to find solid Chinese restaurants, this is a bright spot. Many of the city's big critics (Frank Bruni, et al.) glommed onto this Flushing Szechuan when it opened a Midtown Manhattan branch in 2004, praising its fresh ingredients, authentic preparation, and firepower. It's still a hot ticket for folks searching out flavorful, well-prepared Szechuan dishes like double-cooked pork belly, mapo tofu, cold sesame noodles—even old reliable Kung Pao chicken is just the way it should be.

Tir na nÓg, 5 Penn Plaza, Eighth Ave. at 33rd St.; (212) 630-0249; tirnanognyc.com; Subway: A, C, E to 34th St./Penn Station; Irish/ American; $$. A food-and-drink oasis amid the boisterous blocks surrounding Madison Square Garden and Penn Station, this atmospheric Irish pub is located on the first floor of a nondescript office building. It may be the best thing going in a restaurant-challenged neighborhood. Inside is a flavorful reconstruction of a classic Celtic pub straight out of the Victorian era, with fancifully carved dark wood and vintage china on the walls. The food is straightforward and flavorful—the kitchen demonstrates a sure hand and a light touch. Dine on traditional Irish specialties like shepherd's pie filled with Guinness-braised lamb, or American bistro favorites, like burgers, roast chicken, and New York strip.

Totto Ramen, 366 W. 52nd St., btw. Eighth and Ninth Aves.; (212) 582-0052; tottoramen.com; Subway: C, E to 50th St.; Ramen Shop; $. First, the rules: Do not sit on the stoop while waiting for a table. Do not block the sidewalk. Bring cash. And you may have to share a table or elbow room at the bar with a stranger. No problem. It's all worth it at this tiny, insanely popular below-street-level Japanese ramen shop on a slightly scruffy Hell's Kitchen street. Finally, you're seated: What to order? There's the basic Paitan Ramen soup, a big, steaming bowl of straight noodles cooked in homemade chicken broth and soy sauce and topped with scallions, onions, and nori (get it with chicken or pork). (It also comes in spicy or extra-spicy—with a kick of spicy sesame oil.) Vegetarians can opt for the ramen cooked in a kelp-based broth brimming with seasonal raw veggies, seaweed, slices of avocado, yuzu paste, and sesame oil. Our favorite is probably the miso ramen, wavy noodles cooked in chicken broth and miso and topped with a scoop of ground pork/soybean paste, half-boiled egg, bean sprouts, onions, and scallions. Ordering takes a minute, and it's all of 5 minutes before a hot bowl of ramen is set down before you, as the background music swings between Mexican cocktail samba and funk. Dig in: It's indescribably delicious.

Landmarks & Old-School Faves

Keens, 72 W. 36th St., at Sixth Ave.; (212) 947-3636; keens.com; Subway: 1, 2, 3, to 34th St./Penn Station; Chophouse; $$$–$$$$. Two blocks from the hubbub of Macy's and Madison Square Garden, this old-time chophouse from 1885 is a wonderful relic from the circa-1890s Herald Square Theater District. (Before that the area was lined with dance halls and bordellos and known as the Tenderloin.) A collection of vintage clay churchwarden pipes lines the walls, and the warren of intimate, low-ceilinged rooms harken back to the days of gas lamps and horse-drawn carriages clip-clopping down Sixth Avenue. Sitting square and solid amid button and bead shops and transient wholesalers, Keens is an anomaly in a city that has a short attention span. But what a beaut it is. Keens is cooking in the food department as well—in fact, some claim (that would include us) that Keens serves the best char-grilled steaks in town.

The "21" Club, 21 W. 52nd St., btw. Fifth and Sixth Aves.; (212) 582-7200; 21club.com; Subway: N, R to 49th St.; American/Continental; $$–$$$. One of Manhattan's last surviving Prohibition-era watering holes, this former speakeasy opened in an 1872 brownstone as Jack and Charlie's "21" Club on West 52nd Street in 1929. It quickly became a drinking establishment favored by New York writers like Damon Runyon, Ben Hecht, and Charlie MacArthur. Later, show-biz types, sports luminaries, high-powered agents, and media stars jockeyed for the best tables. President John Kennedy dined at "21" the night before his inauguration, and scenes from movies like *All About Eve* and *The Sweet Smell of Success* were filmed here. These days the "21" Club, now owned by Orient-Express Hotels, may be lousy with respectability, but it's a still great place to marinate in the ambience of raucous old New York. Vintage toys and sports stuff hang from the ceiling, the playthings of patrons in thrall to eternal boyhood. Patrons also contributed many of the 33 cast-iron racing jockeys that line the restaurant entrance. Does the food live up to the dazzling clientele? It's perfectly fine, bistro comfort food, well prepared. The vaunted **"21" Burger** comes on a toasted Parker House bun, and the restaurant still serves the famous **"21" Chicken Hash** (see

Restaurant Row: West 46th Street

Theatergoers searching for sustenance have only to stroll down West 46th Street between Eighth and Ninth Avenues and pick the spot that suits them. The block is a smorgasbord of some 25 restaurants, a number of them worthy destination restaurants in their own right. Restaurant Row is such a fixture that it even has its own promotional website (restaurantrownyc .com). Our recommended favorites include **Orso** (322 W. 46th St.; orsorestaurant.com), a classy Italian on the south side of the street. Next door is **Joe Allen** (326 W. 46th St.; joeallenrestaurant.com), the famed theater boîte hung with posters of Broadway flops and a kitchen serving classic American bistro food. Across the street is **Barbetta** (321 W. 46th St.; barbettarestaurant.com), the century-old Italian where you dine in the rococo salmon-tinged interior of a fancy town house. To the west is **Sushi of Gari** (347 W. 46th St.; sushiofgari.com), one of the city's top-ranked sushi restaurants. Farther west still is the Roman-Jewish cuisine of **Lattanzi** (361 W. 46th St.; lattanzinyc.com), served in an atmosphere of elegant rusticity, and the refined Russian cuisine of **FireBird** (365 W. 46th St.; firebirdrestaurant.com), a tapestry of opulence, czar-style, enveloping diners in jewel-box rooms, an homage to the good old days of prerevolutionary Russia.

recipe, p. 209), a rich, creamy chicken mush that many powerful men had their wives (and mistresses) replicate at home.

Amy's Bread, 672 Ninth Ave., btw. 46th and 47th Sts.; (212) 977-2670; amysbread.com; Subway: N, R to 49th St.; Bakery. In the waning years of the 20th century, the city saw a return to small-batch, artisanal baking, the pioneering work of folks like Amy Scherber and her partner Toy Kim Dupree, who opened Amy's Bread in this Hell's Kitchen location in 1992. Today Amy's Bread has a sprinkling of outposts all over the city, notably Chelsea Market, but this little 1896 storefront, its wood façade painted a cheery Marseilles blue, was where it all began. Sample hearty breads made using traditional European baking methods, like semolina with golden raisins and fennel or big and small loaves of walnut raisin, as well as house-made pastries, scones, biscuits, cookies, cakes, cupcakes, sandwiches, and more. This location has a cafe section with a smattering of tables.

Le Maraís, 150 W. 46th St., btw. Sixth and Seventh Aves.; (212) 869-0900; lemarais.net; Subway: N, R, S, 7, 1, 2, 3 to 42nd St.; Kosher Butcher. This atmospheric little glatt-kosher (nondairy) French steak house in the Theater District also has a top-notch butcher shop selling prime kosher meats aged on the premises. It has a butcher case filled with quality French-cut steaks as well as specialized meats like veal sausage and lamb roast.

Little Pie Company, 424 W. 43rd St., btw. Ninth and Tenth Aves.; little piecompany.com; (212) 736-4780; amysbread.com; Subway: A, C, E to 42nd St./Port Authority; Bakery. You can smell the pies cooking blocks away, and that's a big part of the appeal of this throwback to the days when Mama put her pies out on the back porch to cool. If you're in the neighborhood and find yourself enraptured with the perfume of fresh-baked fruit pies, follow the scent to this little shop, baking house-made pies with fresh ingredients and no preservatives since 1985. The menu includes a Mississippi mud pie, banana coconut cream, Southern pecan, and Little Pie's signature creation, a sour cream apple walnut pie, as well as cakes, muffins, brownies, even chicken pot pies.

Sea Breeze Fish Market,
541 Ninth Ave., at W. 40th St.; (212) 563-7537; seabreezefish markets.com; Subway: A, C, E to 42nd St./Port Authority; Fish Market. This no-nonsense retail fishmonger close to the Port Authority has some of the

freshest fish in the city at some of the best prices.

Sullivan St. Bakery, **533 W. 47th St., btw. Tenth and Eleventh Aves.; (212) 265-5583; sullivanstreetbakery.com; Subway: A, C, E to 42nd St.; Bakery/Pizza.** It's no longer in its little spot on Sullivan Street, but no matter: Sullivan Street Bakery and its wondrous breads, pizzas, and panini live on, blessedly, in the western wilds of Hell's Kitchen. (It also has another retail location in Chelsea at 236 Ninth Ave.) Baker Jim Lahey is a brilliant small-batch baker, and his rustic loaves of bread are ethereal, no question. But we keep coming back for the square-cut slices of Roman-style pizza, a thin-crust wonder of sea salt, olive oil, and herbs. The signature *pizza bianca* is both light and chewy; the *pizza zucchini* ultra-delicious, especially when the gruyère and bread crumbs have a slight char. The *pizza funghi* is topped with a savory mix of cremini mushrooms, onions, and thyme. Don't leave without sampling a bomboloni, the bakery's delectable Italian doughnut.

Midtown East: Kips Bay, Murray Hill & Grand Central

Manhattan's geographical midsection is where you'll find its most iconic buildings, with the Empire State Building and the Chrysler Building ably anchoring the city skyline. Fifth Avenue, perhaps the most celebrated boulevard of commerce on the planet, slices through Midtown, where storied department stores share precious real estate with the flagship shops of international brands. Here too are Rockefeller Center (with a dining arcade below ground level), Grand Central Station (and its terrific Dining Concourse downstairs), and the New York Public Library Main Building, the green oasis of Bryant Park at its back door. Some of the city's most elegant, historic hotels are here too, from the Plaza to the St. Regis to the Carlyle, each with correspondingly rarefied dining experiences. On the eastern fringes of Midtown are the residential enclaves of Kips Bay and Murray Hill, with a sprinkling of destination restaurants and a thriving Little India along Lexington Avenue between 26th and 30th Streets, known as "Curry Hill." Farther east still stands the United Nations, which towers over the East River and the traditionally affluent neighborhoods of Sutton Place, Beekman Place, and Turtle Bay.

Ai Fiori, Langham Place Fifth Avenue Hotel, 400 Fifth Ave., btw. 36th and 37th Sts.; (212) 613-8660; aifiorinyc.com; Subway: N, Q, R to 34th St./Herald Square or 6 to 33rd St./Lexington Ave.; Italian/ Seafood; $$$$. If the polished corporate look of this Midtown spot is calculated to make suits feel right at home, then they're doing something right, because on a recent midsummer day, the place was filled with white-collar working stiffs. Not that this was an expense-account crowd necessarily; it was Restaurant Week and plenty of cubicle dwellers who don't regularly spring for $50 lunches were out in force. Opened in 2010, Ai Fiori is part of Chef Michael White's growing empire of Manhattan restaurants. Its location on the second floor of Langham Place Hotel, a mini Time-Warner complex near the Empire State Building, puts it squarely in a business-centric frame of mind, so you can't fault the determinedly unsplashy decor, with walls in teal and black, massive columns wrapped in a nubby mint fabric, and stolid suede banquettes against the wall. The sheer breadth of space is luxury itself. The food—White's homage to the Italian and French Riviera—is pricey but often transcendent. Sample silky *crudo,* a wonderful lobster velouté (bisque), or the White Label burger, specially customized for the restaurant by celebrity meat purveyor Pat La Frieda. Agnolotti arrive here as parcels of braised veal with a squash puree and black truffle *sugo*. The *trofie nero* encapsulate the simple elegance and balanced flavors of White's cooking: the *trofie*—tightly curled ribbons of pasta—here made with black squid ink, come in a Ligurian crustacean *ragù* of *seppia* (cuttlefish), scallops, spiced *mollica* (bread crumbs), white wine, olive oil, and garlic. The many levels of service people swirl around the room; all but the top level—the suited fellows who take your order with a withering impassiveness—are warm and welcoming.

Bluebell Cafe, 293 Third Ave., btw. 22nd and 23rd Sts.; (646) 649-2389; thebluebellcafenyc.com; Subway: 6 to 23rd St.; $–$$;

Country Cafe. This little rustic cafe is a fresh breath of country air amid the characterless apartment complexes east of Gramercy Park. The reasonably priced bistro menu has a few high points, with a solid roster of burgers, salads (tuna niçoise, roasted beets), and soups, but this is really more a happy neighborhood spot with a peaceful vibe. The straightforward entrees might be a chicken and vegetable crock pie with a pastry lid or a hearty beef bourguignon or a maple-braised pork shank. A grilled cheese sandwich here comes with gruyère cheese, honey-smoked ham, and caramelized onions. If you're an early riser, you can order up a traditional country breakfast and sip a cup of coffee at a leisurely pace. It's that kind of neighborly place.

Enoteca i Trulli, 122 E. 27th St., btw. Park and Lexington Aves.; (646) 649-2389; itrulli .com; Subway: 6 to 23rd St.; Italian Wine Bar; $$. Although we've had some disjointed meals of late at the mother ship next door, i Trulli, this  little *enoteca* is well worth a stop. It's a sweet spot to sample a flight of carefully curated Italian varietals at the marble-topped bar or do a little grazing on the foods of Puglia. The menu features house-marinated olives, platters of *affettati,* including Calabrese salami and prosciutto di Parma, and some interesting bruschetta (fava bean puree with pecorino; asparagus and egg salad; chicken liver pâté). On Sunday, the *enoteca* has a list of half-priced wines.

Forcella Pizza, 377 Park Ave. S., btw. 26th and 27th Sts.; (212) 448-1116; forcellaeatery.com; Subway: 6 to 28th St.; Pizza; $$. It takes about 2 minutes to crank out a perfect pizza in the Naples-made wood-fired brick ovens of Forcella Pizza. Forcella is one of the newest traditional Neapolitan-style pizzerias to hit town, with a pizza master in Giulio Adriani at the helm. Forcella may be the new kid in town—with a non–Olde Italy decor that is sleekly a la mode—but its pizza technique is strictly old school. What you get is simple and simply

fantastic: chewy crust, bright and piquant tomato sauce, mozz with a whisper of heat. The pizzeria's flagship location is located at 334 Bowery (btw. Bond and E. 3rd Sts.; 212-466-3300).

Juni, 12 E. 31st St., btw. 5th and Madison Aves.; (212) 995-8599; juninyc.com; Subway: 6 to 33rd St.; New American; $$. Although officially part of the trendy new NoMad neighborhood, Juni just nicks the edges on an off-the-beaten-path street, if one can even be off the beaten track in Manhattan anymore. It's set in the small but gracious confines of the Hotel Chandler—bet you didn't even know that such an animal existed in the city. To add to the puzzle, consider that Juni's highly regarded chef, Shaun Hergatt, was last seen cooking up a storm at SHO, his sort-of-eponymous restaurant located in another strangely off-the-radar pocket of Manhattan, the recession- and storm-battered Financial District, without so much as a sign on the window. Then SHO, well, disappeared. Here Hergatt emerges again, cool as a cucumber in a coolly bland room, doing wondrous things with the food on your plate in a slightly out-of-the-way neighborhood in a slightly under-the-radar hotel. Well, if it's a dream, hope you don't wake up, 'cause Hergatt may be doing some of the best cooking in the city. It's food so lovely and easy to love that it belies the work it took to make it all seem so effort- less. A constantly evolving menu of contemporary American dishes shows off Hergatt's continued love of high fusion. On a recent visit, we dined on salmon so exquisitely tender that it did a slo-mo dissolve on the tongue. Glazed beef cheek came with parsnip puree. Even the fresh salads are masterworks of flavor and balance. Don't let the civilized but vapid look of the place keep you away—even with plush carpeting, Champagne banquettes, and creamy vaulted ceilings, Juni has the feel of a luxe dentist's office. But with food this good, does it matter?

Riverpark, 450 E. 29th St., btw. First Ave. and the East River; (212) 481-7372; riverparknyc.com; Subway: 6 to 28th St.; New American;

$$$$. New Yorkers know a thing or two about space, or the lack of it, so rooms as expansive as these are not only embraced but practically become medicinal balm for cubiclized Manhattanites. Set on the bottom floor of a sleek glass-and-steel NYU bioscience complex, Riverpark is overseen by *Top Chef* Tom Colicchio and Executive Chef Sisha Ortúzar, and it's quite a spread, with a large outdoor terrace overlooking the East River and soaring ceilings inside. Running along the outer edge of the plaza is a garden they call the Farm, and it feels like the urban gentry have landed. On a summer visit rows of Sungold cherry tomatoes, Brandywine heirloom tomatoes, Fairy Tale baby eggplants, peppers, okra, you name it, were preening for the sun as helicopters zoomed above and traffic buzzed below. Inside, the luxury of space makes for a wonderfully serene experience—even the restaurant floor, a type of composite granite, is so rubbery that dropped silverware barely makes a clang. The modern American menu is seasonal and local, prepared with produce straight from the Farm and farmers elsewhere. When the weather's nice, opt for a seat on the outdoor terrace—hard to believe on an island surrounded by water that so few places have great water views. Riverpark is one of them.

Sakagura, 211 E. 43rd St., B1F, near Third Ave.; (212) 953-7253; sakagura.com; Subway: 4, 5, 6 to 42nd St./Grand Central; Japanese Soba; $$. First off, many make the mistake (including yours truly) of going into Totto Soba, the Japanese soba joint that sits streetside—although its handmade soba, yakitori, and *donburi* rice bowls are actually quite good. But Sakagura is reached by entering the lobby at 211 E. 43rd St. and following signs around, down, and down again into what appears to be the subterranean basement of the office tower. Open the door into an enchanting, traditional Japanese *izakaya,* with a full menu of homemade soba (buckwheat) noodles, yakitori, sushi, and *donburi*— and some 200 varieties of sake imported from Japan. It's a sake lover's dream, in fact, with a long wooden bar lined with sake bottles and a special thermostatically controlled sake refrigerator. Come for lunch

for the special soba sets, tasting courses, and bento boxes, where you can sample an assortment of pickled Japanese appetizers, salads, sashimi, soba noodles, tempura, and sashimi. Complement your meal with a glass of chilled sake or belly up to the bar, where certified "sake advisors" lead you through sake tastings.

Second Avenue Deli, 162 E. 33rd St., btw. Lexington and Third Aves.; (212) 689-9000; 2ndavedeli.com; Subway: 6 to 33rd St.; Deli; $$. One of the last of the red-hot delis still standing in Manhattan, the Second Avenue Deli is, alas, no longer on Second Avenue (in its place is a Chase bank); in fact, it's tucked off of Third Avenue on a nondescript street on the fringes of Curry Hill. Nor is this 65-seat kosher deli anywhere near the size it was in its original location, when it grew from a 10-seat luncheonette (circa 1954) to a 128-seat neighborhood fixture. (A newer location on the Upper East Side, at 1442 First Ave., is bigger.) Size, schmize: It matters little when you breathe in the aroma of matzoh ball soup and see the classic deli salads aligned in the dairy case. The old-fashioned tile floor is here, as is the Hebrew-style lettering of 2NDAVEDELI on the frosted glass throughout. Stuffed sandwiches—pastrami, corned beef, brisket—remain a challenge to wrap your jaws around, and that matzoh ball soup is just like you like it.

Wolfgang's Steakhouse, 4 Park Ave. at 33rd St.; (212) 889-3369; wolfgangssteakhouse.net; Subway: 6 to 33rd St.; Steak House; $$$–$$$$. Wolfgang Zwiener, a waiter at Peter Luger's in Williamsburg for 40 years, opened his eponymous fine steak house in this space in 2004. Since then, the franchise has mushroomed to six (including locations in Waikiki, Beverly Hills, and Miami), but not one can claim a space as sublime as this. You dine in the shadows of flickering candlelight beneath vaulted terra-cotta tiles crafted in 1912 by Rafael Guastavino for a very, very rich member of a tribe known as Vanderbilt, who built a posh hotel here back in the Gilded Age. The Wolfgang steak house is in the Vanderbilt's ground-level "crypt" and the former hotel drinking hole, the Della Robbia Bar, is embellished not only with Guastavino tile but decorative ceramics from Rookwood Pottery. Today, in Gilded Age II, patrons swarm to Wolfgang's for the buttery sliced porterhouse made famous at Peter Luger's, as well as a roundelay of exquisitely grilled meats. Yes, you can get a lobster or two, or grilled fish, or the typical steakhouse shrimp cocktail, but this is a chophouse, dear readers. And with candlelight playing on those century-old tiles, it's got Olde New York spirits to boot.

Landmarks & Old-School Faves

Four Seasons, 99 E. 52nd St., at Park Ave.; (212) 754-9494; fourseasonsrestaurant.com; Subway: E, V to 53rd St; New American; $$$$. Few restaurants feel as fully New York as this smart, assured ode to classic minimalism. Designed by architect Philip Johnson to fully integrate with the Seagram Building, the Four Seasons has long been a power hot spot, a stage set for moguls and media titans. The restaurant has two main rooms. With tables set around a pool wrapped in Cararra marble and 20-foot ceilings, the Pool Room mixes "moxie and restraint," in the words of architect Allan Greenberg. It's pretty swelle-gant, with four towering trees and massive floor-to-ceiling windows shadowed by shimmering curtains of aluminum chains. The Grill Room is equally impressive, a lunchtime powerhouse with 20-foot ceilings and walls paneled in walnut. Expect to pony up top dollar for food and drink—and the New American food is quite good, blessedly—but what you're really paying for is time spent in a romantically retro version of moneyed Manhattan.

Grand Central Oyster Bar, Lower Level, Grand Central Station; (212) 490-6650; oysterbarny.com; Subway: S, 4, 5, 6 to Grand

With spiffy renovations to its 1950s-era interiors expected to be completed in 2014, the United Nations is a fascinating place to tour. If renovations to the UN's Delegates' Dining Room have been finished by the time of your visit, be sure to reserve a spot. The buffet-style food may not be haute cuisine, but each week the kitchen cooks a different international cuisine, and the setting—with dazzling floor-to-ceiling East River views and a colorful assortment of world citizens chattering about you—makes this a memorable experience.

Central/42nd St.; Seafood; $$$–$$$$. In a space as inspiring as this, the food doesn't have to work that hard, right? Wrong. This is New York City, bub. Some people, curmudgeons and otherwise, grouse that the Oyster Bar is overpriced and underperforming in the food department. We know few locals who actually eat in the main restaurant anymore, in fact, although we love the retro feel of the old saloon and the red-checkered tablecloths, and the fresh oysters at the Oyster Bar are sublime. The beautiful landmark space alone is a must-see. Opened in 1913, the Oyster Bar sprawls beneath the exposed vaulted tile ceiling created by Rafael Guastavino. It's breathtaking, and a 2014 restoration has given the century-old tiles a gleaming fresh polish. So here's your strategy for dining in the Grand Central Oyster Bar: Have lunch with the locals at one of the Oyster Bar counters or in the saloon. Stick to the basics, like samplings from the raw bar; one of the excellent soups, stews, or pan-roasts; or the catch of the day simply prepared.

La Grenouille, 3 E. 52nd St., btw. Fifth and Madison Aves.; (212) 752-1495; la-grenouille.com; Subway: E, V to 53rd St; French;

$$$$. Lutèce and La Côte Basque have departed, but this flower-filled bastion of classic French cuisine still stands, a beautiful relic from the early 1960s, when fancy French dining rooms were the height of chic. This is where you still whisper of *velouté* (here a yellow tomato bisque with aioli), creamy *quenelles* (here a pike Lyonnaise with caviar), Grand Marnier soufflés, *tartes, fromage.* The classics are ably represented, from a lightly grilled Dover sole to the *poulet rôti* (roast chicken) to the beef tournedos, in a swoony room where table lamps give off an amber glow. It's a big-ticket night out, no doubt, but this grande dame still rocks.

Specialty Stores, Markets & Producers

Ess-a-Bagel, 831 Third Ave., btw. 50th and 51st Sts.; (212) 980-1010; ess-a-bagel.com; Subway: 6 to 51st St. or E, M to Lexington Ave./53rd St.; Bagels. Now that the chewy behemoths of H&H are fading into the sunset, this may be the borough's pre-eminent bagel factory, making hand-rolled bagels that *New York* magazine says "rank among the city's best." This store, along with the original Ess-a-Bagel, which opened in 1976 on First Avenue and 21st Street (212-260-2252), offers bagels in all flavors along with the works: spreads, smoked fish, deli meats, cheeses, and salads.

Grand Central Dining Concourse, Lower Level, Grand Central Station; Subway: S, 4, 5, 6 to Grand Central/42nd St.; Food Arcade. Amid the hurly-burly of commuters swarming in and out of Grand Central is this terrific assortment of food vendors, with plenty of seating in the center of the concourse. Three spots—**Two Boots** (pizza and Cajun food), **Shake Shack** (hamburgers), and **Junior's** (classic deli)—even offer their own sit-down table-service areas. We highly recommend a stop if you're in the Grand Central area around lunchtime—it's a quality assemblage of some of the city's best food vendors, including **Hale and Hearty Soups** (212-983-2845), **Mendy's Kosher Delicatessen and Dairy** (212-856-9399), **Magnolia Bakery** (212-682-3588), **Thai Toon** (212-883-0400), and **Manhattan Chili Company** (212-682-6644). The **Grand Central Oyster Bar** (212-856-9399) is just across a hallway, with a little takeout window where you can order up excellent seafood soups (New England and Manhattan clam chowder; Maryland crab; rock shrimp and corn), po' boys, and more.

Grand Central Market, Grand Central Station, Lexington Ave. entrance; grandcentralterminal.com/market; Subway: S, 4, 5, 6 to Grand Central/42nd St.; Food Arcade. This fine little upscale market was designed to give Grand Central commuters a convenient place to buy a full roster of dinner fixings or simply select from a full roster of prepared dishes—dinner to go, soup to nuts. But we know plenty of locals for whom this is a go-to shopping stop. Grand Central Market has two excellent seafood markets in **Wild Edibles** (212-687-4255) and **Pescatore Seafood Co.** (212-557-4466), both offering impeccably fresh (if pricey) selections of fish, shellfish, caviar, smoked fish, and prepared seafood dishes. The ever-popular **Murray's Cheese** (212-922-1540) sells a smart selection of cheeses, dairy, *salumi,* and crackers. **Ceriello** (212-972-4266), a high-end butcher shop, has prime-aged beef, organic poultry, Italian sausages, prepared foods, dry pasta, and pasta sauces. Artisanal breads are sold at **Eli Zabar's Bakery** (646-503-3534). Vendors selling fresh vegetables, fruits, and packaged nuts bookend the market. If you don't feel like cooking at all, go directly to **Dishes** (212-370-5511), for wonderful gourmet prepared foods. The market is right next door to **Grande Harvest Wines** (Graybar Passage; 212-682-5855), where you can pick out a nice wine complement.

L. Simchick & Co. Meats, 988 First Ave., btw. 54th and 55th Sts.; (212) 888-2299; lsimchick.com; Subway: 6 to 51st St.; Butcher.

DINING THE DEPARTMENT STORES

In 2012, visitors spent $7.4 billion on dining out in New York City. That number was only bested by hotel spending (no surprise at $10 billion) and shopping (a whopping $8 billion!). It would appear, then, that mixing shopping and dining is a recipe for pure gold. Little wonder that the classic ladies-who-lunch tearooms tucked inside Manhattan's illustrious department stores have morphed into real dining destinations. The newest is **Stella 34 Trattoria** at Macy's Herald Square, serving pizzas made from wood-burning ovens and house-made pasta. Even better: The restaurant's takeout counter is the first place in the US to serve gelato from Florence, Italy's famed Vivoli. For winner of most restaurants in a store, Bloomingdale's takes the prize hands down, with six eateries, including a branch of **Magnolia Bakery,** the stalwart **40 Carrots** (more grab-and-go than table dining, but the tunafish has rejuvenated shoppers for years), and the very elegant **Le Train Bleu,** a replica of a 19th-century French dining car. At Saks, **Cafe SFA,** on the store's eighth floor, serves a limited menu of nutritious soups, salads, and sandwiches along with restorative views of St. Patrick's Cathedral. The best of the bunch? We say it's a toss-up between **Goodman's** at Bergdorf-Goodman and **Fred's** of Barney's—we'd gladly go out of our way to lunch at either. Bergdorf's signature restaurant, **BG,** is fancier, with Central Park views and a design by Kelly Wearstler, but our heart is with Goodman's, even if it's been relegated to the basement. Goodman's sweet pea soup alone will warm the cockles of your acquisitive heart. Fred's of Barney's feeds its chic clientele with a menu of modern Italian fare.

In a neighborhood where the local butcher has gone the way of the dodo bird, L. Simchick is a terrific, full-service source for fresh meat and poultry. You can also buy such prepared foods as roast chicken, chicken pot pie, lasagna, and beef brisket; oven-ready meals like meat loaf, stuffed pork chops, and fruited pork roast; not to mention deli meats, meat sauces, vegetable sides and salads, and homemade soups.

Pisacane Seafood, 940 First Ave., btw. 51st and 52nd Sts.; (212) 758-1525; pisacanefishandseafood.com; Subway: 6 to 51st St.; Fish Market. This longtime fishmonger has been selling wholesale and retail fish and seafood for more than 50 years. You don't last that long in the seafood trade if you aren't selling fresh, quality goods.

Ralph's Famous Italian Ices, 144 E. 24th St., near Lexington Ave.; (212) 533-3333; ralphsices.com; Subway: 6 to 23rd St.; Italian Ices. It's eternal summertime at Ralph's, where old-fashioned Italian ices are dispensed from this window storefront. The Manhattan location of Ralph's opened in 2011, dispensing many of the flavors that Grandpa Ralph Silvestro first made on Staten Island in 1928. But many more have been conjured up since, and now the menu offers some 100 flavors for water ices and creme ices (sherbets). Flavors for water ices include black raspberry, bubble gum, and watermelon. Flavors for creme ices are more extensive, with chocolate peanut butter, strawberry cheesecake, cannoli, and cherry jubilee on the roster.

Sherry-Lehman Wine & Spirits, 505 Park Ave., at 59th St.; (212) 838-7500; sherry-lehmann.com; Subway: N, R, 4, 5, 6 to 59th St.; Wine Shop. In business for nearly 80 years, this is one of the city's premier wine shops, with excellent tastings and plenty of quality quaffs at both the high and low end of the price range. It's been offering a sensational low-priced French sparkling wine, Boyer Brut, since the 1940s—and selling plenty of it; a bottle of Boyer bubbly currently goes for $10.95.

Uptown

Upper East Side & Carnegie Hill

The traditional nesting site for society bluebloods and titled Europeans, the Upper East Side still entertains a moneyed class with high-end shops and designer boutiques. No, the Upper East Side may not be the top culinary district in Manhattan, but it has plenty of clubby boîtes to feed the ladies-who-lunch crowd, cashmere-clad gossip girls, and those quasi-continental types quaintly known as jet-setters. It's also a grand place to feed your head: The Upper East Side is home to Museum Mile, that magnificent stretch of art and culture that is upper Fifth Avenue. It's a lineup of some of the greatest collections of art on the planet, cultural institutions such as the Guggenheim, the Frick, the Metropolitan Museum of Art, the Museum of the City of New York, and the Cooper-Hewitt National Museum of Design. The neighborhood also has a glorious front yard: Central Park, which follows Fifth Avenue from 60th Street to 110th Street, a 2½-mile swath of shady green.

 Foodie Faves

Daniel, 60 E. 65th St., at Park Ave.; (212) 288-0033; danielnyc .com; Subway: N, R to Fifth Ave.; French; $$$$. For our money, this, the flagship restaurant of Chef Daniel Boulud, is the most beautiful dining room in all of Manhattan. You enter, like Cinderella at the ball, at the top of a short flight of stairs. Facing you at the other end is a neo-classical dining room framed by pillars in creamy tones and luminescent panels. The landmark space was given a contemporary overhaul by restaurant designer Adam Tihany in 2008. Eighteen-foot ceilings are lit by custom chandeliers crafted with Limoges tiles from the legendary porcelain company Bernardaud. Swirls of brown and tan in the lush carpet mimic the swirling stars that are the restaurant motif throughout. The laser attention to detail has been carried over to the plate, where the seasonal French food reaches for the stars—and is very often transcendent. Ingredients have been meticulously sourced: Sea scallops come with a crust of Sicilian pistachios and licorice; a divine butter-poached jade tiger abalone is prepared with a sake beurre blanc. Wild Alaskan red king salmon is baked in clay, and a grilled swordfish comes with sweet Georgia stewed corn. Some folks—*Times* critic Pete Wells, for one—have lamented an unnecessary complexity in spots and what Wells called the intrusion of too many "dollhouse garnishes." If we have a complaint, it's a slight underseasoning. (Maybe our taste buds have been corrupted by all those nacho cheese chips, but would it hurt some of these high-end joints to put salt and pepper on the table?) Ultimately, is a visit to Daniel worth the considerable price tag? We say: Oh *yeah*. Even if it's only once, a meal at Daniel is a food experience you don't want to miss. And may we say that we found the service at Daniel to be as gracious as if we were the king of Siam. Note that you can dine a la carte in the more casual bar area; many regulars request seating in the bar's clubby upper lounge, where cheese steward Pascal has been taking exceptional care of diners for years.

E.A.T., 1064 Madison Ave., btw. 80th and 81st Sts.; (212) 772-0022; elizabar.com; Subway: 6 to 77th St./Lexington Ave.; New

American; $$–$$$. The Upper East Side is Eli Zabar's world, and welcome to it. This was Zabar's first business foray after breaking away from the family business: Zabar's, the Upper West Side home of sublime smoked fish and much more. E.A.T. is part market but mostly cafe (140 seats), with a menu reflecting Eli Zabar's unerring feel for the culinary zeitgeist and passion for thoughtfully made food. It's gourmet comfort food (including traditional Jewish deli fixings) fashioned with meticulously sourced ingredients and built for maximum flavor. E.A.T. bustles all day long with diners sampling Dagwood-size sandwiches on Zabar's artisanal breads, smoked fish, quiche, salads, and desserts. The house-made soups are truly excellent, from chicken vegetable to matzoh ball to Tuscan vegetable. The informal cafe environment may make E.A.T. a more natural choice for breakfast and lunch, although the dinner menu expands to include well-executed American standards like roast chicken, meat loaf, and pot roast as well as grilled fish and a smattering of pasta entrees.

Farinella Italian Bakery, Pizza & Panini, 1132 Lexington Ave., btw. 78th and 79th Sts.; (212) 327-2702; farinellabakery.com; Subway: 6 to 77th St./Lexington Ave.;

Pizza; $. This small storefront with a sprinkling of tables sells some of our favorite pizza in the city. The pizza master is a former hip-hop artist from Naples who sells his pizza by the square slice, or Roman style, in 4-foot-long palams or half-palams (a half-palam has about eight square slices). The thin-crust pizza is built with high-quality (and often organic) ingredients, with the perfect balance of sea salt and extra-virgin olive oil. We love the primavera pizza with zucchini, mushrooms, and fresh mozzarella, but it's all good. Farinella also bakes loaves of rustic bread and calzone.

Maison Kayser/Eric Kayser Artisan Boulanger, 1294 Third Ave., at 74th St.; (212) 744-3100; maison-kayser-usa.com;

Noshing in Central Park

An undulating sprawl of 840 acres, Central Park separates the Upper West Side from the Upper East Side, bookended by the high-rises of Midtown to the south and Harlem to the north. It's Manhattan's all-purpose playground. It's also a fine place to relax and defuse, and, when the weather's nice, pack a park picnic. You can find excellent fixings from gourmet markets like **Zabar's** (see p. 149; zabars.com), although a number of high-end restaurants and hotel eateries offer seasonal picnic boxes. From April to November the **Loeb Boathouse** (thecentralpark boathouse.com) opens up its full-service restaurant overlooking the Central Park Lake as well as a cafe/takeout (burgers, french fries, salads) and an outdoor bar. (You can rent a boat here as well.) The boathouse complex and lake are reached via the Fifth Avenue/72nd Street park entrance. Other snack bars/lunch spots in the park can be found at the Sheep Meadow (**Pain Quotidien,** near 69th St.), the Conservatory Water Boat Pond, Columbus Circle, the Ballplayers House at Heckscher Ballfields, and the Central Park Zoo (centralparkzoo.com), where the **Dancing Crane Cafe** has indoor and outdoor seating and serves burgers, hot dogs, pizzas, and sandwiches.

Subway: 6 to 77th St./Lexington Ave.; Bakery/French; $$. French master baker Eric Kayser has invaded New York with his chemical-yeast-free leavened breads and much, much more. This, his first American outpost (two more will be open at press time), is both a boulangerie/patisserie and a full-service, 100-seat cafe, served by a waitstaff in saucy French stripes. Kayser's celebrated breads include *pains aromatiques* (fig bread, olive bread, turmeric bread), *pains de mie* (chocolate loaf, apple-cinnamon, and maple-syrup loaf), croissants, and brioche. The interesting menu at the cafe takes full advantage of those wonderful breads with a range of tartines (sourdough baguettes), including a chicken tartine with artichoke and green olive tapenade, and a crab and avocado tartine. Hearty entrees include a rich boeuf bourguignon and a vegetable *cocotte,* lush with sweet peas, potatoes, artichoke, asparagus, carrots, and onion.

Maya, 1191 First Ave., btw. 64th and 65th Sts.; (212) 585-1818; richardsandoval.com/mayany; Subway: N, R, 4, 5, 6 to 59th St./ Lexington Ave.; Mexican; $$$. We love Maya, a "Modern Mexican" restaurant in a sprawling, low-ceilinged Upper East Side space. Okay, the room is somewhat generic, even though adobe-hued leather banquettes and carved wooden chairs spruce it up a bit, but no matter. What we love about Maya is Chef Richard Sandoval's food. Sandoval lets the ingredients lead, and the result is fresh, unfussy, and utterly delicious. You probably will, and should, start with a seasonal fruit drink known as *agua fresca,* or go full-tilt with a house margarita: a Mercado, say, with jalapeño-infused Agavales tequila with passion fruit, or a Yucatan, Agavales blanco infused with habañero and blood orange. The made-to-order guacamole is state of the art—you can choose the basic (excellent) or go rogue with spicy crab guacamole, bacon guacamole, or tuna tartare guacamole. The wild-mushroom flatbread is sprinkled with goat cheese, a black-bean puree, and caramelized onions, and the quesadilla is topped with squash blossoms and chile poblano. A smoked-brisket taco with creamy cole slaw is a mashup that really works. But even those weary of mashups will be happy; the kitchen does straightforward—a simple grilled salmon on a bed of roasted zucchini and spinach, say—just fine and dandy.

San Matteo Pizza, 1739 Second Ave., at 90th St.; (212) 426-6943; sanmatteopanuozzo.com; Subway: 6 to 86th St. or 96th St.; Pizza; $$. Home to what the *New York Times* praised as "tender, crisp and flavorful" Neapolitan-style pizzas, not to mention calzone, salads, and a handful of gnocchi and pasta dishes, San Matteo made its bones on its *panuozzo*, a Southern Italian specialty (Campania region) that's a delicious fusion of pizza and panini, where the dough is baked, filled and then toasted. The result is a bulging sandwich, more or less, all brittle, charred crust on the outside, chewy moistness on the inside. The *panuozzo* comes with your choice of fillings, like prosciutto, bufala mozzarella, and roast peppers; homemade mozzarella, sausage, and broccoli rabe; or mozzarella, eggplant, and tomato sauce. At press time it was reported that San Matteo was opening a downtown location in the East Village.

Landmarks & Old-School Faves

The Carlyle/Bemelmans Bar, In the Carlyle Hotel, 35 E. 76th St., at Madison Ave.; (212) 570-7192; thecarlyle.com; Subway: 6 to 77th St./Lexington Ave.; American/Continental; $$$–$$$$. The Carlyle feels like a royal drawing room, where suited maitre d's emerge from behind swooping drapes and diners settle into velvet banquettes the color of cognac. It's a pretty starchy place, really—at these prices we could be sampling the sun and the stars at Daniel, nearby. (How about $75 for a lunch of Dover sole, prepared tableside?) But baby, that old-school glamour is fun to swaddle yourself in for a few hours. (Tip: It's a great deal during Restaurant Week!) The throwback menu could be described as the upper-rung "gout diet"—foie gras, beef Wellington, beef tournedos Rossini, lobster Thermidor, all delicious—but it also offers plenty of lighter choices for the social X-ray set, including a flavorful Carlyle lobster bisque with tomato and tarragon and a raft of salads, including niçoise, cobb, and Greek. Next door enchantment reigns at Bemelmans Bar, wrapped in the ethereal murals by Ludwig Bemelmans (creator of the Madeline children's books) and topped with a ceiling of gold leaf. This is a wonderful place to have a cocktail and sample a snappy bar menu that includes mini burgers, lobster mac 'n' cheese, cheese platters, and more. Keep in mind that the witching hour is 9:30 p.m., when everyone in the bar must pony up a $30 cover ($15 if you're sitting at the bar) for the evening's musical accompaniment. Just off Bemelmans Bar is a storybook tea room where English tea is a civilized afternoon repast.

Heidelberg Restaurant, 1648 Second Ave., btw. 85th and 86th Sts.; (212) 628-2332; heidelbergrestaurant.com; Subway: 4, 5, 6 to 86th St./Lexington Ave; German; $$. It's eternal Oktoberfest at this retro German restaurant, which has been serving food since 1936 and is one of the last surviving Yorkville eateries in what used to be a vibrant German enclave on the Upper East Side. With waitresses clad in traditional German garb, and a *Biergarten* downstairs serving frothy German beer in liter mugs and two-liter *stiefels* (boots), Heidelberg lays the Bavarian shtick on thick. Call it corny; dismiss it as theme-parky— just don't diss the food until you try it. Heidelberg is sure-footed in preparing German specialties like sauerbraten, spinach strudel, wiener schnitzel, and goulash. The atmosphere is fun and fizzy, so order up a boot of beer and join the oom-pah-pah celebration.

Lexington Candy Shop Luncheonette, 1226 Lexington Ave., at 83rd St.; (212) 288-0057; Subway: 4, 5, 6 to 86th St.; Luncheonette; $. They sure don't make 'em anymore like this fabled circa-1925 luncheonette, where you can sit on a chrome-rimmed stool at the soda fountain and order an old-fashioned New York egg cream. The Lexington Candy Shop hasn't been "done" to look vintage; it *is* vintage, and hurrah that at least one little piece of Upper Manhattan managed to dodge gentrification over the years. The menu is classic soda-jerk cuisine: milk shakes made with "super premium" Bassett's ice cream; malteds and fresh lemonade; grilled-cheese, tuna melts, BLTs, and club sandwiches; full breakfasts including pancakes, french toast, and egg sandwiches.

Manhattan's Best Hotel Restaurants

In Manhattan, the moldy old cliché of tired, uninspired hotel dining has been turned on its head. These days, some of the city's most innovative chefs have set up shop in hotels all over the city. Here are a few of the best, from downtown to uptown.

CO-OP Food & Drink, Hotel Rivington (107 Rivington St.; co-oprestaurant.com). Executive Chef James London's Southern roots—combined with his passion for Japanese food—makes for an inventive "East meets South" menu at this Lower East Side brasserie on the first floor of the Hotel Rivington.

The Breslin & John Dory, Ace Hotel (20 W. 29th St.; ace hotel.com/newyork). British Chef April Bloomfield shows she can cook just about anything at her two Ace Hotel restaurants: the meat-heavy Breslin and the seafood-centric John Dory.

NoMad, NoMad Hotel (1170 Broadway; thenomadhotel.com). It's a sumptuous stage set, the kind of place the Addams Family would call home if they had good taste. But with Daniel Humm's food firing on all cylinders, this is serious dining as well.

Jean-Georges, Trump Hotel Central Park (1 Central Park West; jean-georges.com). Some call it perfection on earth, and few would disagree that the food at Vongerichten's flagship restaurant is righteously magnificent.

Cafe Boulud, Hotel Surrey (20 E. 76th St.; cafeboulud.com). In the equally elegant Surrey Hotel, this dining room of understated elegance manages to serve top-flight cuisine and be a proper neighborhood joint in the bargain.

Eli's Manhattan/TASTE, 1411 Third Ave., at 80th St.; (212) 717-8100; elizabar.com; Subway: 6 to 77th St./Lexington Ave.; **Specialty Market/Cafe.** A warren of rooms filled with gourmet foods, produce, meats and seafood, coffees, artisanal breads, exotica sourced from all over the world—even magazines, newspapers, and party paraphernalia—this two-level marketplace is foodie ambrosia. You can sample many of Eli Zabar's greatest hits on the weekdays at the self-serve TASTE cafe, including a lineup of his fabulous soups, from chicken vegetable to Tuscan peasant, as well as sandwiches, salads, and hearty mains like lasagna. Prices are at the high end, but the quality is impeccable, and everything is fresh and flavorful. TASTE becomes a full-service dinner spot at night, with a menu that might include an olive-oil-poached halibut with artichokes and brussels sprouts or lamb shank with polenta.

Eli's Vinegar Factory, 431 E. 91st St., btw. First and York Aves.; (212) 987-0885; elizabar.com; Subway: 4, 5, 6 to 86th or 96th St.; **Specialty Market.** This Carnegie Hill warehouse is 9,000 square feet of top-quality food goods, produce, meats, seafoods, breads—you name it, it's here. The prepared foods section is one of the city's best, with savory, freshly made meats, entrees, pastas, and soups mostly made on the premises and good to go (you can also nosh in a little cafe). A rooftop greenhouse ensures that plenty of vegetables and herbs are fresh-picked.

FP Patisserie, 1293 Third Ave., at 74th St.; (212) 717-5252; payard.com; Subway: 6 to 77th St./Lexington Ave.; **Bakery/Patisserie.** James Beard Award–winning pastry chef François Payard may not have invented *macarons,* but he certainly helped start the craze—now everybody and his mother has colored *macarons* on their patisserie menu. But Payard has taken it a step farther and in the process raised the bar on ice-cream sandwiches: His marry ice cream and *macarons,* with flavors like raspberry-pistachio and strawberry cheesecake. But Payard is also a master with chocolate, cakes, and cookies; I would move heaven and earth to keep a ready supply of his flourless chocolate walnut cookies in my home. No longer in its elegant flagship location on Lexington Avenue (with a much-missed full-service restaurant), Payard Patisserie & Cafe landed at this some-what sterile spot on Third Avenue. *Note:* Payard also has bakery/patis-serie locations at 1 W. 58th St., 210 Murray St., 116 W. Houston St., and 3 Columbus Circle.

La Maison du Chocolat, 1018 Madison Ave., at 78th St.; (212) 744-7117; lamaisonduchocolat.com; Subway: 6 to 77th St./Lexington Ave.; Chocolate. Ooh-la-la: This French chocolate boutique is da bomb. The first La Maison du Chocolat shop was opened by a master-craftsman chocolatier known as "the Wizard of Ganache" on the rue du Faubourg Saint-Honoré in Paris in 1977. La Maison du Chocolat today has shops all over the world, and this is the main store in Manhattan (La Maison du Chocolat also has locations at 30 Rockefeller Center, the Plaza Food Hall, and 63 Wall Street). The elegant, delicately made chocolates include signature ganaches, fruited chocolates, éclairs, *macarons,* and tartes.

Lobel's Prime Meats, 1096 Madison Ave., at 82nd St.; (212) 737-1372; lobels.com; Subway: 6 to 77th St./Lexington Ave. or 86th St.; Butcher. This storied family-owned butcher shop has been selling high-quality meats from this location for more than 50 years. The Lobel family sells dry-aged USDA high-Prime beef and Wagyu beef as well as Kurobuta and Berkshire pork, artisanal sausages, heritage meats, all-natural veal, lamb, and poultry, and heat-and-serve ribs, brisket, and other barbecued meats. In late 2012, the Lobel family opened a second location, Lobel's Kitchen, specializing in high-end take-out food, meats, and specialty items in the Trump Plaza apartment building (1030 Third Ave., at 61st St.; 212-317-0200).

The Plaza Food Hall, The Plaza Hotel, Concourse Level, 1 W. 59th St., at Central Park West; (212) 986-9260; theplazany.com; Subway: N, R to Fifth Ave.; Food Arcade. In a chic space of gleaming marble and polished tile, this European-style food court on the basement level of the Plaza Hotel is an elegant stop for an eat-in or takeout gourmet lunch. The selection of food vendors is solid and includes Luke's Lobster (famed for its lobster rolls); the artisanal breads of Pain d'Avignon; Sushi of Gari (some say producing the best sushi in Manhattan); the ganaches of La Maison du Chocolat, the *macarons* of Payard (FP Patisserie), and the cupcakes of Billy's Bakery. Food porn of the highest order.

Two Little Red Hens, 1652 Second Ave., at 86th St.; (212) 452-0476; twolittleredhens.com; Subway: 4, 5, 6 to 86th St./Lexington Ave.; Bakery.  Dreamy cakes of all flavors, fillings, and frostings are the specialty of this boutique bakery in Yorkville. Its cupcakes are some of the city's best—including red velvet, gingerbread, marble (made with a "swirl   of fudge and Swiss vanilla buttercream"), and our favorite, banana peanut butter.

Upper West Side & Harlem

Home to folks and families in a range of ethnicities and religions, the Upper West Side has an egalitarian feel. It's a beautiful, sprawling, largely residential neighborhood, bracketed by Central Park on its eastern flank and the sparkling Hudson River to the west. Luxury pre-war apartment buildings stretch along the neighborhood's outer edges (Central Park West, Riverside Drive), and brawny brownstones fill the cross streets running east and west. Most of the restaurants are congregated along Broadway, a four-lane ribbon of asphalt that slices through the center of the neighborhood. Farther uptown, Harlem stretches east and west above Central Park. The surprising thing about this traditional African-American enclave is the lack of high-rises; there's a lot of blue sky in Harlem. There's a lot of excitement on the restaurant scene as well, with a growing number of eateries popping up in pockets around Lenox Avenue and Frederick Douglass Boulevard.

Foodie Faves

Bar Boulud, 1900 Broadway, btw. 63rd and 64th Sts.; (212) 595-0303; barboulud.com/nyc; Subway: 1 to 64th St.; French Country;

$$$–$$$$. Home to Daniel Boulud's seasonal riffs on French country classics, Bar Boulud has a buzzing, more casual feel than its starchier Upper East Side counterparts. At night the place practically vibrates with electric energy; this is one happy crowd. Maybe they're on their way to a performance at Lincoln Center, practically across the street, or maybe they're here for a post-concert bite. Maybe they've come, as we do, for the spot-on bistro food, like a velvety hanger steak braised in red wine or the seared sea scallops in an almond vermouth broth. Bar Boulud specializes in classic nose-to-tail charcuterie; order up some finely sliced *jambon* or a plate of country pâtés and terrines from Parisian charcutier Gilles Verot—or go whole hog with a tasting platter. The long, tunnel-like space (designed to resemble a wine cavern) may lack the classic proportions of the Boulud flagship, Daniel, or the clubby intimacy of the Surrey Hotel location, Cafe Boulud. But mirrored walls and high ceilings add to the illusion of more space, and the fizziness is contagious, making a meal here feel like a celebration.

Cafe Luxembourg, 200 W. 70th St., btw. Amsterdam and West End Aves.; (212) 873-7411; cafeluxembourg.com; Subway: 1, 2, 3 to 72nd St./Broadway; New American/French Bistro; $$–$$$. It's barely mentioned in the press anymore, the fanfare of its 1983 opening long faded into the urban gestalt. But 30 years later, Cafe Luxembourg is still quietly sending out flawlessly prepared brasserie standards—*poulet rôti* (roast chicken), steak tartare, *moules-frites*—in a great-looking retro space, from the McNally brother who helped create the Odeon in Tribeca. Luxembourg in fact is something of an uptown Odeon, but less starry-eyed and more intimate. It, like many of the McNally brothers' creations, is an artful impersonation, here of a turn-of-the-century Parisian bistro, all antique mirrors, classic bistro tile floor, and red leather banquettes. The place looks great, and food-wise, it has long had its steps down. (Is this the "blueprint," as critic Hal Rubenstein once suggested, "for a faultless urban restaurant"?) Faux Parisian bistro, urban blueprint, whatever: More than anything, Luxembourg today feels like a genuine neighborhood joint.

Good Enough to Eat, 483 Amsterdam Ave., btw. 83rd and 84th Sts.; (212) 496-0163; goodenoughtoeat.com; Subway: 1 to 86th St.; American Comfort Food; $$. A country-style bastion of American comfort food, this restaurant has been serving Upper West Siders what's good for 'em since 1981. It's a menu crammed with wholesome all-American classics given a healthy, locavore spin. That would be house-made baked goods, hefty farmhouse breakfasts, and dishes like meat loaf, tuna melt, and mac 'n' cheese, with plenty of vegetarian entrees (the "vegetable mountain" is veggie stir-fry on steroids, served over brown sticky rice), salads, and soups.

Henry's, 2745 Broadway, at 105th St.; (212) 866-0600; henrysnyc .com; Subway: 1 to 103rd St.; American; $$. The very essence of a neighborhood restaurant, Henry's is located on a tree-shaded corner of Amsterdam Avenue, in a relatively peaceful stretch of urban Manhattan a few blocks south of the Cathedral of St. John the Divine. It's a sprawling, sunny spot serving American standards in a woody dining room with Arts and Crafts fixtures. Henry's does double duty as both a casual, inexpensive neighborhood eatery and the kind of special-occasion spot to which a student from nearby Columbia University might take the 'rents for a quite comfortable and (culinarily speaking) very reliable night out. The chops and steaks are quite good, the pastas (hand-cut pappardelle with Bolognese sauce; seafood tagiolini) delicious, and seasonal soups, salads, and appetizers perfectly satisfying. *Tip:* Week-end brunches can be busy.

Jean-Georges, 1 Central Park West, at 60th St.; (212) 299-3900; jean-georges.com; Subway: 1, A, B, C, D to 59th St./Broadway; Modern French; $$$$. In the riveting theater that is fine dining in New York, this Michelin-three-star room remains one of the greats.

Like fellow heavyweights Daniel and Per Se, it's the flagship restaurant of one of the world's super-chefs, in this case, Jean-Georges Vongerichten, whose quest for global domination rivals only that of Google. In spite of overseeing a culinary empire upon which the sun never sets, Jean-Georges and company keep the plates flawlessly spinning in this ultra-civilized stage set, located on the ground floor of the Trump Hotel Central Park. It's a virtuoso performance in every way, and if you can snag a reservation—and that's a big if—be prepared to be dazzled. (And if you can snag a seat at lunch, do so, because the two-course $38 prix-fixe is an excellent value.) The dinner prix-fixe and tasting menus lean heavily on seasonal, market-driven ingredients with a light and flavorful Asian bent. A lobster tartine is drizzled in a lemongrass and fenugreek broth, for example, and a crispy confit of suckling pig comes with rutabaga pudding. Just put yourself in Chef's capable hands, bring a tub of money, and prepare to stay a leisurely while to appreciate every exquisite bite. And gentlemen, don't forget your jackets.

Loi, 208 W. 70th St., near Amsterdam Ave.; (212) 875-8600; loirestaurant.com; Subway: 1, 2, 3 to 72nd St./Broadway; Greek; $$$–$$$$. Nouvelle Greek served in a crisply elegant space: It's a combination that's been packing them in ever since colorful and charismatic Chef Maria Loi hit town in the former Compass space in 2011. Loi, a cookbook author who once had her own cooking show in Greece (she's been called the "Martha Stewart of Greece"), takes a market-driven, health-minded approach to preparing the food of her native country. That means that butter is kept to a minimum, and fish, scented with fennel and leeks, more often than not comes grilled, sautéed, or baked in sea salt. Lamb might show up in a lean stew of Santorini tomatoes, potatoes, and onions, flavored with little more than Greek olive oil, garlic, and bay leaves. Vegetable sides are plentiful, from seasonal wild steamed greens to rainbow caulifower cooked in caramelized tomato sauce to roasted marinated beets. When she's not behind the stove, Chef Loi often takes a sweep through the restaurant dining rooms, spreading a little Greek sunshine.

Ouest, 2315 Broadway, at 84th St.; (212) 580-8700; ouestny.com; Subway: 1, 9 to 86th St.; American Bistro; $$$. This good-looking restaurant has a sexy retro sheen, with curvy red leather banquettes and ceilings up to there (you can dine at a table up on the mezzanine for optimum spying of the chattering crowds down below). Tom Valenti's American bistro has been hitting the pedal to the metal since Ouest opened in 2001, a testament to a winning formula of refined American classics served in a casually sophisticated setting. More than anything, though, this is a comfortable trough for grownups who appreciate the smart service and a menu that acknowledges, channels, and often transcends the great neighborhood joints of the Upper West Side past, like the Museum Cafe and Teacher's. You can go upscale or basic here, from porcini-crusted halibut with white-bean puree to simple grilled steaks or salmon. The food is fresh, seasonal, thoughtfully sourced, and inventive when it needs to be. If you're on the Upper West Side, Ouest is the place to be.

Patsy's Pizzeria, 2287 First Ave., at 118th St.; (212) 534-9783; thepatsyspizza.com; Subway: 6 to 116th St.; Pizza; $$. This 80-year-old landmark is a living relic from the days when East Harlem was an enclave for Italian immigrants. The classic coal-fired brick oven is still cooking up thin-crust pizza, some of the best in town, but the menu comprises a full complement of Italian specialties, from *zuppa di fagioli* and *linguine alle vongole* to chicken scarpariello or a hefty *bistecca* (steak).

Per Se, 10 Columbus Circle, at 60th St.; (212) 823-9335; perseny .com; Subway: A, B, C, D, 1 to Columbus Circle/59th St.; New

MANHATTAN'S BEST
MUSEUM RESTAURANTS

Some of the best food in Manhattan is found inside museums—
and we don't mean the 5,000-year-old bread found in the tombs
of Egyptian mummies. Here are some of our favorites.

**The Morgan Dining Room/Morgan Cafe at the Morgan
Library (225 Madison Ave.; themorgan.org).** You can't beat
breaking bread with the ghosts of turn-of-the-century one-per-
centers in the original Morgan family dining room. We also
love the light and airy museum cafe, in a glass atrium with lots
of greenery.

**Robert, Museum of Arts & Design (2 Columbus Circle;
robertnyc.com).** With a fizzy '60s pop palette and a creative
contemporary menu, Robert also has something you don't usu-
ally find at your corner pizzeria: dazzling views of Central Park.

**The Modern, Museum of Modern Art (9 W. 53rd St.; the
modernnyc.com).** This sleek and urbane restaurant has elegant food to match. The Modern bar room has a more casual
ambience but the food is just as exemplary.

**Untitled, the Whitney (945 Madison Ave.; untitledat
thewhitney.com).** It's another Danny Meyer hit, this time in
the crisply smart environs of the Whitney. It's described as a
farm-to-table reimagining of coffee-shop classics.

**Porterhouse Brewing Co., Fraunces Tavern (54 Pearl
Street; frauncestavern.com).** Little that is authentic remains
of the colonial-era tavern where George Washington said farewell to his troops in 1783. But this sunny spot has a real period
feel, and the menu offers solid versions of tavern classics.

American; $$$$. When it opened in 2003, the glass-and-steel sky-scraper that is the Time Warner Center wrestled the architectural hodgepodge that was Columbus Circle to the ground. The glossy façade now reigns over a more pedestrian-friendly traffic roundabout, while inside, silvery escalators whiz consumers into a retail stratosphere of marble floors and high-end gewgaws. If it feels suburban (and it does, if your suburb is Tysons Corner), don't let that stop you from heading upstairs to sample the mighty fine vittles of Tom Keller at Per Se. The tiered room has a modern spareness, but the views over Central Park are glittery extravagance. Tables wrapped in smooth linens are much more than an arm's length apart. Keller's nine-course prix-fixe tasting menus are a hosanna of earthly delights, exquisitely sourced and prepared, singing of seasonality (one is a vegetarian tasting). (Note the top billing Keller gives the farms he sources from.) Start with "oysters and pearls"—pearl tapioca with fresh oysters and caviar. Mains include Four Story Hill Farm's shoulder of rabbit with Oregon chanterelle mushrooms, Royal Blenheim apricot puree, and a Dijon sauce or a butter-poached Nova Scotia salmon. You will pay a bundle to dine here, but save your pennies—it's a dream.

Red Rooster, 310 Lenox Ave., (212) 792-9001; redroosterharlem .com; Subway: 2, 3 to 125th St./Lenox Ave.; American/Soul Food; $$–$$$. You gotta love a place where the cooks yell "Two yardbirds!" when an order for fried chicken comes in. Red Rooster has that kind of folksy spirit. We love Red Rooster's expansive room, with the original tile floor and energetic chalkboard graph-ics framing the open kitchen. The big black-and-white photos of Harlem residents are the work of Swedish photographer Pontus Höök, and a number of other artists are represented here, including the legendary self-taught artist Thornton Dial. We love that the name, Red Rooster, is an homage to a legendary speakeasy nearby that once entertained greats like Willie Mays and Nat King Cole. We love the friendly, easygoing service. We love a lot of the food, updated soul food classics, including those yardbirds (crispy fried chicken), shrimp and grits, and mac 'n' greens, baked with collards. The star chef behind Red Rooster, Marcus Samuelsson, has even put his Swedish mother's excellent meatballs on the menu. But sometimes, as with true soul food, it's the sides that shine. A summer succotash was so much more than the usual butterbeans and corn—Red Rooster's come in a small cast-iron dish, baked with cherry tomatoes, peppers, and small shreds of turkey bacon; we can still taste that sweet-and-sassy bite.

Shun Lee West, 43 W. 65th St., btw. Columbus Ave. and Central Park West; (212) 769-3888; shunleewest.com; Subway: 1 to 66th St./Lincoln Center; Chinese; $$$. The sumptuous room still has the power to jolt, all gleaming black lacquer and dramatic lighting. It's a special-occasion spot as much for the elegantly prepared "haute Chinese" food and formal white-linen service as for the nosebleed prices. Shun Lee's food is, we admit, a guilty pleasure, but we defy you not to love it too. Just taste the decadent Grand Marnier prawns, the Beijing duck, the lobster Cantonese, the grilled scallops that come topped with a whisper of baked meringue—wonderful, all. A Midtown East location (155 E. 55th St., near Lexington Ave.), Shun Lee Palace, is equally good, but we prefer the sexy aesthetics here. Shun Lee West also has a more casual and less expensive cafe counterpart just next door, which serves dim sum during the day.

Landmarks & Old-School Faves

Barney Greengrass, 541 Amsterdam Ave., at 86th St.; (212) 724-4707; barneygreengrass.com; Subway: 1 to 86th St.; Deli; $$. A

Tourist Traps We Secretly Love: Boat Basin Cafe

For a borough more or less surrounded by water, Manhattan has a shocking paucity of waterfront restaurants and cafes. We suspect it has something to do with the tangle of highways and beltways built along Manhattan's outer edges on the orders of deranged city planner Robert Moses. In any event, those few places with water views are predictably popular. The Boat Basin Cafe overlooks the Hudson River houseboat marina in lower Riverside Park near 79th Street. It's an open-air structure of vaulted limestone arches, and when the wind is right, you can smell the burgers grilling from Riverside Drive. It's not gourmet fare, just burgers and salads and sandwiches. You sit at tables (if you can get a table) with green plastic chairs, and at happy hour the place gets crazy with frat boys and girls. But it's outside! Overlooking the river! And when it opens, in March, and the wind off the Hudson can still pierce like an icy knife, it means that summer can't be far behind, right? (W. 79th St. at the Hudson River, in Riverside Park; 212-496-5542; boatbasin cafe.com)

West Side institution since 1908, Barney Greengrass is a relic from the New York of a century past. The front room holds vintage dairy cases filled with classic deli food—nova, lox, chopped liver, cold borscht, whitefish salad—that you can take out. Or you can eat in; Barney Greengrass has a full menu of breakfast eggs, smoked fish platters, soups, salads, and sandwiches (keep in mind that weekend brunch can be busy so you might have a wait).

Sylvia's, 328 Lenox Ave., btw. 126th and 127th Sts.; (212) 996-0660; sylviassoulfood.com; Subway: 2, 3 to 125th St.; Soul Food; $$.

South Carolina native Sylvia Woods died in 2012, but her empire lives on. You can buy Sylvia's canned Southern-style vegetables, fry mixes, even aprons and oven mitts right here in her eponymous restaurant. This Harlem institution has been serving up Southern soul food since 1962, and it's got a real community vibe, with locals hugging waitstaff and barstools at the counter filled with a ravenous lunchtime crowd. But many lament that the brand has overtaken what was once the best soul food in town. (In Sylvia's defense, and those like it, even in the South it's a challenge to replicate what at heart is a highly personal, largely intuitive style of home cooking, traditionally dependent on fresh market ingredients. We can't tell you how deflating it is to be served a plate of tired, tasteless collards, frozen fried okra, or canned green beans in a so-called "soul-food" restaurant.) But back to Sylvia's. Okay, the place looks like it hasn't seen an update since the 1960s, but the fried chicken and catfish and barbecue ribs are still pretty great. And in one dining room the first thing you see is a luminous painting of Barack and Michelle Obama entwined as they walk down Pennsylvania Avenue after the first inauguration. Don't miss the whoop-and-holler Sunday gospel brunch, featuring live music.

Specialty Stores, Markets & Producers

Absolute Bagels, 2788 Broadway, near 108th St.; (212) 932-2052; absolutebagels.com; Subway: 1 to Cathedral Pkwy. or 103rd St.; Bagels. It's been a long time since we went out of our way to hit a bagel shop. But we would go back again and again for the tasty, chewy bagels of Absolute Bagels. Get in line at this small, no-frills shop close to Columbia University for what some say are the city's best bagels. Who are we to argue? The bagels are baked on premises, and you can choose flavored cream cheeses to go with. And lo and behold,

Absolute's bagels stay fresh and chewy even after hanging around the house for a day or two.

Acker Merrall & Condit, 160 W. 72nd St., btw. Broadway and Columbus Ave.; (212) 787-0222; acker wines.com; Subway: 1, 2, 3 to 72nd St./Broadway or B, C to 72nd/Central Park West; Wine. This legendary wine merchant touts itself as "America's oldest wine shop," having been merchants in the grocery/wine business since 1820. It has its hands in all things wine, including offering a Wine Every Month Club, regular Wine Workshops and in-store tastings. It's also currently the world's leading wine auctioneer, securing and selling rare, collectible, and old wines (Acker Auctions). A recent 2013 Acker Auction of rare Bordeaux (including three double-magnums of 1990 Château Petrus) in Hong Kong set sales records. The wine shop is relatively small, but the staff knows its stuff.

Bouchon Bakery, Time Warner Center, 10 Columbus Circle, 3rd Fl.; (212) 823-9366; bouchonbakery.com; Subway; 1, A, B, C, D to Columbus Circle/59th St.; Bakery. This retail bakery and 60-seat cafe is the work of Chef Thomas Keller, and the wonderful housemade breads, pastries, and sweets are crafted around French baking techniques. The bakery also has a few savory items, like quiche, sandwiches, and salads, to balance what is sure to be a carb overload. It all looks beautiful, too.

Citarella, 2135 Broadway, at 75th St.; (212) 874-0383; citarella .com; Subway: 1, 2, 3 to 72nd St./Broadway; Gourmet Grocery. What started as a small family-run seafood shop a century ago in Harlem has grown into a full-service gourmet-grocery business, with five locations in the city and the Hamptons. Unlike Fairway, the mega-store next door, Citarella is at heart a small-scale food boutique offering fresh seafood, meats, produce, and gourmet foods and exotica. Citarella's seafood is a tad more expensive than you'll find elsewhere in town, but it's reliably fresh, and these days it's a sad truth that good seafood comes at a premium. Citarella's meat department is the real revelation, with some of the finest prime aged steaks, cuts of beef, and Italian sausages in the city. The produce guy in our neighborhood Citarella is a stickler for freshness, and he mans his post with the vigilance of a PT boat captain. We like to think there is one of him in every store. Citarella's prepared foods can be pricey, and much of it is made off-premises (unlike the prepared foods in, say, Eli Zabar's Vinegar Factory). Some is good; others, meh. All in all, however, Citarella's overall commitment to quality and personal service is admirable.

Fairway, 2127 Broadway, at 74th St.; (212) 595-1888; fairway market.com; Subway: 1, 2, 3 to 72nd St./Broadway; Food Market. Fairway, it seems, is now practically everywhere, but for many years this store *was* the business. Fairway was the creation of Nathan Glickberg, who opened a little fruit and vegetable store in this location 80 years ago. Stuff happens, and the store now sprawls over 22,000 feet, with piles and piles of fruits and vegetables, meats, seafood, prepared foods, and Fairway's own label of just about everything—including good dips, jams, chocolates, even organic eggs and milk. Not to mention urbanites clawing and pawing their way through the narrow aisles. Now, almost overnight it seems, what had forever been an uptown business has infiltrated downtown, with gigantic stores opening in Kips Bay (550 Second Ave., at E. 30th St.) and Chelsea (766 Sixth Ave., btw. 25th and 26th Sts.). We have little doubt that these behemoths will undercut everyone else price-wise with regards to basic foodstuffs; where Fairway gets its clock cleaned is fresh-off-the-farm produce (try the farmers' markets instead) and artisanal meats and seafood. Otherwise, Fairway is for many an indispensable resource.

Harlem Shambles, 2141 Frederick Douglass Blvd., at 116th St.; (646) 476-4650; harlemshambles.com; Subway: B, C to 118th St.; **Butcher.** Don't let the old-school fedoras worn by the butchers at this West Harlem give you a hipster shudder. This boutique butcher shop partners with locals farms like Kinderhook Farms (a Hudson Valley farm that raises 100-percent grass-fed beef and lamb) and Arcadian Pastures (producing hormone- and antibiotic-free heritage breeds).

Levain Bakery, 167 W. 74th St., at Amsterdam Ave.; (212) 874-6080; levainbakery.com; Subway: 1, 2, 3 to 72nd St./Broadway; **Bakery.** Cookies! That's the ticket at this little bakery on Amsterdam Avenue. These suckers are big, good, and gooey, from the signature chocolate chip walnut to dark chocolate peanut butter chip to oatmeal raisin. You can also buy good breads and rolls, brioche, and pastries. Also at 2167 Frederick Douglass Blvd. (646-455-0952).

Mondel Chocolates, 2913 Broadway, at 114th St.; (212) 864-2111; mondelchocolates.com; Subway: 1 to 116th St.; **Chocolate.** Katharine Hepburn was a fan of the chocolates at this little old-fashioned shop (opened in 1943) in the Columbia University area, crammed with beautiful handmade chocolates. Choose from chocolate truffles and cream, chocolate fruits and cordials, chocolate nuts and chews, and more. It's a great place to pick up a gaily wrapped gift box of chocolates.

Schatzie the Butcher, 555 Amsterdam Ave., at 87th St.; (212) 410-1555; schatziethebutcher.com; Subway: A, C to 86th St.; **Butcher.** Bronx-born Schatzie has been in the meat business since he was a cashier in his father's butcher shop, some 50 years ago. He has been in this location since 2010, having been a favorite butcher for Upper East Siders at his Madison Avenue shop for some 30 years. So

HARLEM RENAISSANCE

The Harlem food scene, it appears, is buzzing. *New York* magazine even proclaimed it the "new new Harlem." Whatever is happening, it seems to be going on in the Lenox Avenue (Malcolm X Boulevard) vicinity of **Red Rooster,** Chef Marcus Samuelsson's popular restaurant, and its neighbor a block away, the longtime soul-food institution, **Sylvia's** (see reviews of both, pp. 141 and 143). The most promising newcomer is **Corner Social** (321 Lenox Avenue, at 126th St.; cornersocialnyc.com), a handsome, high-ceilinged spot across Lenox Avenue from Sylvia's that touts farm-to-table, made-from-scratch American classics. Head south down Lenox to **Harlem Shake** (100 W. 124th St., at Lenox Ave.; harlemshakenyc.com), with a serious 1950s-diner look and an all-American diner menu to match: burgers, handcrafted milk shakes, fries, da works. Down on 116th Street, between Lenox Avenue and Adam Clayton Powell Jr. Boulevard, **Amy Ruth's** (113 W. 116th St.; amyruthsharlem .com) serves classic soul food, but the place was looking a little bedraggled (and full of foreign tourists) when we last visited. Harlem's self-described "Restaurant Row" lies farther just west and a few blocks farther south, around West 112th and 113th Streets along Fredrick Douglass Boulevard. We particularly like the New American menu at **5 and Diamond** (2072 Frederick Douglass Blvd.; 5anddiamondrestaurant.com) and the smart bistro food of **Harlem Food Bar** (2111 Frederick Douglass Blvd.; hfbnyc.com).

Schatzie knows meat. The shop sells top-quality USDA Prime beef, free-range poultry, milk-fed veal, Colorado lamb, cheeses, and heat-and-eat prepared foods like brisket, roast loin of pork, and meat loaf.

Zabar's, 2245 Broadway, at 80th St.; (212) 496-1234; zabars.com; Subway: 1, 9 to 79th St.; Food Market/Deli. This legendary epicurean marketplace is everything it's cracked up to be. The 20,000-square-foot store is crammed with food, not only the unparalleled smoked fish it's famous for, but vast sections of delicious prepared foods, gourmet edibles, coffees, chocolates, bread, juices, you name it. Cheeses fill one whole section of the store, and upstairs on the mezzanine is a terrific selection of coffeemakers, food processors, bakeware, pots, pans, knives, housewares, and gifty things. Prepared foods are dazzling: It's every salad you can think of, house-made soups, mouthwatering entrees, and cooked meats. But Zabar's built its business and its reputation for quality and exacting standards on smoked fish and classic deli accompaniments. When we head down to the Southland for a spell, we pull into Zabar's on our way out and order up some nice Gaspé nova, cream cheese, a handful of whitefish chubs, maybe some pickled herring. We hope it will be ever thus. Unlike its competitors and neighboring markets, Zabar's hasn't branched off into other locations—this is the one and only, and it's a beaut.

Manhattan Culinary Salons, Cooking Classes & Food Tours

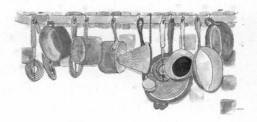

City Grit. During the day, the vintage schoolhouse is a furniture showroom for WRK Design. At night, it is transformed into a culinary salon retrofitted with communal farmhouse tables and flickering candles. This Nolita supper club is the informal version of the James Beard House chef series, where visiting chefs prepare food for what function as multicourse intimate dinner parties with strangers, prepared by chefs from all over the world. Here both famous and emerging guest chefs ramble through on a regular basis, but many of the food events/dinners are created by City Grit founder and Carolina native Sarah Simmons around her sexy Southern repertoire. Dinners can accommodate up to 70 guests. At press time, a Kickstarter campaign was under way to lock in a new, more permanent location; stay tuned. Go to citygritnyc .com to subscribe, or call (646) 580-5720.

James Beard House. The former town house home of legendary chef James Beard is immersed in everything food, from holding food conferences to hosting multicourse dinners cooked by visiting chefs in Beard's kitchen at 167 W. 12th St. (near 7th Ave.). The James Beard Foundation Awards are the food world's version of the Oscars, awarded annually in spring. Go to jamesbeard.org or call (212) 675-4984.

Small-Group Cooking Classes

Camaje Bistro Cooking Classes. You'll feel like a real chef when you sign up for a hands-on cooking class at this small, charming MacDougal Street bistro; classes are taught by the talented chef Abigail Hitchcock while the restaurant is open. Classes have included "Soul Food," "Shop and Cook: Chinatown for Fish," and "A Taste of Maine in Greenwich Village." Classes are held at the restaurant on 85 MacDougal Street, between Houston and Bleecker streets. Go to camaje.com/ cooking-classes or call (212) 673-8184.

Haven's Kitchen Recreational Cooking School. In Chelsea, Haven's Kitchen recreational cooking classes are more like intimate parties, where small groups are treated to thoroughly enjoyable, hands-on cooking instruction in a full-service kitchen and then dine on the finished dishes at a rustic farm table. This is a fun choice for a birthday party or a gathering of friends. Haven's is located at 109 W. 17th St., between Sixth and Seventh Avenues. Call (212) 929-7900 or go to havenskitchen.com.

Home Cooking New York. Small-group cooking classes covering cuisines that span the globe (or the city's ethnic enclaves) are offered in a Chelsea loft at 236 W. 26th St. (Ste. 601), between Seventh and Eighth Avenues. Call (917) 803-6857 or go to homecookingny.com.

Miette Culinary Studios. Led by the Belgium-born chef of that charming little slice of France in the West Village, Tartine restaurant, this MacDougal Street "culinary studio" is located in a vintage Village town house. Each of the wide-ranging, hands-on cooking classes is limited to 12 persons; topics have included "New French Country Classics," "New Steak House Favorite Classics," "Dim Sum Brunch," "Indian Restaurant Favorites," and "Mexican Classics." Classes are held at 109 MacDougal St., between Bleecker and W. 3rd Streets (Ste. 2). Register at mietteculinarystudio.com or call (212) 460-9322.

Rustico Cooking. This big, bright Midtown cooking loft is the brainchild of the Milan-born former editor of *La Cucina Italiana* who realized her dream in 2002 when she started teaching Italian cooking classes. The philosophy at Rustico hews closely to the elegant simplicity of rustic Italian cuisine: "Fresh ingredients, treated simply and with respect, are the foundation of memorable meals." That means straightforward, interactive cooking classes such as "The 10 Best Pasta Sauces," "Tuscan Harvest Feast," "Neapolitan Classics," and "Summer in an Italian Herb Garden." Yum. Rustico is located at 40 W. 39th St., between Fifth and Sixth Avenues, on the 3rd floor. Go to rustico cooking.com or call (917) 602-1519.

Group Cooking Classes & Chef Demonstrations

The Bouley Test Kitchen. Chef David Bouley is a downtown institution, and the Bouley Test Kitchen is a food lab and home cook's dream. Bouley and his team now offer "interactive" cooking demonstrations, such as crafting a tasting menu with ideal wine pairings. Bouley even employs a nutritionist to teach participants how to replace your kitchen pantry with healthy, unprocessed alternatives in "Building a Healthy Pantry." Classes in 2013 included "The Basics of Seafood Cookery," a tapas preparation class with Barcelona guest chef Roger Martinez, and a Union Square Greenmarket tour and Test Kitchen vegetarian lunch class. The test kitchen is located at 163 Duane St. Go to davidbouley.com to register or call (212) 964-2525 for information.

DeGustibus—The School of Good Taste, at Macy's. Now we know that Macy's has everything. This mega department store DeGustibus has been offering chef demonstration classes and wine tastings for more than 30 years—not to mention operating hands-on cooking classes on location with top chefs in restaurants around the city. Renowned chefs on the ticket have included Alfred Portale of Gotham Bar & Grill, Gabrielle Hamilton of Prune, and Dan Kluger of ABC Kitchen. DeGustibus is located on the eighth floor of Macy's Herald Square. Check it out at degustibusnyc.com or call (212) 239-1652.

La Scuola at Eataly. This sprawling Italian marketplace is about much more than just buying and eating; it's about learning about buying and eating. Part of Eataly's La Scuola, the Chef Kitchen showcases cooking demos by both in-house and guest chefs. Eataly's Chef's Tables are communal dinners paired with regional wines. Eataly also offers a food and language course. It's all at 200 Fifth Ave., between 23rd and 24th Streets. Go to eataly.com to sign up for the La Scuola newsletter.

Cooking Classes:
Professional Cooking Schools

Institute of Culinary Education (ICE). ICE, the city's preeminent vocational cooking school, runs the largest program of hands-on recreational cooking courses in the country, some 1,500 courses a year. Classes in the recent past have included "The Soulful Fatty Pig," "Cuban Surf and Turf," and "Authentic Hong Kong Dim Sum." ICE is located at 50 W. 23rd St., between Fifth and Sixth Avenues. Go to recreational.ice.edu or call (800) 522-4610.

The International Culinary Center (formerly the French Culinary Institute). This vocational cooking school offers one-day culinary, baking, and wine-and beverage classes to nonmatriculated students. Typical classes would be "French Classics: Bouillabaisse, Crème Caramel, and Other Favorites," "Macarons and Madeleines," "The Secret of Spices," and "Introduction to Mixology." The International Culinary Center is located at 462 Broadway, at Grand Street. Go to internationalculinarycenter.com or call (888) 318-2433.

Natural Gourmet Institute. Eating healthy means cooking healthy, and the National Gourmet Institute is a champion of "health-supported culinary arts." It's all about utilizing quality (largely organic) ingredients and whole-food traditions for optimal nutrition and flavor. Classes include "Vegetarian Soups, Stews, and Salad Suppers," "Fish without Fuss," "9 Secrets of Healthy Aging," "A Traditional South Indian Supper." The Natural Gourmet Institute is located at 48 W. 21st St., between Fifth and Sixth Avenues, on the second floor. Call (212) 645-5170 or check the details on public classes at naturalgourmetinstitute .com.

Cheese Classes & Tastings

Artisanal Cheese Center. A wide range of cheese-tasting classes, from "Cheese and Wine 101" to courses with regional themes, are offered by this artisanal cheese purveyor. Call about locations. Call (212) 239-1200 or go to artisanalcheese.com.

Murray's Cheese: The Cheese Course.
Offering a range of award-winning cheese classes or 3-day Cheese Boot Camps. Most classes are held in Murray's Village location at 254 Bleecker St., but a number of wine and cheese classes are held at City Winery or the Chelsea Wine Vault. Call (212) 243-3289, ext. 42, or go to murrayscheese.com.

Wine Workshops/Dinners

Astor Center. One of the city's largest wine retailers, Astor Wines & Spirits offers an interesting schedule of wine/spirits classes and tastings. Recent classes included a "Whiskey Master Class," "French Wine: Discoveries from the Astor Cellar," and "The Elements of Wine" with Andrew Fisher, longtime president of Astor Wines. The wine store is located at 399 Lafayette St., near East 4th Street. Go to astorwines.com or call (212) 674-7501.

Otto Enoteca Tuesday Wine Nights. Every Tuesday at 6:30 p.m., the restaurant Otto holds 90-minute wine-tasting classes in its handsome *enoteca,* led by the restaurant's sommelier. The classes are often accompanied by a selection of artisanal cheeses and house-cured meats. Otto also offers wine classes on weekend afternoons at 2 p.m.

The restaurant is located at 1 Fifth Ave. (entrance on 8th Street). For details, call (212) 995-9559, ext. 102, or go to ottopizzeria.com.

Wine Workshops, Acker Merrall & Condit. Sip and sample wines with some of the best in the business at these wine and food extravaganzas. Previous workshops have included Burgundy seminars with Pierre Rovani (for years the associate of wine critic Robert Parker), Barolo wine dinners, and Bordeaux blind tastings with Bordeaux expert Bill Blatch. Call (212) 875-0222 or go to ackerwines.com.

Food & Tasting Tours

Big Onion Walking Tours. Offering smart, entertaining public walking tours at competitive prices, the Big Onion offers a history-centric Multi-Ethnic Eating Tour. It's 2 hours of noshing the Lower East Side, Little Italy, and Chinatown, sampling a wide range of ethnic bites, mainly vegetarian and dairy. Go to bigonion.com or call the Big Onion Hotline at (888) 606-9255 for details.

The Enthusiastic Gourmet. Susan Rosenbaum's downtown food tours come highly recommended not only by those who take them, but from the merchants she visits. Unlike some of the more fly-by-night tour guides, who swoop their groups into businesses like they own the place and speak nary a word to proprietors, Rosenbaum has a genuine relationship with the places and people on the tour route. Rosenbaum offers three highly touted eight-person walking tours: "Chinatown Discovered," "Melting Pot Tour" (including Chinatown, Lower East Side, and Little Italy), and "NY Nosh" (a food tour of the Jewish Lower East Side of yesteryear). Book your tour at enthusiasticgourmet.com.

Foods of New York Tours. The entertaining, personable guides on these downtown walking tours know their stuff, and the tours offer a fascinating immersion in some of New York's most flavorful enclaves. The most popular tours are the Original Greenwich Village Food and Culture Tour and the Chelsea Market/Meatpacking District Food Tasting Tour. Book early: These tours sell out fast. Go to foodsofny.com or call (917) 408-9539.

Scott's Pizza Tours. When the first New York Travel Fest was held in 2013, this tour quickly sold out among travel and food journalists. When you meet the pizza Ph.D. that is Scott Wiener, you'll understand why. Scott's Pizza Tours are easily among the most entertaining and enlightening food tours in New York. This is no mere pizza tasting; it's a cram course in the historical, sociological, and cultural intricacies of pizza. It's tactile, too: You get to feel the heat of a 100-year-old coal-fired oven (Scott is such a pizza nerd he was even invited to climb inside the oven during its last full cleaning, back in 2011; "I had to do it," grins Scott. "It was a once-in-a-lifetime experience"). Finally, Scott Wiener makes you really think about the elemental power of a little flour, salt, yeast, and good old New York water. Book at scottspizzatours.com or call (212) 913-9903. (See Scott's recipe for **Homemade Pizza** on p. 220.)

Harlem Spirituals. Get into the swing of historic Harlem with the Soul Food & Jazz Tour, an evening tour that includes dinner at **Sylvia's** (see p. 143), the famous soul-food spot on Lenox Avenue, and listening to music in a local jazz club. The Sunday-morning Harlem Gospel Tour includes a bus tour of Harlem (including the Apollo Theater and the Cotton Club) and a Sunday morning gospel church service. Go to harlem spirituals.com or call (212) 391-0900.

Home Cooking New York Tasting Tours. Guided and private tasting tours from the folks who offer intimate cooking classes in a Chelsea loft include 3-hour food forays into Chinatown and informational shopping trips to the Union Square farmers' market. Call (917) 803-6857 or go to homecookingny.com.

Institute of Culinary Education (ICE). ICE, the city's top vocational cooking school, also gives excellent culinary walking tours. Past tours have included a "Little Italy Walking Tour," "Chinatown Dim Sum Tour," and "A Cheese Lover's Romp." Go to recreational.ice.edu/Home/ToursAndOffsites or call (800) 522-4610.

MCNY Tours. These Bronx-based neighborhood tours take you to the flavorful markets and red-sauce restaurants of Bronx's Little Italy (Arthur Avenue, Belmont Avenue) and the Irish pubs and taverns in Little Ireland (Woodlawn). Go to mcnytours.com or call (646) 831-1078.

NoshWalks. "Nosh your way from Odessa to Bombay and never leave New York" is the NoshWalks slogan, and these custom walking tours indeed go deep in the search for a good nosh. It has a lot to work with: NoshWalks covers the rich tapestry of Washington Heights, Inwood, Harlem, and the Bronx, not to mention traditional ethnic enclaves in Brooklyn, Queens, and Manhattan. Discover the only distillery in the Bronx (Tirado, making rum and whiskey); hand-pulled noodles in a Flushing, Queens food stall; and Caribbean finger foods in Brooklyn. Go to noshwalks.com or call (212) 222-2243.

Turnstile Tours. This community-oriented, civic-minded tour company/benefit corporation is on a mission to "engage the public with the urban landscape." Tours are largely Brooklyn-based, but Turnstile hits Manhattan for engaging and enlightening "Food Cart" tours in the Financial District and Midtown, in and around those streets where street vendors, food carts, and food trucks proliferate and the challenges they face to do business there. Go to turnstiletours.com or call (347) 903-8687.

Urban Oyster. This New York–based tour company is only a few years old, but it's already won high praise (and TripAdvisor's Certificate of Excellence 3 years running) for its innovative tours and celebration of those local businesses that make New York neighborhoods "unique and vibrant." A tour with Urban Oyster is highly recommended. Although many of the company's tours are based in Brooklyn, it offers several Manhattan options, including a "Tenement Tales & Tastes" tour, a walking food tour through the historic tenement streets of the Lower East Side. A "Neighborhood Eats Tour of the New York Waterfront" takes you on a tasting tour of historic South Street Seaport and (via ferry ride) Red Hook, Brooklyn. Check it out at urbanoyster.com or call (347) 618-8687.

Resource Guide

Groceries

BIG-BOX STORES & CHAINS

Aside from Manhattan locations of the big chains most prevalent throughout the New York metropolitan area (D'Agostino, Food Emporium, Gristedes), Manhattan has a number of excellent big-box stores. Here are our favorites.

Fairway, 2127 Broadway, at 74th St.; (212) 595-1888; fairway market.com; Subway: 1, 2, 3 to 72nd St./Broadway. If Fairway doesn't have it, it may not even exist. The 22,000-square-foot flagship store of the growing Fairway empire is still jam-packed with fruits and vegetables, meats, seafood, prepared foods, and Fairway's own label of just about everything—including good dips, jams, chocolates, fresh-squeezed juices, even organic eggs and milk—at competitive prices, especially for pricey Manhattan. You will find better farm-fresh produce at the city's greenmarkets, but if you're looking for a one-stop shop for, well, everything—including quality, well-priced groceries—for many, Fairway is an indispensable resource. In 2007, a majority stake in Fairway was acquired by a private equity firm from Connecticut and the Fairway expansion exploded almost overnight, it seems. Today

Manhattan has four additional Fairway stores, each one truly massive: **Harlem** (2328 12th Ave., at 130th St.); the **Upper East Side** (240 E. 86th St., btw. Second and Third Aves.); **Kips Bay** (550 Second Ave., at E. 30th St.); and **Chelsea** (766 Sixth Ave., btw. 25th and 26th Sts.). At press time, it was announced that Fairway would open a sprawling 52,000-square-foot store in **Tribeca** near the World Trade Center (225 Greenwich St., at Murray St.).

Trader Joe's, traderjoes.com. We love the goofy hippie-goes-to-Hawaii vibe at Trader Joe's, not to mention its ability to undercut other specialty grocers, price-wise, with its own respectable brands of condiments, chips, nuts, chocolates, frozen foods, packaged mixes, vitamins—you name it. Trader Joe's keeps its prices low by buying directly from suppliers, among other savvy innovations. Trader Joe's currently has three locations in Manhattan: **Union Square** (142 E. 14th St., near Third Ave.); **Chelsea** (675 Sixth Ave.); and the **Upper West Side** (2073 Broadway, at 72nd St.). It also has a **wine store,** selling a solid selection of reasonably priced wines—including Two-Buck Chuck (now $3 and change)—next door to the Union Square store (138 E. 14th St.). All Trader Joe's stores can get crazy busy, so try to go at nonpeak times, such as early in the morning or early afternoon.

Whole Foods, wholefoodsmarket.com. The retail arbiter of wholesome, natural, and (often) organic, Whole Foods has been a corporate juggernaut in Manhattan since it opened its first store in Chelsea in 2001. It's a powerful presence among health-savvy New Yorkers, with salad bars laden with nutritious grains and shelves piled with organic/natural foodstuffs. Whole Foods makes a real effort to source sustainable, local seafood and grass-fed, humanely grown, and heritage-breed meats from small-scale farmers and regional producers. Each store offers an different dynamic: The Tribeca store has an Indian

FreshDirect: The Moveable Feast

The traditional Manhattan grocery delivery boy is now a full-service grocery truck, delivering any and every foodstuff you order online straight to your door. That is the concept behind Fresh Direct, a web-only grocer that delivers groceries, meats, seafood, fresh produce, dry goods, and even beer and wine directly to residences throughout the New York metropolitan area. Prices are competitive, and the convenience factor can't be underestimated. Organic, local, and sustainable food choices are even available. But those refrigerated delivery trucks idling during a drop-off can be noticeably noisy in a noisy city.

"dosateria"; the Bowery store has a well-stocked Beer Room and a branch of the wildly popular Brooklyn Smorgasburg of artisanal foodstuffs. The seven Whole Foods locations in Manhattan are **Tribeca** (270 Greenwich St., btw. Murray and Warren Sts.); the **Bowery** (95 E. Houston St., btw. the Bowery and Chrystie St.); **Union Square** (4 Union Square South, btw. University Place and Broadway); **Chelsea** (250 Seventh Ave., btw. 24th and 25th Sts.); **Midtown East** (226 E. 57th St., btw. Second and Third Aves.); **Columbus Circle** (Time-Warner Center, 10 Columbus Circle); and the **Upper West Side** (808 Columbus Ave., at 97th St.).

SMALL GROCERS & GOURMET MARKETS

These small grocers and gourmet markets are the neighborhood go-to stores for Manhattanites and often essential food destinations in themselves. Here are the best of Manhattan's small grocers and gourmet markets.

Agata & Valentina, 1505 First Ave., at 79th St.; (212) 452-0690; agatavalentina.com; Subway: 6 to 78th St./Lexington Ave. A family-owned Italian grocer (one of the owners is from the legendary

Balducci family of grocers), Agata & Valentina emphasizes personalized customer service and shelves stocked with gourmet foods, including a solid produce and meat section; an extensive selection of house-made prepared foods and pizzas; smoked fish, and house-made desserts; and a growing body of A&V-brand items, including pastas and rice, sauces, and condiments. It also has a second location at 64 University Place, between 10th and 11th Streets (212-388-0114).

Balducci's Gourmet on the Go, Hearst Tower, 301 W. 56th St., at Eighth Ave.; (646) 350-4194; balduccis.com; Subway: A, B, C, D to Columbus Circle. It may have impressive signage, but this is a wan representation of what was once the city's greatest gourmet market, the West Village Balducci's, devoured by a big food conglomerate in 1995 and never the same since. This iteration, the only Balducci's in Manhattan, is a small takeout cafe/market that caters to nearby Hearst cubicle dwellers with soup, salad, and sandwich stations—not to mention macaroons, a sushi chef, and crepes. Full-bodied salads are surprisingly good and fresh nonetheless, and the coffee is premium.

Blue Ribbon Market, 14 Bedford St., near Downing St.; (212) 647-0408; blueribbonrestaurants.com; Subway: 1, 9 to Houston St. This wee country-style market (with old-time screen door, no less) showcases a select group of foods and staples often served in the Blue Ribbon restaurants, with an emphasis on breads. It's got a handful of good grain-based salads, such as quinoa with cranberries and slivered almonds or pesto couscous, as well as savories like bacon-tomato-spinach quiche and watercress soup. The market also sells artisanal meats and cheeses and homemade lemonades and sweet iced teas.

Citarella, 2135 Broadway, at 75th St.; (212) 874-0383; citarella .com; Subway: 1, 2, 3 to 72nd St./Broadway. Citarella is at heart a small-scale food boutique with an emphasis on fresh seafood, cut-to-order meat, fresh produce, and gourmet foods and exotica. This gourmet grocery has expanded to five locations in the city and the Hamptons. Although Citarella built its reputation on reliably fresh seafood, it's the meat department that is the real revelation, with some of the finest prime aged steaks, cuts of beef, and Italian sausages in the city. Citarella's overall commitment to quality is admirable, but keep in mind that the pricey prepared foods are largely made offsite, and a fairly steady employee turnover makes us question the happiness of the workplace in general.

Dean & DeLuca, 121 Prince St., at Broadway; (212) 226-6800; deandeluca.com; Subway: N, R to Prince St. Opening its doors in SoHo in 1977, Dean & DeLuca was a pioneer that brought the gourmet/artisanal food concept to downtown. This sprawling space is the company's flagship store, and it's a hushed temple to fine foods, with marble floors and neoclassical columns. It has an exquisite (and exquisitely priced) produce section; an amazing meat department; a coffee bar; and mini-boutique sections selling sushi, smoked fish, ravioli, seafood, cakes and pastries, and more. Come during the lunch hours, when the prepared-foods department is swarmed by a hip local workforce buying up excellent soups, pasta dishes, vegetables, grilled meats, and salads.

Eli's Manhattan/TASTE, 1411 Third Ave., at 80th St.; (212) 717-8100; elizabar.com; Subway: 6 to 77th St./Lexington Ave. A warren of rooms filled with gourmet foods, produce, meats and seafood, coffees, artisanal breads, and exotica sourced from all over the world, this two-level marketplace is foodie ambrosia. Sample or take home many of Eli Zabar's greatest hits: a lineup of his fabulous soups, from chicken vegetable to Tuscan peasant, sandwiches, salads, and hearty mains like lasagna. Prices are at the high end, but the quality is impeccable, and everything is fresh and flavorful.

Eli's Vinegar Factory, 431 E. 91st St., btw. First and York Aves.; (212) 987-0885; elizabar.com; Subway: 4, 5, 6 to 86th or 96th St. This Carnegie Hill warehouse is 9,000 square feet of top-quality food goods, produce, meats, seafoods, breads. The prepared foods section is one of the city's best, with savory, freshly made meats, entrees, pastas, and soups mostly made on the premises and good to go (you can also nosh in a little cafe). A rooftop greenhouse ensures that plenty of vegetables and herbs are fresh-picked.

Grace's Marketplace, 215 E. 68th St., at Third Ave.; (212) 737-0600; gracesmarketplacenyc.com; Subway: 6 to 68th St. Opened by a member of the same Balducci family that ran the legendary Balducci's market in Greenwich Village for more than 50 years, Grace's continues in a similar rustic, colorful, bountiful-Italian-market aesthetic. Even in its new location on East 68th Street (which doubled the space), the place is crammed with gourmet goods, prepared foods, cheeses, dry-aged meats, smoked fish, Italian olive oils, vinegars, and condiments. It's a real neighborhood grocery store, much like its predecessor, but catering to a slightly higher-end customer.

Grand Central Market, Grand Central Station, Lexington Ave. entrance; grandcentralterminal.com/market; Subway: S, 4, 5, 6 to Grand Central/42nd St. This little upscale market is a convenient place to buy lunch to go or dinner fixings. Grand Central Market has two excellent seafood markets in **Wild Edibles** (212-687-4255) and **Pescatore Seafood Co.** (212-557-4466), both offering fresh (if pricey) selections of fish, shellfish, caviar, smoked fish, and prepared seafood dishes. The ever-popular **Murray's Cheese** (212-922-1540) sells a smart selection of cheeses, dairy, *salumi,* and crackers. **Ceriello** (212-972-4266), a high-end butcher shop, has prime-aged beef, organic poultry, Italian sausages, prepared foods, dry pasta and pasta sauces. Artisanal breads are sold at **Eli Zabar's Bakery** (646-503-3534). Vendors selling fresh vegetables, fruits, and packaged nuts bookend the market. If you don't feel like cooking at all, go directly to **Dishes** (212-370-5511) for wonderful gourmet prepared foods. The market is right next door to **Grande Harvest Wines** (Graybar Passage; 212-682-5855), where you can pick out a nice wine complement.

New York Marts, 128 Mott St., btw. Grand and Hester Sts.; (212) 680-0566; Subway: 6 to Spring St. or M, N, R, Z, 6 to Canal St. This Chinatown seafood and vegetable market has prices that are hard to beat. Aisles are crowded with such exotica as conch, lionfish, and barrels of fist-size bullfrogs. Enter on Mott Street to a seafood emporium, which leads to aisles piled high with vegetables, many of them staples in Chinese dishes (bok choy, Chinese broccoli, *sing gua*). Another room contains shelves of sauces, vinegars and oils, freezers filled with ready-made dumplings, and refrigerator cases of fresh wonton wrappers and tofu. It's a great place to stock up on Chinese condiments.

Zabar's, 2245 Broadway, at 80th St.; (212) 496-1234; zabars.com; Subway: 1, 9 to 79th St. You know this legendary epicurean marketplace for its unparalleled smoked fish, but if we lived in the neighborhood we'd be here every day pawing through the dazzling array of prepared foods, cheeses, coffees, chocolates, bread, juices—it all looks scrumptious. Zabar's built its business on smoked fish and classic deli accompaniments, and it's the mother lode for lox and accoutrements.

Food Courts/Emporiums

Combining gourmet aesthetics with the New American propensity for wanting what we want now (food-wise), Manhattan's food courts are state of art and, we would argue, among the best in the world. In the last 5 years alone they've become some of the best places to get good food in the city, constantly raising the culinary stakes with more sublime and creative offerings.

All Good Things, 102 Franklin St., btw. West Broadway and Church St.; allgoodthingsny.com; Subway: 1, 9 to Franklin St. This handsome artisanal market occupies a vintage Tribeca space long held by a family-run business (Freund, Freund & Co.) that had ably supplied mattress and bed ticking to the textile industry since 1845. In that spirit of small-scale, honest toil, All Good Things has a well-chosen smattering of food purveyors, small in number but all top-rate. It's got **Dickson's Farmstand Meats** (dicksonsfarmstand.com), Blue Bottle Coffee (blue bottlecoffee.com), **Blue Marble Ice Cream** (bluemarbleicecream.com), **Cavianola's** gourmet cheese shop (cavaniola.com/tribeca), and a fish and produce stand. Downstairs is a restaurant helmed by Chef Ryan Tate that garnered two stars from the *New York Times* in its rookie year.

Chelsea Market, 75 Ninth Ave., btw. 15th and 16th Sts. chelsea market.com; Subway: A, C, E, L to 14th St./Eighth Ave. This vintage Nabisco factory reborn as a bustling food arcade is a must-do on any food tour of Manhattan. Among fish stores, bakeries, and produce stalls, you'll find top-quality takeout eateries like **Hale and Hearty Soups** (haleandhearty.com), **Dickson's Farmstand Meats** (dicksons farmstand.com), **Amy's Bread** (amysbread .com), **Buon Italia** (buonitalia.com), **Ron-nybrook Dairy Farm** (ronnybrook.com), **Sarabeth's Bakery** (sarabeth.com), **Fat Witch Bakery** (fatwitch.com), **Num Pang** sandwich shop (numpangnyc.com), and the **Lobster Place** (lobsterplace.com), all with cafe tables nearby. The caterer **Cleaver Company** (cleaverco.com) has a terrific sustainable-foods restaurant, the Green Table, and the Lobster Place has a full-service oyster bar, **Cull & Pistol** (cullandpistol .com). **Chelsea Thai** (212-924-2999) is easily one of our favorite Thai take-out restaurants. Chelsea Market is just off the High Line, and when the weather's nice, you can grab picnic fixings from the market and dine on the High Line to Hudson River views.

Eataly, 200 Fifth Ave., btw. 23rd and 24th Sts.; (212) 229-2560; eatalyny.com; Subway: N, R to 23rd St. This 32,000-square-foot Italian emporium is a dream of a food market. In addition to an endless array of artisanal Italian goodies for sale, from pasta to pizza to cheese to bread to *salumi* to fresh produce to beer, Eataly has seven sit-down restaurants with tables and barstools. The rooftop **Birreria** is a brewery where you can sample house-brewed ales and have a bite to eat.

Essex Street Market, 120 Essex St., at Delancey St.; essex streetmarket.com; Subway: F, J, M, Z to Delancey St./Essex St. This warren of small-scale grocery vendors and impassioned food purveyors is located in a landmark 1940s-era building. The **Heritage Meat Shop** (heritagemeatshop.com) sells artisanal, humanely raised and slaughtered meat from heritage and rare breeds. Its neighbor, **Nordic Preserves Fish & Wildlife Company** (nordicpreserves .com) sells all things Scandinavian, from house-cured salmon to Swedish meatballs to an understated potato salad. New **Star Fishmarket** (212-475-8365; no website) sells fresh seafood. Buy delicious handmade chocolates of **Roni-Sue's Chocolates** (roni-sue.com) or artisanal breads of **Pain d'Avignon** (paindavignon-nyc.com). **Shopsin's General Store** (shopsins.com) is the small sit-down eatery of chef Kenny Shopsin and family, capable of whipping up hundreds of dishes from the exhaustive menu. Note that there were rumblings at press time that a proposed Bloombergian development complex, Essex Street Crossing, plans to absorb the landmark market and relocate it across the street in what the *New York Times* calls a "glitzier building."

Gotham West Market, 600 Eleventh Ave., btw. 44th and 45th Sts.; gothamwestmarket.com; (212) 582-7940; Subway: A, C, E to Eighth Ave. Opening with a bang in late 2013, this way-west market is part of a big new 554-unit apartment complex straddling Hell's Kitchen and Hudson River Park. It's got a fairly sensational roster of food purveyors and little restaurants, but the one that has everyone salivating is **Ivan Orkin's Ramen Slurp Shop,** opened by a self-professed "Jewish kid from Long Island" who through some convoluted career path ended up opening some of the top ramen shops in Tokyo. We hear it's pretty great.

Grand Central Dining Concourse, Lower Level, Grand Central Station; Subway: S, 4, 5, 6 to Grand Central/42nd St. If you're waiting for a train, or simply in the neighborhood, this lower-level concourse offers a fine assortment of top-quality food vendors, with plenty of seating in the center of the concourse. Three spots—**Two Boots** (twoboots.com), for pizza and Cajun food, **Shake Shack** (shakeshack .com), for hamburgers, and **Junior's** (juniorscheesecake.com), a classic deli—even offer their own sit-down table-service areas. Food vendors include **Hale and Hearty Soups** (haleandhearty.com), **Mendy's Kosher Delicatessen and Dairy** (mendysdeli.com), **Magnolia Bakery** (magnolia bakery.com), and **Manhattan Chili Company** (manhattanchili.com). The **Grand Central Oyster Bar** (oysterbarny.com) is just across a hallway, with a little takeout window where you can order up excellent seafood soups (New England and Manhattan clam chowder; Maryland crab; rock shrimp and corn), po' boys, and more.

The Plaza Food Hall, The Plaza Hotel, Concourse Level, 1 W. 59th St., at Central Park West; (212) 986-9260; theplazany.com; Subway: N, R to Fifth Ave. An elegant stop for an eat-in or take-out gourmet lunch. The selection of food vendors includes **Luke's Lobster** (lukeslobster.com), famed for its lobster rolls; the artisanal breads of **Pain d'Avignon** paindavignon-nyc .com; **Sushi of Gari** (sushiofgari.com), producing what some say is the best sushi in Manhattan; and the ganaches of **La Maison du Chocolat** (lamaison duchocolat.com), the *macarons* of **Payard (FP Patisserie)** (payard.com), and the cupcakes of **Billy's Bakery** (billysbakerynyc.com).

Rockefeller Center Concourse Level, **Rockefeller Center, 30 Rockefeller Plaza, between Fifth and Sixth Aves.; rockefellercenter .com; Subway: B, D, F, V to Rockefeller Center.** The pickings may not match those of Chelsea Market or Grand Central, but just nosing around the sleek stairways, the walls a Deco dream of black marble, makes this a pretty swell pit stop. Head down to the concourse level and grab some picnic fixings from **Hale and Hearty** soups (haleandhearty.com); **Pret A Manger** (pret.com/us); and **Just Salad** (justsalad.com) and dine on a bench, alfresco, in Rockefeller Plaza.

Greenmarkets

Since 1976, when the city's first **Greenmarket** (grownyc.org/green market) opened in Union Square, these farmers' markets have been a miracle for city folk and city chefs. Today these year-round farmers' markets have become an essential element in the city's food web, with some 54 Greenmarkets operating somewhere in the city 7 days a week. The biggest, of course, is **Union Square Green- market** (Union Square, between 14th and 17th Sts.), which brings the farm to the city four days a week (Mon, Wed, Fri, and Sat). It's sprawling and colorful, and vendors are required to adhere to the city's strict Greenmarket regulations (they can only sell what they grow or make). It's a year-round market, so even in the dead of winter a few stalwarts show up at the break of morning to sell artisanal meats, Long Island sea- food, free-range eggs, dairy products, muffins and cookies, apples, root and greenhouse vegetables, and more. Here is where and when you can find a Greenmarket in the city. Check out grownyc.org/greenmarket for further details.

W. 175th Street: Thursday

W. 97th Street: Friday

E. 92nd Street: Sunday

E. 82nd Street: Saturday

W. 79th Street: Sunday

W. 57th Street: Saturday and Wednesday

W. 42nd Street: Wednesday

Abingdon Square: Saturday

Bowling Green: Tuesday and Thursday

City Hall: Tuesday and Friday

Columbia: Thursday and Sunday

Dag Hammarskjold Plaza: Wednesday

Downtown PATH (West Broadway btw. Barclay St. and Park Place): Tuesday

Fort Washington: Tuesday

Inwood: Saturday

Mount Sinai: Wednesday

Port Authority Bus Terminal: Thursday

Staten Island Ferry Whitehall Terminal: Tuesday and Friday

St. Mark's Church: Tuesday

SoHo: Tuesday and Wednesday

Stuyvesant Town: Sunday

Tompkins Square Park: Sunday

Tribeca: Wednesday and Saturday

Tucker Square: Thursday and Saturday

Union Square: Monday, Wednesday, Friday, and Saturday

Lower East Side Youthmarket: Thursday

Seasonal Outdoor Markets

Madison Square Eats, Pop-up Market, Worth Square, Fifth Ave. btw. 25th and 26th Sts. Going on 5 years old, this very tasty pop-up market of some 30 food stands sets up in the spring and fall months, when the weather isn't too hot or cold—when baby, it's *just* right. It's the only spot in Manhattan where you can sample the coal-fired pizzas of the acclaimed **Roberta's** of Bushwick. Other of the top-notch vendors include **Calexico** Mexican foods; the **Hong Kong Street Cart;**

ilili for Middle Eastern fare; and treats from **Momofuku Milk Bar.** It's open from 11 a.m. to 9 p.m. daily around the month of May and late September to late October.

New Amsterdam Food Market, the Old Fulton Fish Market, South St. between Beekman St. and Peck Slip; (212) 766-8688; newamsterdammarket.org; Subway: A, C, J, Z, 2, 3, 4, 5 to Fulton St. A self-styled reinvention of the city's public markets, the New Amsterdam Food Market is an award-winning Sunday market in the landmark Old Fulton Fish Market. Look for local and regional food purveyors, farmers, and cooks selling an array of artisanal foods and gourmet foodstuffs—including hand-crafted breads, apple cider, and seafood. At press time, the market was in danger of losing its space as part of a proposed mall/hotel/condo expansion by the Howard Hughes Corporation, the mega-developer responsible for the retail mess that is the Seaport's Pier 17. Cross your fingers. For now, the New Amsterdam Market is open from 11 a.m. to 5 p.m. on designated Sundays from late spring through mid-December.

SmorgasBar at the Seaport, 11 Front St. at Fulton St., South Street Seaport; Subway: A, C, J, Z, 2, 3, 4, 5 to Fulton Street; brooklyn flea.com. The artisanal food movement that smartly nurtured and championed the booming Smorgasburg outdoor food markets on the Brooklyn side of the East River has landed in the South Street Seaport, to hurrahs. It's just a sprinkling of the scores of artisanal food and beverage vendors that set up on seasonal weekends at the Brooklyn Flea in DUMBO and the Brookyn Smorgasburg in Williamsburg—but it's bringing an enviable lineup of food choices to the Seaport at last. From late May to late October, vendors like the **Red Hook Lobster Pound** (Maine lobster rolls, shrimp rolls), the **Brooklyn Oyster Party** (fresh-shucked oysters), **Pizza Moto** (wood-fired pizzas), and **Blue Marble Ice Cream** set up daily on the pedestrian plaza along Front Street.

Specialty Stores

BAGEL SHOPS

Absolute Bagels, 2788 Broadway, near 108th St.; (212) 932-2052; absolutebagels.com; Subway: 1 to Cathedral Pkwy. or 103rd St. Get in line at this small, no-frills shop close to Columbia University for what some say are the city's best bagels. The bagels are baked on premises, and you can choose flavored cream cheeses to go with.

Bantam Bagels, 283 Bleecker St., at Seventh Ave.; (646) 852-3041; bantambagels.com; Subway: A, E, C, D, F to W. Fourth St. It's a gimmick, all right, but what a concept: your favorite bagels (and even some combos you've never considered) shrunk down to mini filled bagel balls.

Ess-a-Bagel, 831 Third Ave., btw. 50th and 51st Sts.; (212) 980-1010; ess-a-bagel.com; Subway: 6 to 23rd St. This may be the borough's preeminent bagel factory, making hand-rolled bagels that *New York* magazine says "rank among the city's best." This store, along with the original Ess-a-Bagel, which opened in 1976 on First Avenue and 21st Street (212-260-2252), offers bagels in all flavors along with the works: spreads, smoked fish, deli meats, cheeses, and salads.

Kossar's Bialys, 367 Grand St., just east of Essex St.; (212) 253-2138; Subway: F, J, M, Z to Delancey St./Essex St. Kossar's Bialys has been making bialys (flat bagels made with high-gluten flour, brewers' yeast, salt, onions, and water) since 1936. Today they're still baked fresh here on the premises (along with fresh bagels) and sold for about $12 a dozen.

Murray's Bagels, 500 Sixth Ave., btw. 12th and 13th Sts.; (212) 627-5054; murraysbagels.com; Subway: F, V, L to 14th St./Sixth Ave., 1, 2, 3 to 14th St./Seventh Ave., or 4, 5, 6 to Union Square. Making 15 fresh, hand-rolled varieties, including pumpernickel, garlic, and sesame seed, Murray's makes fine New York bagels. It also has the requisite accompaniments, including terrific smoked salmon, cream cheese, pastries, and coffee.

BAKERIES & PASTRY SHOPS

Amy's Bread, 672 Ninth Ave., btw. 46th and 47th Sts.; (212) 977-2670; amysbread.com; Subway: N, R to 49th St. A pioneer in small-batch, artisanal baking, Amy's Bread opened in this little 1896 Hell's Kitchen storefront in 1992. Sample hearty breads made using traditional European baking methods, like semolina with golden raisins and fennel or big and small loaves of walnut raisin, as well as house-made pastries, scones, biscuits, cookies, cakes, cupcakes, sandwiches, and more. Today Amy's Bread has locations in **Chelsea Market** (75 Ninth Ave., btw. 15th and 16th Sts.) and **Greenwich Village** (250 Bleecker St., at Leroy St.), but you can also find Amy's breads at retailers throughout the city; check the website for one near you.

Babycakes, 248 Broome St., btw. Orchard and Ludlow Sts.; (855) 462-2292; babycakesnyc.com; Subway: F, J, M, Z to Delancey St./Essex St. This cute-as-a-button shop looks and smells like a dream of a

bakery—and baby, it is—but it goes the extra healthful mile for people with food sensitivities and strict dietary requirements. All of its tasty cupcakes, cookies, brownies, muffins, and other baked goods are 100 percent vegan and wheat-, gluten-, egg-, and dairy-free. Agave nectar and evaporated cane juice substitute for refined sugar—and everything is certified kosher.

Balthazar Bakery, 80 Spring St., at Crosby St.; (212) 965-1785; balthazarbakery.com; Subway: 6 to Spring St. Selling the sublime artisanal breads and pastries offered at Balthazar restaurant next door, this bakery has a cozy Parisian feel. It also sells sandwiches, breakfast foods, soups, and desserts.

Beurre & Sel, 120 Essex St., btw. Delancey and Rivington Sts.; (917) 623-3239; nycedc.com/project/la-marqueta; Subway: 6 to Spring St. These exquisite cookies are the work of James Beard Award–winning baker and cookbook author Dorie Greenspan. It also has a stall in **La Marqueta** in East Harlem (1590 Park Ave., at 115th St.; nycedc .com/project/la-marqueta).

Birdbath Bakery, 160 Spring St., btw. West Broadway and Thompson St.; (646) 556-7720; thecitybakery.com/birdbath; Subway: 6 to Spring St. The ultra-green arm of the celebrated business that is already steeped in eco-consciousness, the **City Bakery** (see p. 177), Birdbath strives to be as carbon-footprint-light, sustainable, and locavore (and organic) as possible. You can see the Birdbath bikes all over town. You'll find many of the same excellent bakery treats that City Bakery makes, including raspberry bran muffins, maple-bacon biscuits, and oversize chocolate-chip cookies. The SoHo location is in the Vesuvio Bakery, one of the most photogenic old storefronts in town, a circa-1920 wooden storefront painted a distinctive green.

Bouchon Bakery, Time Warner Center, 10 Columbus Circle, 3rd fl.; (212) 823-9366; bouchonbakery.com; Subway; 1, A, B, C, D to Columbus Circle/59th St. This retail bakery and 60-seat cafe is the work of Chef Thomas Keller, and the wonderful house-made breads, pastries, and sweets are crafted around French baking techniques. The bakery also has a few savories, like quiche, sandwiches, and salads.

Caffè Dante, 79–81 MacDougal St., btw. Bleecker and Houston Sts.; (866) 681-0299; caffe-dante.com; Subway: 1, 9 to Houston St. This vintage Italian cafe sells a range of Italian pastries with espresso and cappuccino.

Caffè Roma, 385 Broome St., at Mulberry St.; (212) 226-8413; Subway: 6 to Spring St. This atmospheric slice of old Little Italy has a genuine tin ceiling and tile floors. Sit at one of the little wrought-iron cafe tables and sip cappuccino and nibble on Italian cookies or cannoli.

The City Bakery, 3 W. 18th St.; btw. Fifth and Sixth Aves.; (212) 366-1414; thecity bakery.com; Subway: L, N, R, 4, 5, 6 to Union Square/14th St. Yes, it's a gourmet salad bar, but it's also really a bakery, fashioning house-made delicacies such as ginormous cookies, blueberry corn muffins, artisansal pizzas, pretzel croissants, and maple bacon biscuits. Warm up in winter with a cup of decadent City Bakery hot chocolate.

DeRobertis Pasticceria, 176 First Ave., between 10th and 11th Sts.; (212) 674-7137; derobertiscaffe.com; Subway: 6 to Astor Place. An old-fashioned, unfancy pastry shop selling creamy cannoli and cheesecake along with anise cookies and fruit tarts.

Doughnut Plant, 379 Grand St.; (212) 505-3700; doughnutplant .com; Subway: F, J, M, Z to Delancey St./Essex St. This is one of those culinary miracles that make us glad to be living in 21st-century Manhattan. We would hang out at the Doughnut Plant all day long, inhaling its ethereal gourmet doughnuts, if only we had an extra pancreas or two. On a recent fall Saturday, a quietly reverent queue of doughnut fans was musing over the day's autumnal flavors, among them cinnamon apple, vanilla bean, and pumpkin (the latter studded with a honeyed glaze of roasted nuts). Buy it to go, or take your bag with a cup of French press coffee. The Doughnut Plant also has a location at the revamped **Hotel Chelsea** (220 W. 23rd St., btw. Seventh and Eighth Aves.; 212-505-3700).

Duane Park Patisserie, 179 Duane St., near Greenwich St.; (212) 274-8447; duaneparkpatisserie.com; Subway: 1, 2, 3, 4, 5, 6, J, A, C, Z to Chambers St. This charming bakery has a turn-of-the-century Parisian-patisserie aesthetic, with white-tile floors and high ceilings. Inside the bakery case are fruit pies and berry tarts, not to mention an assortment of cakes. It's a great place to stop for breakfast croissants, scones, Danishes, and muffins in the morning or an afternoon snack of freshly baked cookies or cupcakes and homemade lemonade.

FP Patisserie, 1293 Third Ave., at 74th St.; (212) 717-5252; payard.com; Subway: 6 to 77th St./Lexington Ave. Award-winning pastry chef François Payard is a master of chocolate, cakes, and cookies, with divine *macarons* and decadent double-chocolate cookies. The flagship Payard Patisserie & Cafe is a somewhat sterile spot on Third Avenue, but Payard also has livelier bakery/patisserie locations at 1 West 58th St., 210 Murray St., 116 W. Houston St., and 3 Columbus Circle.

Hungarian Pastry Shop, 1030 Amsterdam Ave., at 111th St.; (212) 866-4230; Subway: 1 to Cathedral Pkwy. This old-fashioned Morningside Heights cafe and bakery is everything Starbucks is not, slightly down at the heels but full of dim, cozy nooks crammed with Columbia students inhaling the good coffee, the fresh strudels and croissants, and delicious walnut macaroons.

Il Buco Alimentari & Vineria, 53 Great Jones St., btw. the Bowery and Lafayette St.; (212) 837-2622; ilbucovineria.com; Subway: 6 to Bleecker St. Master baker Kamel Saci starts his day around 3 a.m. making some of the city's best bread. It's sold daily, fresh made, in the restaurant's splendid market/cafe up front, as are cured meats, gelato, olives, biscotti, and seasonal salads.

Little Cupcake Bakeshop, 30 Prince St., at Mott St.; (212) 941-9100; littlecupcakebakeshop.com; Subway: N, R to Prince St. or 6 to Spring St. This corner bakeshop is as cute as a button, a sweet little slice of Main Street USA plunked down in groovy Nolita. It's actually a Brooklyn transplant specializing in small-batch baked goods, making downright righteous cupcakes (and cakes and banana pudding and cookies, pies, and pudding), using ingredients that are as locally and sustainably sourced as possible. The cupcakes are hand-crafted beauties, with that imperfect-looking artisanal perfection, coming in such tantalizing flavors as Blue Velvet, Brooklyn Blackout, and Coconut Cloud.

Little Pie Company, 424 W. 43rd St., btw. Ninth and Tenth Aves.; (212) 736-4780; littlepiecompany.com; Subway: A, C, E to 42nd St./Port Authority. This little shop has been baking house-made pies with fresh ingredients (no preservatives) since 1985. The menu includes a Mississippi mud pie, banana coconut cream, Southern pecan, and Little Pie's signature creation, a sour cream apple walnut pie, as well as cakes, muffins, brownies, even chicken pot pies.

Maison Kayser/Eric Kayser Artisan Boulanger, 1294 Third Ave., at 74th St.; (212) 744-3100; maison-kayser-usa.com; Subway: 6 to 77th St./Lexington Ave. French master baker Eric Kayser has invaded New York with his chemical-yeast-free leaven breads and pastries. This, his first American outpost (two more will be open at press time), is both a boulangerie/patisserie and a full-service, 100-seat cafe.

Make My Cake, 121 St. Nicholas Ave., at 116th St.; (212) 932-0833; makemycake.com; Subway: 2, 3 to 116th St. Expats from the American South dreaming of Southern-style pies and cakes better hustle on up to Harlem for this shop's endearing favorites and updated twists from the Alabama/Mississippi school. Look for instant classics like sweet potato cheesecake, red velvet cake with toasted pecans, and lemon meringue pie. Cakes are pretty as a picture. Make My Cake has another location at 2380 Adam Clayton Powell Blvd. (at 139th St.; 212-234-2344).

Parisi Bakery, 198 Mott St., btw. Spring and Kenmare Sts.; (212) 460-8750; parisibakery.com; Subway: N, R to Prince St., 6 to Bleecker/Lafayette or Spring St. Frank Sinatra loved Parisi bread, and we used to love meandering by Parisi's open-door bakery just to trail the scent of fresh-baked bread down Elizabeth Street. Nowadays, this century-old family-owned shop has two locations: The bakery is at 290 Elizabeth Street (btw. Houston and Bleecker Sts.) and the delicatessen is at 198 Mott Street, the site of the original bakery. Both offer fresh Parisi bread baked daily.

Rocco's, 243 Bleecker St., btw. Carmine and Leroy Sts.; (212) 242-6031; pasticceriarocco.com; Subway: A, B, C, D, E, F, M to W. 4th St. This is the last of the old-fashioned Italian *pasticceria* (pastry shops) on the traditional Italian strip of Bleecker Street between Sixth and Seventh Avenues. This is the place to buy pound boxes of fancy Italian cookies and biscotti; or pastries like chocolate éclairs or babas au rhum; or classic Italian desserts, such as house-made tiramisu, gelato, and Rocco's cannoli, a made-to-order treat and the creation of pastry chef Rocco Generoso, whose family has owned the pastry shop since 1974.

Sugar Sweet Sunshine, 126 Rivington St., btw. Essex and Norfolk Sts.; (212) 995-1960; sugarsweetsunshine.com; Subway: F, J, M, Z to Delancey St./Essex St. Our favorite cupcake shop is everything you want a cupcake shop to be: warm and inviting and slightly messy in that homegrown, hands-on fashion where the kitchen and the shop are practically one. As you pay for your sweet stuff, you'll be mere feet from bakers bustling about in kerchiefs amid trays of fresh-baked cupcakes.

Sullivan St. Bakery, 533 W. 47th St., btw. Tenth and Eleventh Aves.; (212) 265-5583; sullivanstreetbakery.com; Subway: A, C, E to 42nd St. Sullivan Street Bakery and its wondrous breads, pizzas, and panini can be found in its flagship shop on the city's western edges in Hell's Kitchen or in its newer (and likely more convenient) retail location in Chelsea at 236 Ninth Ave. Sample rustic loaves of bread, square-cut slices of Roman-style pizza, or a bomboloni, the bakery's Italian doughnut. The *pizza bianca,* brushed with olive oil and sea salt, has crispy bubbles of heavenly char.

Veniero's, 342 E. 11th St., between First and Second Aves.; (212) 674-7070; venierospastry.com; Subway: L to 14th St./Second Ave. or 6 to Astor Place. The scent of sugary things almost makes your teeth ache in this marble-floored cafe. Get in line and order up a box of classic Italian pastries or cookies, plus cappuccino and espresso made with a flourish.

Zucker Bakery, 433 E. 9th St., between First Ave. and Ave. A; (646) 559-8425; zuckerbakery.com; Subway: 6 to Astor Place. Just when you think the Village has overdosed on adorable little bakeshops, you stumble upon this homey spot, and it's a heartbreaker. The owner/ baker customizes Eastern European and Middle Eastern classics from personal family recipes. All are beautifully crafted, including a rugelach made with almonds and scented dates, chocolate "snowballs" flavored with coffee and rolled in coconut flakes, and sticky buns called "Roses."

BUTCHERS/MEAT SHOPS

The Cannibal, 113 E. 29th St., btw. Park and Lexington Aves.; (212) 686-5480; thecannibalnyc.com; Subway: 6 to 28th St./Lexington Ave. The retail  arm of the Murray Hill restaurant of the same name, the Cannibal sells choice cuts of meat as well as bike paraphernalia for its cycling-loving owners/clientele (it was named for a celebrated Grand Tour cyclist who ruled the pro circuit 50 years ago).

Ceriello, Grand Central Market, Grand Central Station, 43rd St. and Lexington Ave.; (212) 972-4266; ceriellofinefoods.com; Subway: S, 4, 5, 6 to Grand Central/42nd St. This high-end butcher has an excellent array of prime-aged beef, organic poultry, Italian sausages, prepared foods, dry pasta, and pasta sauces.

Faicco's Pork Shop, 260 Bleecker St., near Leroy St.; (212) 243-1974; Subway: A, B, C, D, E, F, M to W. 4th St. A century-old Italian market run by the same family since 1898, Faicco's sells Italian sausages, trimmed meats, ready-made meatballs and ziti, as well as sauces, pastas, cheeses, olives, oils, and vinegars.

Florence Prime Meat Market, 5 Jones St., at Bleecker St.; (212) 242-6531; Subway: 1 to Christopher St. or A, B, C, D, E, F, M to W. 4th St. This classic butcher shop in the heart of the Village gets a lot of local love for its hand-cut steaks, fresh ground meat, fresh poultry, and personal service.

Harlem Shambles, 2141 Frederick Douglass Blvd., at 116th St.; (646) 476-4650; harlemshambles.com; Subway: B, C to 118th St. This boutique butcher shop partners with locals farms like Kinderhook Farms (a Hudson Valley farm that raises 100-percent grass-fed beef and lamb) and Arcadian Pastures (producing hormone- and antibiotic-free heritage breeds).

The Heritage Meat Shop, 120 Essex St., at Delancey St.; (212) 539-1111; heritagemeatshop.com; Subway: F, J, M, Z to Delancey St./Essex St. This little butcher stall is a wonder, selling artisanal, humanely raised and slaughtered meat from heritage and rare breeds as well as some of the nation's top country hams.

L. Simchick & Co. Meats, 988 First Ave., btw. 54th and 55th Sts.; (212) 888-2299; lsimchick.com; Subway: 6 to 51st St. A full-service source for fresh meat and poultry that also sells prepared foods such as roast chicken, chicken pot pie, lasagna, and beef brisket; oven-ready meals like meat loaf, stuffed pork chops, and fruited pork roast; not to mention deli meats, meat sauces, vegetable sides and salads, and homemade soups.

Le Marais, 150 W. 46th St., btw. Sixth and Seventh Aves.; (212) 869-0900; lemarais.net; Subway: N, R, S, 7, 1, 2, 3 to 42nd St. A butcher shop selling prime kosher meats aged on the premises is situated in a glatt-kosher (non-dairy) French steak house in the Theater District. Look for quality French-cut steaks as well as specialized meats like veal sausage and lamb roast.

Schatzie the Butcher, 555 Amsterdam Ave., at 87th St.; (212) 410-1555; schatziethebutcher

.com; **Subway: A, C to 86th St.** Schatzie has been in the meat business some 50 years, and this shop sells top-quality USDA Prime beef, free-range poultry, milk-fed veal, Colorado lamb, cheeses, and heat-and-eat prepared foods like brisket, roast loin of pork, and meat loaf.

Union Square Greenmarket, Union Square, btw. 14th and 17th Sts.; L, N, R, 4, 5, 6 to Union Square/14th St. Cut out the middleman entirely and buy your fresh meat direct from the farmers themselves at the city's greenmarkets. Union Square (Mon, Wed, Fri, and Sat) has a number of regular meat purveyors, with an emphasis on sustainability, humane practices, and rare or heritage breeds. Among them, **Flying Pigs Farms** (flyingpigsfarm.com) is at the Union Square farmers' market every Friday and Saturday selling pork—chops, ham steaks, cutlets, slab bacon, artisanal sausages—from rare heritage breeds. **Quattro's Game Farm** sells poultry, venison, and fresh eggs raised in Dutchess County, New York, at the Saturday greenmarket. **Tamarack Hollow Farm** (tamarackhollowfarm.com) sells heritage-breed pork and poultry in Union Square every Wednesday. Piedmontese beef is the specialty of the 28-acre family-owned **Stony Mountain Ranch** (stonymountainranch.net), which has a stand at Union Square every Wednesday. For farm-fresh eggs from "free-running" chickens raised on vegetarian-only feed and no hormones or antibiotics, you can't do better than Dutchess County–based **Knoll Krest Farm** (v3test.com/knollkrestfarm).

CHEESE/DAIRY SHOPS

Alleva, 188 Grand St., at Mulberry St.; (212) 226-7990; allevadairy.com; Subway: 6 to Spring St. This Little Italy old-timer is a favorite on the food-tour circuit, a genuine window onto turn-of-the-20th-century immigrant life. Family-owned and -operated since 1892, Alleva sells homemade mozzarella in several iterations, including fresh and smoked. It's a good place to get quality ricotta, shaved Parmesan,

Asiago, pecorino, as well as fresh-made Italian sausages, breads, olives, pastas, and sliced-to-order *salumi*.

Artisanal Bistro Cheese Shop, 2 Park Ave., at 32nd St.; (212) 532-4033; artisanalbistro.com; Subway: 6 to 33rd St. It's a small selection, but the cheese counter at Artisanal Bistro sells many of the same hand-crafted, artisanal cheeses you dine on in the restaurant, and more.

Bedford Cheese Shop, 67 Irving Place, btw. 18th and 19th Sts.; (718) 599-7588; bedfordcheeseshop.com; Subway: L, N, R, 4, 5, 6 to Union Square/14th St. This welcoming neighborhood *fromagerie* is a Williamsburg outpost with a genuine country-store aesthetic: wooden floors, barrels of cheese, and a big dairy case crammed with cheese.

Culture: An American Yogurt Company, 60 W. 8th St., near MacDougal St.; (646) 823-9715; cultureny.com; Subway: 1 to Christopher St. or A, B, C, D, E, F, M to W. 4th St. Cultivating its own yogurt onsite using milk from Hudson Valley Fresh and Organic Valley farms, Culture makes stuffing your gut with bacteria (the good kind) an addictive pleasure. Look for fresh-made, probiotic-rich yogurt with artisanal fruit toppings as well as frozen yogurt in a seasonally changing medley of flavors. And yes, it started in Brooklyn.

East Village Cheese Shop, 40 Third Ave., btw. 10th and 11th Sts.; (212) 477-2601; Subway: 6 to Astor Place. With little to no ambience, and windows plastered in white paper signs advertising the shop's low, low prices, East Village Cheese has been selling cheeses from all over the world for what feels like forever. The decor hasn't changed in years, but the prices for quality cheese undercut pretty much everyone else.

5 Oz. Factory, 24 W. 8th St., btw. Fifth Ave. and MacDougal St.; (212) 777-MILK [777-6455]; 5ozfactory.com; Subway: 1 to Christopher St. or A, B, C, D, E, F, M to W. 4th St. The Wisconsin dairy farm comes to the Big Apple at this Village shop, which opened in 2013 (on an increasingly interesting food block). The shop specializes in gooey cheese melts and densely creamy Midwestern frozen custard made from dairy products sourced from the great state of Wisconsin. To go or eat in.

Ideal Cheese Shop, 942 First Ave., at 52nd St.; (800) 382-0109; idealcheese.com; Subway: 6 to 51st St. Offering some 250 cheese varieties from 17 countries, this gourmet cheese shop and specialty market is going on 60 years old.

Murray's Cheese Shop, 254 Bleecker St., btw. Sixth and Seventh Aves.; (212) 243-3289; murrayscheese.com; Subway: 1 to Christopher St. or A, B, C, D, E, F, M to W. 4th St. This smart-looking Village cheese shop is the city's premier cheese purveyor; it has an excellent selection of *salumi,* olives, nuts, pastas, and crackers and even artisanal beers. Sandwiches and soups are made daily at the front of the store, and if they whet your appetite for more, Murray's now has a next-door restaurant, **Murray's Cheese Bar** (264 Bleecker St.; 646-476-8882), serving up cheesy standards like mac 'n' cheese, spaghetti *cacio e pepe,* cheese melts, and cheeseburgers. Murray's has a second location in **Grand Central Market** (Grand Central Station, 43rd St. and Lexington Ave; 212-922-1542).

Union Square Greenmarket, Union Square, btw. 14th and 17th Sts.; L, N, R, 4, 5, 6 to Union Square/14th St. Buy premium milk, butter, yogurt, and cheese every Saturday from **Ronnybrook Dairy Farm** (ronnybrook.com), out of Ancramdale, New York. (Ronnybrook also has a cafe in Chelsea Market.) Selling a wide range of goat cheese (feta, chèvre, and blue cheese), goat's milk, and yogurt from its herd of Nubian and Saanen goats, the **Butterfield Farm Company** (promotethe goat.com) is at Union Square every Monday and Saturday.

COOKBOOKS, VINTAGE & NEW

Bonnie Slotnick Cookbooks, 163 W. 10th St., btw. Seventh Ave. and Waverly Place; (212) 989-8962; bonnieslotnickcookbooks .com; Subway: 1 to Christopher St. This inviting nook of a store is crammed with vintage cookbooks of every stripe—from community cookbooks to rare collectibles to antiquarian gems—with a sprinkling of vintage kitchenware like Pyrex bowls and old-fashioned aprons. The warm, engaging owner, Bonnie Slotnick, is a real champion of the neighborhood. Closed Mon.

Greenwich Street Cookbooks, 488 Greenwich St., btw. Spring and Canal Sts.; (212) 226-5731; greenwichstreetcookbooks .com or joannehendrickscookbooks.com; Subway: A to Spring St. We like to think that once upon a time the city was filled with little enchantments like this antique-cookbook shop on the fringes of Canal Street. In a vintage townhouse, behind a rusticated wooden door that whispers cookbooks is this sweet shop with lots of wondrous old things—antique cookbooks, vintage jelly glasses, teapots, and tea cozies.

Kitchen Arts & Letters, 1435 Lexington Ave., btw. Seventh Ave. and Waverly Place; (212) 876-5550; kitchenartsandletters.com; Subway: 8 to 96th St. Sprawling and comprehensive, this Upper East Side store has a stock of some 13,000 cookbook titles, including brand-new, foreign, and out-of-print books.

COOKWARE/KITCHEN SHOPS

ABC Carpet & Home, 888 Broadway, at 18th St.; (212) 473-3000; abchome.com; Subway: L, N, R, 4, 5, 6 to Union Square/14th St. Much to covet here, from state-of-the-art cookware to vintage-style glassware to artisanal table linens beyond your wildest dreams. It may expand further by selling foodstuffs from the store's celebrated restaurants, ABC Kitchen and ABC Cocina.

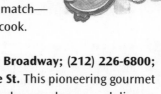

Broadway Panhandler, 65 E. 8th St., near Mercer St.; (212) 966-3434; broadway panhandler.com; Subway: N, R to 8th St. or 6 to Astor Place. A smart selection of gourmet cookware and commercial-quality kitchen tools—with often discounted prices to match—make this an essential stop for the home cook.

Dean & DeLuca, 121 Prince St., at Broadway; (212) 226-6800; deandeluca.com; Subway: N, R to Prince St. This pioneering gourmet food market has a selection of high-end cookware, glasses, and dinnerware in the back of its Prince Street flagship store.

Eataly, 200 Fifth Ave., btw. 23rd and 24th Sts.; (212) 229-2560; eatalyny.com; Subway: N, R to 23rd St. This mammoth Italian-food emporium has a small but select section of cookware, kitchen gadgets, and culinary doo-dads, pretty much all of it Italian made. You'll covet the exquisite designs from Alessi, incuding a stainless-steel-and-glass sugar jar in a beehive shape, or the wonderful glass tableware from Guzzini.

MoMA Design and Book Store, 11 W. 53rd St., btw. Fifth and Sixth Aves.; (212) 708-9700; momastore.org; Subway: N, R to 57th St. or Fifth Ave. If you're looking for uniquely designed everyday kitchenware and housewares, the MoMA shop is tops. From smartly fashioned bread boxes to whimsical glassware to elegant enamelware to measuring cups and chopping knives, the selection here exemplifies the form-follows-function aesthetic. It also has a location in SoHo (81 Spring St., btw. Crosby St. and Broadway; 646-613-1367).

N.Y. Cake & Baking Distributor, 56 W. 22nd St., btw. Fifth and Sixth Aves.; (212) 675-CAKE [675-2253]; nycake.com; Subway: N, R to 23rd St. This unfussy, old-fashioned baking supply store is somewhat under the radar, but real home cooks and bakers are all over it. Its 5,000 square feet are jammed with baking pans, cake stands, cake molds, cake toppers, and all manner of decorations, including edible sugar diamonds.

Sur la Table, 306 W. 57th St., at Eighth Ave.; (212) 574-8334; surlatable.com; Subway: A, B, C, D, 1 to Columbus Circle/59th St. This chain gourmet kitchenware shop has cookware, cook's tools, dinnerware, linens, and more, and is always stocked with nifty gift gadgets. Look for good prices and even better ongoing sales. It has two other locations in Manhattan: SoHo (75 Spring St., at Crosby St.; 212-966-3375); and Upper East Side (1320 Third Ave., at 75th St.; 646-843-7984).

Zabar's, 2245 Broadway, at 80th St.; (212) 496-1234; zabars.com; Subway: 1, 9 to 79th St. In the upstairs mezzanine at Zabar's is a top-notch selection of coffeemakers, food processors, bakeware, pots, pans, knives, housewares, and gifty things.

CUPCAKE/CAKE SHOPS

Baked by Melissa, 7 E. 14th St., btw. Fifth Ave. and University Place, and 10 more locations in Manhattan; bakedbymelissa.com. Less traditional cupcake and more bite-size morsels, Baked by Melissa's shrunken-down versions are as cute as buttons and not much bigger.

They taste great, too, coming in such creative flavors as Tie-Dye, Peanut Butter Cup, and Candy Corn (a Halloween special).

Buttercup Bake Shop, 973 Second Ave., at 51st St.; (212) 350-4144; buttercupbakeshop.com; Subway: 6 to 51st St. Buttercup makes fetching fresh-from-scratch cakes and cupcakes in the Magnolia Bakery mold (which makes sense; owner/baker Jennifer Appel cofounded Magnolia back in 1996).

Crumbs, multiple locations; crumbs.com. If you must have a (big) cupcake *this very minute,* Crumbs sells fist-size versions at 20 Manhattan locations. They're plenty sweet. And Crumbs even has a **gluten- and peanut-free shop** (37 E. 8th St., between University Place and Broadway).

Cupcake Cafe, 545 Ninth Ave., at 40th St.; (212) 465-1530; cupcakecafe-nyc.com; Subway: N, R, 1, 2, 3, 9 to 42nd St. Cupcake Cafe makes some of the prettiest flower-bedecked cakes and cupcakes you can imagine, decorated with sugary sprays of purple violets, pink roses, and yellow sunflowers.

Dessert Club, ChikaLicious, 204 E. 10th St., btw. First and Second Aves.; (212) 475-0929; dessertclubchikalicious.com; Subway: 6 to Astor Place. When pitted in cupcake-tasting competitions against the big boys, ChickaLicious's cupcakes consistently rake in the top honors. They're silken beauties, tautly elegant, and come in a variety of interesting flavors, from red velvet to s'mores to key lime.

Little Cupcake Bakeshop, 30 Prince St., at Mott St.; (212) 941-9100; littlecupcakebakeshop.com; Subway: N, R to Prince St. This Brooklyn transplant is an old-fashioned pocket of Main Street USA plunked down on the aggressively trendy streets of Nolita. Its handmade cupcakes are a model of beautiful imperfection, topped with artful swoops of frosting. Among the flavors are Blue Velvet, Coconut Cloud, and Brooklyn Blackout, and look for a raft of other bakery classics (banana pudding, muffins, cakes).

Magnolia Bakery, 401 Bleecker St., at W. 11th St.; (212) 462-2572; magnoliabakery.com; Subway: 1 to Christopher St. Perhaps the most famous cupcake shop in Manhattan, a celebrity from its telegenic work in *Sex and the City,* the flagship store of Magnolia Bakery is a winning bit of homespun fancy, a Village shop with lacy curtains in the windows and a genuine screen door. *Sex and the City* tours stop here for cupcake breaks on a regular basis, but even after the tour buses have blasted away, tourists from all over the globe fill the little store, sampling Magnolia's big, pastel-hued cupcakes. (We actually prefer the Southern-style banana pudding.) Magnolia has been on an expansion kick of late and now has four other locations in Manhattan: **Grand Central Station Lower Dining Concourse** (212-682-3588); **Rockefeller Center,** 1240 Ave. of the Americas, at 49th St. (212-767-1123); **Bloomingdale's,** 1000 Third Ave., btw. 59th and 60th Sts. (212-265-5320); and the **Upper West Side,** 200 Columbus Ave., at 69th St. (212-724-8101).

Tribeca Treats, 94 Reade St., btw. Church St. and West Broadway; tribecatreats.com; (212) 571-0500; Subway: 1, 2, 3, 4, 5, 6, J, A, C, Z to Chambers St. This specialty bakery makes lovely cakes and cupcakes in flavors ranging from black velvet to s'mores.

Two Little Red Hens, 1652 Second Ave., at 86th St.; (212) 452-0476; twolittleredhens.com; Subway: 4, 5, 6 to 86th St./Lexington Ave. This boutique bakery makes some of the city's best cupcakes in flavors like gingerbread and banana peanut butter.

DELICATESSENS/SMOKED FISH

Barney Greengrass, 541 Amsterdam Ave., at 86th St.; (212) 724-4707; barneygreengrass.com; Subway: 1 to 86th St. A West Side institution since 1908, Barney Greengrass offers top-notch smoked fish and accoutrements—nova, lox, chopped liver, cold borscht, whitefish salad—to take out or eat in.

Katz's, 205 E. Houston St., at Ludlow St.; (212) 254-2246; katzsdeli catessen.com; Subway: F to Second Ave. It's crowded, you bet, and the overcaffeinated deli guys keep things moving. But up on the coun- ter plops a fresh-cut slice of meaty wonderfulness on a piece of wax paper. Snap it up before the wolves all around you do. It's pearlescent with fat, all velvety perfection. And that's just the pastrami! Ask for it, or the tender brisket sandwich, or the corned beef on rye.

Pastrami Queen, 1125 Lexington Ave., near 78th St.; (212) 734- 1500; pastramiqueen.com; Subway: 6 to 77th St. A Queens classic that moved to Manhattan back in 1998 (talk about a reverse commute) and, curiously, changed its gender in the process (from Pastrami King to Pastrami Queen), this kosher deli is old school right down to its tile floor and deli case crammed with salads and meats. It may be on the small side, but step inside for an irresistible onslaught of pastrami perfume.

Russ & Daughters, 179 E. Houston St., btw. Orchard and Lud- low Sts.; (212) 475-4880; russanddaughters.com; Subway: F to Sec- ond Ave. What began as a family-owned pushcart in 1911 celebrated its 100th year in business in 2014, still run by the same family, whose patriarch, Joel Russ, named the shop for his three daughters in 1933. Inside are creamy white dairy cases holding an assortment of smoked or cured lox and nova, sable, whitefish, herring, chopped liver, and an intuitive selection of newfangled stuff, like smoked salmon tartare. And by the time you read this, Russ & Daughters will have opened its first business offshoot, a 65-seat **cafe at 127 Orchard St.**, serving the good stuff that made them famous.

Sarge's, 548 Third Ave., btw. 36th and 37th Sts.; (212) 679-0442; sargesdeli.com; Subway: 6 to Lexington Ave./33rd St. This slightly under-the-radar neighborhood delicatessen has been quietly selling and serving top-notch smoked fish by the platter or pound (not to mention sandwiches, burgers, salads, soups, cheesecake—the whole deli oeuvre) since 1964—and it's open 24 hours!

Second Avenue Deli, 162 E. 33rd St., btw. Lexington and Third Aves.; (212) 689-9000; 2ndavedeli.com; Subway: 6 to 33rd St. No longer in its downtown location on Second Avenue, this blessedly old-school deli now has two locations (the other is at 1442 First Ave., at 75th St.; 212-737-1700). Give it up for "Jewish penicillin"—classic matzoh ball soup—deli salads, and overstuffed sandwiches, including pastrami, corned beef, and brisket.

Zabar's, 2245 Broadway, at 80th St.; (212) 496-1234; zabars .com; Subway: 1, 9 to 79th St. This legendary epicurean marketplace is everything it's cracked up to be. The 20,000-square-foot store is crammed with food, not only the unparalleled smoked fish it's famous for, but vast sections of delicious prepared foods, gourmet edibles, coffees, chocolates, bread, juices, you name it. Cheeses fill one whole section of the store, and upstairs on the mezzanine is a terrific selection of coffeemakers, food processors, bakeware, pots, pans, knives, housewares, and gifty things. Prepared foods are dazzling: It's every salad you can think of, house-made soups, mouthwatering entrees, and cooked meats. But Zabar's built its business and its reputation for

Food-Related Charities and Nonprofits

Perhaps nowhere in New York is Mayor Bill de Blasio's "tale of two cities" more readily apparent than in Manhattan. With Wall Street firms soaring following the financial crisis in 2008 and the UBS Global Billionaire Census 2013 reporting that New York City can claim the world's largest number of billionaires, the moneyed class is a vivid and powerful presence in the borough. The skyscraping luxury buildings belie the very real struggles of the city's lower and middle classes and society's most vulnerable citizens. A number of food-related charities continue to carry on the noble tradition of helping the needy. If you're looking into charity giving, consider the following:

Citymeals-on-Wheels (citymeals.org): Provides meals to thousands of elderly New Yorkers annually.

City Harvest (cityharvest.org): This 30-year-old charity "rescues" excess food (from restaurants, farmers' markets, corporate cafeterias) and delivers it to some 400 community food programs in the city.

God's Love We Deliver (glwd.org): This organization prepares and delivers nutritious meals to people who are unable to provide for themselves because of illness.

New York Food Bank (foodbanknyc.org): A 30-year-old hunger-relief organization finds and distributes food to hundreds of community-based member programs.

exacting standards on smoked fish and classic deli accompaniments, and theirs may be the city's best.

FISH MARKETS

In addition to the following, the stores of **Whole Foods** (wholefoods market.com) and **Citarella** (citarella.com) have excellent seafood sections.

Chinatown, Subway: N, R, 4, 5, 6 to Canal Street. Chinatown's seafood markets are famous for selling the most inexpensive seafood in town. You can buy a pound of shrimp for half the price you'd pay anywhere else in the city. In Chinatown, it's about volume (the locals like their seafood) and what the local market can bear. It's also about competition: The neighborhood has scores of seafood markets, often side by side. Many of the best seafood markets are found on Grand Street and Chrystie; on Mulberry between Bayard and Canal Streets; and along Elizabeth Street. Fresh seafood—including live fish—are found at larger seafood emporiums like New York Marts at 128 Mott Street. Keep in mind that Chinatown's seafood markets are often interspersed with vegetable stands selling vegetables and fruits often at prices much cheaper than you'll find elsewhere in the city.

The Lobster Place, Chelsea Market, 75 Ninth Ave., btw. 15th and 16th Sts.; (212) 255-5672; lobsterplace.com; Subway: A, C, E, L to 14th St. Newly expanded, smartly reconfigured, and dazzlingly comprehensive, this is not just a seafood market; it's a seafood shack, raw bar, sushi bar, and lobster bar. Next door is the Lobster Place's sit-down seafood eatery, Cull & Pistol, complete with its own oyster bar. If you love seafood, and we do, this is a jewel of a fish market.

Pescatore, Grand Central Market, Grand Central Station, 43rd St. and Lexington Ave.; (212) 557-4466; pescatoreny.com; Subway: S, 4, 5, 6 to Grand Central/42nd St. An outstanding seafood market, with quality fish, prepared seafood dishes, and ready-to-cook prepared foods. As with its Grand Central Market neighbor **Wild Edibles** (below), the high-rent location means inflated prices, some of the highest you'll pay for raw seafood in the city, but the quality is high as well.

Pisacane Seafood, 940 First Ave., btw. 51st and 52nd Sts.; (212) 758-1525; pisacanefishandseafood.com; Subway: 6 to 51st St. This longtime fishmonger has been selling wholesale and retail fish and seafood for more than 50 years.

Sea Breeze Fish Market, 541 Ninth Ave., at W. 40th St.; (212) 563-7537; seabreezefishmarkets.com; Subway: A, C, E to 42nd St./ Port Authority. This no-frills retail fishmonger close to the Port Authority has some of the city's freshest, most reasonably priced fish.

Union Square Greenmarket, Union Square, between 14th and 17th Sts.; Subway: L, N, R, 4, 5, 6 to Union Square/14th St. Long Island fish purveyors sell fresh-off-the-boat seafood at the Union Square farmers' market (Mon, Wed, Fri, and Sat). A dry-erase board at the **Blue Moon Fish** farm stand (bluemoonfish.com) lets you know where—and often on which boat—your fish was caught; look for Long Island–based Blue Moon in Union Square every Wednesday. On Saturday look for the fresh regional fish and shellfish from the fishmongers of **P.E. & D.D. Fish,** out of Riverhead, Long Island.

Wild Edibles, Grand Central Market, Grand Central Station, 43rd St. and Lexington Ave.; (212) 687-4255; wildedibles.com; Subway:

S, 4, 5, 6 to Grand Central/42nd St. With a longtime commitment to sustainable fisheries, Wild Edibles is one of two excellent seafood markets in Grand Central Market (the competition can't hurt). It sells fresh, glistening seafood as well as prepared seafood dishes, chowders, seafood salads, and smoked fish. Again, prices are higher than you'll find at other markets, but the quality is impeccable—an essential when it comes to seafood.

PASTA/RAVIOLI SHOPS

Piemonte, 190 Grand St., at Mulberry St.; (212) 226-0475; piemonteravioli.com; Subway: 6 to Spring St. Piemonte has been making fresh ravioli, tortellini, and pasta since 1920.

Raffetto's, 144 W. Houston St., at Mac-Dougal St.; (212) 777-1261; raffettos pasta.com; Subway: 1 to Houston St. In business since 1906, this old-school ravioli shop is one of the last of the city's custom-made pasta shops. Raffetto's is still run by the Raffetto family, but the menu of ravioli and egg noodles has grown to include some 50 kinds of pastas, including ravioli filled with eggplant *pomodoro,* seafood in black squid, and Gorgonzola and walnut.

PICKLES

The Pickle Guys, 49 Essex St., btw. Grand and Hester Sts.; (212) 656-9739; pickleguys.com; Subway: F, J, M, Z to Essex St./Delancey St. Yes, you can still buy kosher pickles on the Lower East Side, and, even better, you can buy them from some of the same people who worked at the legendary Guss' Pickles over on Orchard Street. In this largely open-air market are barrels filled with classic kosher pickles as well as olives, pickled peppers, pickled vegetables, and pickled *arriv-istes* such as sun-dried tomato and watermelon.

SMOKED FISH

See Delicatessens, p. 192.

SPICES

Lior Lev Sercarz's La Boîte, 724 Eleventh Ave., btw. 51st and 52nd Sts.; (212) 247-4407; laboiteny.com; Subway: C, E to 59th St. Spicemaster to the star (chefs), Lior Lev Sercarz makes custom blends of spices and sells them at his Clinton Hill/Hell's Kitchen shop. Sercarz recently partnered with Le Bernardin chef Eric Ripert to create three spice blends for sale: a pepper blend, a gray sea salt, and Riviera herbal mashup.

Spices and Tease, 2580 Broadway, at 97th St.; (347) 470-8327; spicesandtease.com; Subway: 1, 2, 3 to West 96th St. With its roots in Naples, Italy, some four generations past, and following a blazing detour through France, Spices and Tease opened its first shop in New York in 2003, selling beautiful homemade blends of spices, pure spices, and several varieties of teas. You can see their distinctive displays of open bowls of spices at locations in Chelsea Market (75 Ninth Ave., btw. 15th and 16th Sts.) and the Grand Central Market (78 Grand Central Terminal, at Lexington Ave.).

TEAS

Kusmi Tea, 1037 Third Ave., at 61st St.; (212) 355-5580; us.kusmi tea.com; Subway: 4, 5, 6 to 59th St./Lexington Ave. A Gilded Age tea empire founded by a Russian peasant, Kusmi is enjoying a 21st-century revival. You can buy its celebrated teas, sold loose or in muslin sachets, at this, its first shop in the US, opened in 2010. Kusmi also has a cafe in the Plaza Food Hall at the Plaza Hotel.

McNulty's Rare Teas & Choice Coffees, 109 Christopher St., btw. Bleecker & Hudson Sts.; (212) 242-5351; mcnultys .com; Subway 1, 9 to Christopher St. Looking like an old-fashioned general store, all well-worn wood floors and vintage scales and apothecary glass jars filled with aromatic loose teas, McNulty's is a small, vivid slice of the village that once was Greenwich. This circa-1895 shop is packed with shelves, glass jars, burlap bags, and exotic Oriental tea chests.

Porto Rico, 201 Bleecker St., btw. MacDougal St. and Sixth Ave.; (212) 477-5421; portorico.com; Subway: A, B, C, D, E, F, M to W. 4th St. Established in 1907, this family-owned and -operated coffee and tea importer sells a wide range of teas, including green, black, oolong, scented and flavored, house blends, chai, rooibos, and herbal blends. (It also has locations at Essex Market on the Lower East Side, St. Mark's Place, and Brooklyn).

Spices and Tease, 2580 Broadway, at 97th St.; (347) 470-8327; spicesandtease.com; Subway: 1, 2, 3 to West 96th St. With its roots in Naples, Italy, some four generations past, and following a blazing detour through France, Spices and Tease opened its first shop in New York in 2003, selling beautiful homemade blends of spices, pure spices, and several varieties of teas. It has locations in Chelsea Market (75 Ninth Ave., btw. 15th and 16th Sts.) and the Grand Central Market (78 Grand Central Terminal, at Lexington Ave.).

Sun's Organic Garden Tea Shop, 79 Bayard St., at Mott St.; (212) 566-3260; Subway: 4, 5, 6 to Canal St. One of the city's best

MANHATTAN, THE GLOBAL MARKETPLACE

Homesick expats, take heart: If you look hard enough, you will locate the foodstuffs of your childhood. Keep in mind that Manhattan's **Chinatown** is loaded with places to find Chinese everything, and Korean markets can be found in the heart of **Koreatown,** along 32nd Street between Fifth and Sixth Avenues. Here are some other markets and shops that offer a taste of home.

Despaña SoHo, 408 Broome St., at Center St.; (212) 219-5050; despanabrandfoods.com; Subway: 6 to Spring St. A gourmet food shop selling the food and wine of Spain, including hand-carved meats (Serrano and Ibérico ham), sandwiches, cheeses, and Spanish condiments and olive oils, vinegars, olives, and vegetable and fruit preserves. It also includes a tapas cafe on the premises and a Spanish wine shop next door.

Di Palo's Fine Foods, 200 Grand St.; (212) 226-1033; dipaloselects .com; Subway: 6 to Spring St. or M, N, R, Z, 6 to Canal St. Only a handful of markets selling Italian foodstuffs are left in Little Italy, including this old-world shop, which opened in 1925 as a traditional *latteria* (dairy shop). Today the same family runs the shop, offering Italian cheeses, *salumi,* sauces, pasta, bread, olives, and prepared foods. Next door the family *enoteca* sells Italian wines.

Kalustyan's, 123 Lexington Ave., btw. 27th and 28th Sts.; (212) 685-3451; kalustyans.com; Subway: F to Second Ave. A Middle Eastern market, where the downstairs is filled with wooden barrels containing nuts, grains, and spices, and shelves are stocked with every kind of cooking oil, vinegar, and condiment known to humankind. Upstairs is a modest little cafe where trays are steaming with all manner of house-made Middle Eastern specialties, including a sublime *mujadarra* (lentils and bulghur wheat cooked with caramelized onions), fresh lentil soup, and stuffed samosas.

Myers of Keswick, 634 Hudson St., btw. Horatio and Jane Sts.; (212) 691-4194; myersofkeswick.com; Subway: A, C, E to 14th St./ Eighth Ave. Savor a handmade pork pie and cross the ocean to merry old. It's more than a little bit of England, what with fresh-made Cumberland sausage, Branston baked beans, cans of mushy peas, and jars of marmalade. Not to mention Union Jack teapots and lots of royal souvenirs.

Puro Chile, 161 Grand St., at Centre St.; (212) 925-0090; puro-chile.com; Subway: 6. One side of this shop sells Chilean wines from some 50 wineries, and the other sells Chilean goods, including edible treats, all organic. Look for Chilean olive oils, salts, jellies, spicy chutney, and a popular white-milk caramel sauce known as *manjar blanco.*

Sockerbit, 89 Christopher St., btw. 7th Avenue and Bleecker St.; (212) 206-8170; sockerbit.com; Subway: 1/9 to Christopher St. Swedish candies, in delicious flavors like hazelnut and framboise, colorfully wrapped and ready for stocking (or goody bag) stuffing.

Sunrise Mart, 29 Third Ave., near 9th St.; (212) 598-3040; Subway: 6 to Astor Place or N/R to 8th St. In an area of the East Village known as Little Tokyo, this upstairs Japanese grocery is the place to find frozen shumai and gyoza at a fraction of what you'll pay in restaurants; Japanese condiments; ramen, soba, and udon noodles; Japanese sodas and snacks; fish and produce; and even bento boxes to go. You can also find Sunrise Marts in Midtown East (12 E. 41st St., btw. Fifth and Sixth Aves.; 646-380-9280) and SoHo (494 Broome St., at West Broadway; 212-219-0033).

sources for Chinese, Taiwanese, and Japanese specialty teas and hand-blended herbal teas, with a warm, helpful owner (more "tea sommelier than merchant," says SeriousEats.com).

Ten Ren Tea & Ginseng Co., 75 Mott St., btw. Canal & Bayard Sts.; (212) 349-2286; tenrenusa.com; Subway: 4, 5, 6 to Canal St. Taiwanese tea maker Ten Ren has a store on Mott Street that's a must-stop for tea lovers. The tea cafe next door, Ten Ren Tea Time, is the spot to sip pearl, tapioca, and bubble tea, among other varieties.

WINE SHOPS

Acker Merrall & Condit, 160 72nd St., btw. Broadway and Columbus Ave.; (212) 787-0222; ackerwines.com; Subway: 1, 2, 3 to 72nd St./Broadway or B, C to 72nd/Central Park West. "America's oldest wine shop" has been in the grocery/wine business since 1820. It has its hands in all things wine, including offering a Wine Every Month Club, regular Wine Workshops and in-store tastings. It's also currently the world's leading wine auctioneer, securing and selling rare, collectible, and old wines (Acker Auctions). A 2013 Acker Auction of rare Bordeaux (including three double-magnums of 1990 Château Petrus) in Hong Kong set sales records. The wine shop is relatively small, but the staff knows its stuff.

Astor Wines & Spirits, 399 Lafayette St., at E. 4th St.; (212) 674-7500; astorwines.com; Subway: 6 to Astor Place. Located in a handsome landmark NoHo building, this sprawling wine shop is the biggest in the city. It's stocked with plenty of delectable wines at reasonable prices, but we sometimes find staff recommendations and advertised "employee selections" to be spotty. But if you know what you want, you have a very good chance of getting it—or something very similar—here. Astor Place has a number of ongoing tastings and big-time wine events; check the calendar online for the latest.

Bottle Rocket Wines, 5 W. 19th St., btw. Fifth and Sixth Aves.; (212) 929-2323; bottlerocket.com; Subway: N, R to 23rd St. This 2,500-square-foot Flatiron store takes the mystique out of buying wines with its helpful, unstuffy staff, easy layout, and highly drinkable wines that won't break the bank.

Chambers Street Wines, 148 Chambers St., btw. Greenwich St. and West Broadway; (212) 227-1434; chambersstwines.com; Subway: 1, 2, 3, 4, 5, 6, J, A, C, Z to Chambers St. One of the city's best little wine shops, with an erudite, passionate staff and an "anti-brand" commitment to naturally made wines from small, artisanal producers. That means you will discover wines here you simply won't find anywhere else, like a nifty little Cerdon Bugey. (And the shop has a coveted "Slow Food Snail of Approval" from Slow Food NYC.) It's in a classic loft space with rustic wood floors.

Chelsea Wine Vault, 75 Ninth Ave., btw. 15th and 16th Sts.; (212) 462-4244; chelseawinevault.com; Subway: A, C, E, L to 14th St./Eighth Ave. No kitchen-sink wine shop this, Chelsea Wine Vault has a select stock of choice wines that is ever fluid but always interesting. We find the selection (and recommendations) practically fail-safe for that perfect host or hostess gift bottle of wine. The staff is knowledgeable, and the shop entertains an ongoing rotation of tastings and events.

Crush Wine & Spirits, 153 E. 57th St., btw. Lexington and Third Aves.; (212) 980-WINE [980-9463]; crushwineco.com; Subway: N, R, 4, 5, 6 to Lexington Ave./59th St. This snazzy, stylish 3,200-square-foot wine shop debuted nearly 9 years ago to much fanfare (it won "Best New Wine Shop" honors at *Food & Wine*'s American Wine Awards the year it opened, in 2005). It's co-owned by Drew Nieporent, the well-known Manhattan restaurateur. Look for collectibles, high-end indulgences, and highly drinkable good buys amid the shop's meticulously curated selection.

Garnet Wines & Liquors, 929 Lexington Ave, btw. 68th and 69th Sts.; (212) 772-3211; garnetwine.com; Subway: 6 to 68th St.

One of the stalwarts of the Upper East Side, Garnet is stocked with a broad selection of wines—from heavyweight high end to tasty lower end—at competitive prices.

Eataly Wine Shop, 200 Fifth Ave., btw. 23rd and 24th Sts.; (646) 398-5102; eatalyny.com; Subway: N, R to 23rd St.

With a roster of some 1,000 bottles of Italian varietals (including owner Joe Bastianich's own line of wines, Bastianich), Eataly's wine shop is a bastion of high-quality, thoughtfully curated artisanal wines. The entrance to the wine shop is on 23rd Street.

Italian Wine Merchants, 108 E. 16th St., btw. Irving Place and Park Ave.; (212) 473-2323; italianwinemerchants.com; Subway: L, N, R, 4, 5, 6 to Union Square/14th St.

A terrific resource for Italian wines, this Union Square shop is stocked with both ready-to-drink and collectible wines. The handsome space hosts a rotating calendar of public and private tastings—but you can also arrange indulgent "at-home" food-and-wine tastings in the comfort of your own easy chair, guided by a sommelier from the shop.

Moore Brothers Wine Company, 33 E. 20th St., btw. Broadway and Park Ave.; (866) 986-6673; moorebrothers.com; Subway: L, N, R, 4, 5, 6 to Union Square/14th St.

Moore Brothers buys its wines

straight from the source, working with (largely) European wine growers to develop quality vineyard-to-table wines and using temperature-controlled distribution systems to bring the finished product home. The splendid staff is passionate about wines.

Morrell & Co., **1 Rockefeller Plaza, Rockefeller Center; (212) 688-9370; morrellwine.com; Subway: B, D, F, V to Rockefeller Center.** With a sturdy motto of "Taste You Can Trust," this is one of the city's most venerable wine merchants, family-owned and -run since 1947.

Pasanella and Son Vintner, **115 South St.; (212) 233-8383; pasanellaandson.com; Subway: A, C, J, Z, 2, 3, 4, 5 to Fulton Street.** This wonderful Seaport wine shop is on the ground floor of a five-story 1839 Federal town house in the Seaport. Be sure to take home a bottle or two of the Pasanella-brand house red or white, a flavorful quaff and terrific bargain at $10.99. (And have staff show you where the waters from Hurricane Sandy crested in 2012.)

Sherry-Lehman Wine & Spirits, **505 Park Ave., at 59th St.; (212) 838-7500; sherry-lehmann .com; Subway: N, R, 4, 5, 6 to 59th St.** In business for nearly 80 years, this is the Rolls-Royce of Manhattan wine shops, selling premier wines and hosting a regular roster of top-flight tastings. The shocker is that you can find plenty of quality quaffs at both the high and reasonable end of the price range.

67 Wine & Spirits, **179 Columbus Ave., at 68th St.; (212) 724-6767; 67wine.com; Subway: 1, 9 to 64th St./Lincoln Center.** Selling wines in the neighborhood since 1941, with a helpful, discerning staff and wooden shelves groaning with wines, this has long been one of the top go-to wine shops in the city.

Trader Joe's, 138 E. 14th St., near Irving Place; (212) 529-6326; traderjoes.com; Subway: 4, 5, 6, L to 14th St./Union Square. Purveyor of Charles Shaw's incredibly successful Two-Buck Chuck, Trader Joe's Manhattan stand-alone wine store sells a solid selection of well-priced wines right next door to its eponymous Union Square food store.

Union Square Wines, 140 Fourth Ave., at 13th St.; (212) 673-8100; unionsquarewines.com; Subway: 4, 5, 6, L to 14th St./Union Square. This wine shop has a thoughtful selection of wines and a well-attended calendar of tastings and events.

Recipes

The following compilation of recipes is, like Manhattan itself, a jazzy, muscular mix of old and new. Classic dishes were born here and continue to be born here. They are the progeny of chefs of boundless creativity and drive who operate in a theater of unlimited possibility. We offer our deep and humble thanks to all those who generously shared their recipes—giving home cooks a taste of that ever-protean and often rapturous Manhattan adventure, dining out.

"21" Club Chicken Hash

"21" Club

The "21" Club Chicken Hash is arguably the most classic dish at this venerable 1929 drinking and eating establishment. It's a rich, creamy concoction that's the ultimate comfort food, beloved by regulars and a fixture on the menu for years. The béchamel sauce of old has given way to a lighter Mornay sauce, but it's still cooked with spinach and a toasty gruyère crust. The hash is most commonly accompanied by wild rice—although spread on toast it makes a yummy finger food.

Serves 4

- 1½ pounds skinless, boneless chicken breasts
- Salt and freshly ground pepper
- 3 cups chicken stock
- 1 stick unsalted butter, softened
- ½ cup unbleached white flour
- ¼ cup dry sherry
- ¼ cup heavy cream
- 1½ pounds grated gruyère
- ½ teaspoon fresh grated nutmeg

Season the chicken breasts with salt and pepper. In a saucepan, bring the chicken stock to a boil. Add the chicken breasts and lower the heat to a simmer. Poach the chicken breasts for 20 minutes, or until fully cooked.

Remove the chicken from the poaching liquid and cool completely before cutting into 1-inch cubes. Reserve the liquid.

Combined the softened butter with the flour, kneading them together into a paste.

Return the reserved chicken stock to a boil, and, using a wire whisk, add the butter-flour mixture in 1-tablespoon increments.

Cook for 5 minutes, then add the sherry and cream.

Adjust the seasoning with salt and pepper. Whisk in the gruyère cheese and nutmeg. Remove from heat once cheese is melted.

Fold in the diced chicken.

OPTIONAL CRUNCHY TOPPING: *Top with additional cheese, and brown lightly under the broiler.*

Serve the chicken hash with spinach and wild rice. Many patrons prefer the hash served over white toast instead of wild rice.

Seared Spinach

3 tablespoon olive oil

1 pound fresh spinach leaves, thoroughly washed, stems removed

Salt and freshly ground pepper to taste

Heat olive oil in a large skillet over medium heat. Add the spinach leaves and sear quickly on one side.

Add salt and pepper.

Toss/turn with tongs or a spatula to cook the rest of the spinach until just wilted but still bright green (3 to 6 minutes).

Wild Rice

2 cups water

2 bay leaves

Salt and freshly ground pepper to taste

1 cup wild rice

1 tablespoon unsalted butter

½ teaspoon cayenne pepper

½ teaspoon ground cumin

½ teaspoon salt

Combine water, bay leaves, and salt and pepper to taste in a pot with a snug-fitting lid. Bring to a boil. Add the rice, butter, cayenne, cumin, and salt, reduce to a simmer, and cook for 40 to 45 minutes.

Recipe courtesy of the "21" Club

Roasted Carrots with Chipotle, Yogurt & Watercress

Chef Alex Stupak, Empellón Cocina

James Beard Award nominee Alex Stupak is one of the city's most innovative chefs, and this roasted carrots dish is already a classic at his nouveau Mexican East Village restaurant, Empellón Cocina (Stupak's second Manhattan restaurant is Empellón Taco, in the West Village). The restaurant version comes with a complicated mole poblano sauce, but Stupak says it works perfectly well with this simpler salsa negra. Prepare to have guests swoon over this inspired and elegant collaboration of flavors.

Serves 4

- **32 baby carrots, washed thoroughly but not peeled.**
- **3 tablespoons of salsa negra plus a bit more for garnish**
- **Kosher salt**

- **Thick plain Greek yogurt, for serving**
- **32 watercress leaves (approx. 4 oz.)**
- **4 tablespoons toasted sesame seeds**

Roasted Carrots

Preheat an oven to 300°F.

Place the baby carrots in a bowl with the salsa negra and sprinkle with salt. Toss the carrots and make sure they are evenly coated.

Transfer the carrots to a baking sheet and spread them out in an even layer. Place the baking sheet in the oven and allow the carrots to roast for roughly 25 minutes. They should be tender but not mushy. Once the carrots are done roasting, allow them to cool down at room temperature.

Place the yogurt in a bowl and season it to taste with salt.

Using a pastry brush, paint 4 plates with a bit of the salsa negra.

Place a dollop of the yogurt on each plate.

Arrange 8 of the carrots on each plate. Arrange 8 of the watercress leaves on each plate as well.

Garnish each plate with a tablespoon of toasted sesame seeds.

Salsa Negra

Makes approximately 2 cups

10 garlic cloves, unpeeled
oil for fryer
40 chipotle meco chiles
3 cups water

8 ounces piloncillo
2 tablespoons olive oil
1 teaspoon kosher salt

Place a skillet over medium heat. Place the unpeeled garlic cloves in the skillet and allow them to toast, turning the garlic over from time to time and continuing to cook until the garlic has softened and the skin has blackened in spots. Remove the garlic from the skillet and allow it to cool. Once the garlic has cooled, peel away the skins.

Preheat a fryer to 300°F.

Fry the chipotle meco chiles until they are dark brown.

Place the fried chiles in a bowl and cover them with warm water. Allow them to soak for at least an hour.

Slice open the soaked chiles and scrape out as many of the seeds and veins as you can.

Take the prepared chiles and place them in a blender with the measured amount of water, the roasted garlic, and the piloncillo. Blend the mixture to smooth puree and pass it through a fine-mesh strainer.

Heat the olive oil in a large pot until it is just barely smoking. Add the chipotle puree to the pot all at once. Turn down the heat to medium and allow the salsa to simmer until it is very thick and dark. Season the salsa to taste with salt and remove it from the heat. Allow the salsa to cool to room temperature before refrigerating.

Recipe courtesy of Chef Alex Stupak of Empellón Cocina

Gougères (French Cheese Puffs)

Executive Chef Philippe Bertineau, Benoit

Chef Alain Ducasse opened the Manhattan location of the classic Parisian bistro Benoit in 2008. It's a beautiful, frothy spot that feels like a little bit of vintage Paris in Midtown. The food, a collaboration between Ducasse and Executive Chef Philippe Bertineau, takes a light, seasonal approach to French bistro classics. All diners are treated to a little basket of these light and ethereal gougères upon arrival. It's impossible to eat just one. This recipe makes enough for a dinner party gathering or a small cocktail party.

Makes about 80–90 cheese puffs

¾ cup water
¼ cup dry white wine
½ cup butter
1 teaspoon salt
Pinch of freshly ground pepper

1⅓ cups flour
4 large eggs
½ cup aged gruyère cheese, grated

Preheat the oven to 325°F. Line a baking sheet with parchment paper.

Heat the water, wine, butter, salt, and pepper in a saucepan until butter is melted.

Remove from heat and dump in flour all at once and stir vigorously until the mixture pulls away from the sides of the pan into a smooth ball. Remove from heat and let rest 2 minutes.

Add the eggs one at a time, stirring quickly to make sure the eggs don't cook. The batter should appear lumpy at first, but after a minute or so, it will smooth out. (You can transfer the mixture to a bowl before adding eggs, to cool the dough, or do this step in a food processor or electric mixer, if you'd like.)

Add the cheese and stir until well mixed.

Scrape the mixture into a pastry bag with a wide plain tip (or a freezer bag—snip off a corner to create an opening). Another option would be to use two spoons to portion and drop the dough onto the baking sheet.

On a baking sheet, pipe the dough into 1-inch mounds, evenly spaced, making each about the size of a cherry tomato.

Top each puff with a bit of the remaining cheese and place baking sheet in the oven.

Bake in the oven for 5 minutes, then rotate the tray and bake for an additional 5 minutes, until they're golden brown.

Best served warm, and if making them in advance, you can simply pipe the gougères on baking sheets and bake right before your guests arrive, or reheat them in a low oven for 5-10 minutes before serving.

Recipe courtesy of Executive Chef Philippe Bertineau of Benoit

Artichoke & Arugula Salad

Chef Joel Hough, Il Buco

In a room filled with rustic farmhouse tables and flickering candlelight, Il Buco transports diners to the Italian countryside. Dining is a transporting experience as well. For Il Buco chef Joel Hough, the commitment to fresh and seasonal means sourcing from such far-flung places as the Santa Monica Farmers' Market. It means buying fresh wahoo hooked off the Carolina coast or flavorful pork from rare heritage breeds raised upstate. The menu changes daily and seasonally; this simple and elegant artichoke and arugula salad embodies the Il Buco philosophy.

Serves 4

- **4 lemons**
- **2 quarts cold water**
- **12 small artichokes (look for pale green in the leaves and darker green stems; beware of browning in the stems)**
- **1 bunch wild arugula or French arugula, washed**
- **½–¾ cup good quality extra-virgin olive oil (Sicilian is preferable)**
- **Parmigiano Reggiano (sliced into thin strips with a paring knife)**
- **Sea salt**
- **Fresh black pepper**
- **12 fresh mint leaves**

Squeeze the juice of 2 lemons into 2 quarts cold water in a container large enough to hold the 12 artichokes.

Peel back and trim the leaves of the artichokes (wear gloves) until you are left with the tender pale yellow leaves at the base of the artichokes.

Using a peeler, shave off the green, rough part of the stem.

With a sharp knife, slice off the top of the leaves of the artichoke where the color changes from green to pale green/yellow.

Place cleaned artichokes in the lemon water, covered by a few paper towels to keep the artichokes submerged.

Ensure that your arugula is clean by eating a piece to check for sand or grit.

Trim off some of the stem of the arugula, leaving about an inch of stem attached to the leaves. Place your arugula leaves in ice water to wake them up a bit.

Add the juice of 2 lemons to a large mixing bowl. Whisk olive oil into the bowl until you achieve an emulsion; it should take about 8 to 12 tablespoons of oil.

With a (preferably Japanese) mandoline, shave the artichokes into the bowl. You want your shavings to be about ⅛-inch thick.

Dress the artichokes with the lemon-oil emulsion and season with salt, black pepper, and the mint, torn into small pieces.

In a separate mixing bowl, add the remaining dressing left in the artichoke bowl. Add just enough to coat your arugula lightly. Season the arugula to taste with sea salt.

On a platter, arrange arugula leaves in a single layer, followed by the artichokes.

Add a light layer of Parmigiano slices. Repeat this process until all of your ingredients are arranged on the platter.

Top with Parmigiano, cracked black pepper, and more torn mint.

Recipe courtesy of Chef Joel Hough of Il Buco

Roasted Harissa Chicken with Avocado, Sea Beans & Preserved Meyer Lemon

Chef Justin Smillie /
Il Buco Alimentari & Vineria

Few chefs have the kind of in-house resources that Chef Justin Smillie has at his fingertips at Il Buco Alimentari & Vineria. The Italian-made wood-fired stove in the open kitchen is where Chef Smillie roasts meats, among other things. Downstairs in the basement what Bon Appétit magazine calls a "village's worth of food-makers" is bustling about making bread and homemade gelato and curing meats. This delicious roast chicken gets its flavorful kick from harissa, a Tunisian hot chile paste. Brining the chicken beforehand makes the meat more tender and juicy.

Serves 4

1 (3-pound) free-range organic chicken

1 chicken brine recipe (below)

3 ounces harissa, either store-bought or homemade (recipe below)

Sea salt and black pepper to taste

1 avocado (sliced)

2 tablespoons extra-virgin olive oil

1 tablespoon Champagne vinegar

1½ teaspoons water

3 ounces blanched sea beans

1 ounce preserved Meyer lemon

2 ounces mint (picked leaves)

Equipment: 1 cast-iron skillet

Place chicken in chilled brine and refrigerate 4 hours to overnight.

Remove chicken from its brine.

Butcher into four parts (two breasts, two legs). Pat dry. Rub with harissa mixture and refrigerate for 24 hours, uncovered (this allows the marinade to dry).

Preheat oven to 375°F.

Lightly season the chicken skin with salt and pepper.

Heat the skillet to medium-high heat. Place the chicken in the skillet, skin-side down, and cook on stove for about 3 minutes.

Place in oven for approximately 20 to 25 minutes, skin-side down.

Allow to rest for 5 to 10 minutes on a plate.

Cut the chicken into 8 pieces.

Dress the avocado with olive oil, Champagne vinegar, and water. Stir in sea beans and julienned preserved Meyer lemon.

Lightly spoon the avocado mixture over the chicken. Sprinkle with mint.

Harissa

2 ounces crushed Aleppo pepper

1½ ounces nora chiles

½ teaspoon caraway seeds, toasted

½ teaspoon coriander seeds

¼ teaspoon cumin seeds

⅛ teaspoon fennel seeds

2 teaspoon fresh oregano, picked

5 cloves garlic

5 teaspoon extra-virgin olive oil

1 teaspoon sea salt

Juice of 1 lime (to taste)

In a heavy-bottomed skillet, toast the spices over low heat. When aroma is present, remove from heat and allow to dry.

Toast the nora chiles lightly. Remove the seeds and soak chiles for 15 minutes in warm water.

In a mortar and pestle, crush the toasted spices until pulverized into a medium-fine powder. Add the garlic, nora chiles, and Aleppo pepper, and grind into the spices until it forms a fine paste.

Slowly stream the olive oil into the paste while stirring.

Season with salt and lime juice (to taste).

Brine

2 gallons water
2 cups kosher salt
½ cup honey
5 Meyer lemons, sliced
20 bay leaves

1 bunch parsley
1½ head garlic, peeled and crushed
½ cup black peppercorns

Bring water to a simmer. Dissolve salt and honey in water.

Turn off heat and add rest of the ingredients to the solution.

Chill in the refrigerator.

Recipe courtesy Chef Justin Smillie of Il Buco Alimentari & Vineria

Homemade Pizza

Scott Wiener, Scott's Pizza Tours

To say that Scott Wiener is a connoisseur of pizza is like observing that fish sure do like to swim. A serious passion for pizza has driven Scott to drill deeper into the pizza equation than almost anyone we know, and it all spills out in his smart, engaging, and highly entertaining pizza tours (scottspizzatours.com). When Scott is not putting his heart and soul into daily pizza tours, working on his pizza journal, making field reports from pizza outposts, or giving pizza-related interviews, he is at home, firing up the oven to make, well, pizza. There are as many iterations of pizza emanating from Scott's kitchen as there are snowflakes, but Scott's Easy Pizza Dough and Pizza Sauce recipes, below, make a more than fine base from which to create your own perfect pizza. Scott likes baking his homemade pizzas on unglazed terra-cotta floor tiles but is also enamored with his new baking steel (bakingsteel.com).

Scott's Easy Pizza Dough

315 grams water	4 grams yeast
500 grams flour	10 grams salt

Mix all ingredients until a dough is formed. Cover and let rest 20 minutes. Knead until springy and smooth. Split into three 276g balls. Store refrigerated for 1 to 3 days in lightly oiled containers. For faster rise, use warm water and a pinch of sugar and do not refrigerate. About an hour before baking, remove dough from container and poke it lightly with your fingers. If it's ready, the indentation will remain. If it springs back, the dough needs more time to rest. Put flour on your dough and countertop so your hands don't stick, but be careful to wipe away the excess or your crust will taste bitter. Gently stretch out your dough by pushing down on the center and continuing in concentric circles. Starting at the center and working outward, use your palm to flatten out the dough. No throwing! Pick it up with your knuckles close to the rim to stretch it farther, but don't let the center stretch too thin. Pinch the edges slightly to form a lip.

Scott's Pizza Sauce *(makes enough for two pizzas)*

1 (28-ounce) can whole Cali-
fornia tomatoes (Scott
loves Trader Joe's canned
tomatoes)

Salt

Open can and crush tomatoes by hand. Add a big pinch of salt.

Putting it together

Fresh mozzarella (6- to
8-ounce ball)

Slice mozzarella thin and blot with paper towels to rid it of moisture.

When the pizza has been formed, Scott suggests putting the mozzarella on before the sauce. The mozzarella melts right into the crust, and the sauce on top of that sweetens as it bakes. Use a 50/50 ratio of cheese to sauce.

Cook pizza in a 500°F oven on a stone (preheated for 45 minutes) for 7 to 10 minutes or until it's done.

Recipe courtesy of Scott Wiener of Scott's Pizza Tours

Delmonico's Lobster Newberg

Delmonico's Restaurant Group

Lobster Newberg was first introduced to Gilded Age New Yorkers in Delmonico's Restaurant back in the late 1800s. Its provenance remains murky, but supposedly a sea captain named Ben Wenberg, who customarily ate at Delmonico's, brought the recipe home with him in 1876 from a cruise. Calling for a chafing dish, he demonstrated his discovery by cooking the dish at a table in Delmonico's. The restaurant's owner, Charles Delmonico, pronounced it "delicious" and the dish, named Lobster a la Wenberg, became a popular menu entree. By a typographical sleight of hand, the spelling somehow evolved from "Wenberg" to "Newberg" over the years. Delmonico's famous chef, Chef Charles Ranhofer (1836–1899), altered the original recipe to add his own touch. Lobster Newberg is still on the restaurant menu today. The recipe below adds a touch of caviar to both heighten the extravagance and mellow the cream and brandy with some salty brininess—but it's not needed to finish what is by itself a rich and delicious dish.

Serves 4

- 2 (1-pound) live lobsters
- 3 tablespoons unsalted butter
- ½ cup diced carrot
- ½ cup diced onion
- ½ cup diced celery
- 2 tablespoons tomato paste
- ¼ cup plus 1 tablespoon brandy
- 3 cups heavy cream
- Coarse salt and freshly ground white pepper to taste
- 2 shallots, peeled and minced
- Cayenne pepper to taste
- Freshly ground nutmeg to taste
- 1 large egg yolk, at room temperature
- 1 tablespoon freshly squeezed, strained lemon juice
- 1 ounce American sturgeon caviar, optional
- Brioche batons, optional (see recipe below)

Place a lobster on a cutting board. Using a sharp chef's knife held vertically, plunge the point into the lobster's head about 1 inch behind the eyes. Push the knife completely in to touch the cutting board and then move it forward to cut the entire head in half. This is the quickest and easiest method of killing a live lobster. Pull the claws from the body.

Prepare an ice-water bath in a bowl large enough to hold all the lobster parts and set it aside.

Place the claws and bodies in the top half of a steamer over boiling water. Cover and steam the lobster for 4 minutes. Remove the bodies and continue steaming the claws for an additional 3 minutes. Immerse both the bodies and claws in the ice-water bath as soon as you remove them from the steamer to stop the cooking.

Crack the shells on the bodies and claws and carefully remove the meat, keeping it in pieces as large as possible. Separately reserve the meat and the shells.

Preheat the oven to 350°F.

Place the lobster shells in a roasting pan in the preheated oven and roast, turning occasionally, for about 12 minutes, or until nicely colored and fragrant. Remove from the oven and set aside.

Heat 2 tablespoons of the butter in a large saucepan over medium heat. Add the carrot, onion, and celery and sauté for about 4 minutes, or just until the vegetables begin to soften without taking on any color. Add the tomato paste and sauté for about 1 minute, or just until well incorporated. Stir in the reserved lobster shells, followed by ¼ cup of the brandy. Cook for about 3 minutes, stirring to deglaze the pan. Add the cream, stir to blend, and raise the heat. Bring to a simmer and then immediately lower the heat to a gentle simmer. Season with salt and pepper and cook gently for about 1½ hours, or until very thick and well seasoned.

Remove the sauce from the heat and pour it through a fine-mesh sieve into a clean container, pressing on the solids to extract all the flavor.

Discard the solids and set the sauce aside.

Heat the remaining tablespoon of butter in a medium sauté pan over medium-low heat. Add the shallots and season with cayenne and nutmeg.

Cook, stirring constantly, for about 2 minutes, or until the seasonings have colored and are fragrant. Add the reserved lobster meat and sauté for 1 minute. Add the remaining tablespoon of brandy, stirring to deglaze the pan. Add the reserved cream sauce, raise the heat, and bring to a gentle simmer.

Place the egg yolk in a small bowl.

Remove pan from the heat and, using a slotted spoon, transfer an equal portion of the lobster meat to each of 4 shallow soup bowls. Whisk a bit of the hot sauce into the egg yolk to temper it and then whisk the egg mixture into the sauce. Add the lemon juice, taste, and, if necessary, adjust the seasoning with salt and pepper. Pour the sauce over the lobster in each bowl. If using, spoon an equal portion of caviar into the center of each bowl and garnish with brioche batons (recipe below). Serve immediately.

Brioche Batons

1 loaf brioche bread   Sea salt to taste
½ cup (1 stick) melted
   unsalted butter

Preheat oven to 375°F.

Line a rimmed baking sheet with parchment paper. Set aside.

Using a serrated knife, slice the ends from the brioche. Then cut the brioche crosswise into ½-inch-thick slices. Trim the crust from all sides of each slice. Cut each slice into logs about ½-inch wide. You will need 5 pieces for each serving of the lobster.

Using a pastry brush, generously coat all sides of the brioche pieces with butter. Season with sea salt and place in a single layer on the prepared baking sheet.

Bake for about 7 minutes, or until golden and crisp. Remove from the oven and serve warm.

Recipes courtesy of Delmonico's Restaurant Group

Waldorf Salad

The Waldorf Astoria New York

Waldorf Salad is the single most frequently requested recipe at the Waldorf Astoria—and the salad has been served on all of the hotel restaurant menus for a century, with roughly 20,000 sold every year. The original version, with apples and mayonnaise (walnuts were added a bit later), dates back to the 1890s and is credited to Oscar Tschirky, then the Waldorf's maître d'hôtel. The recipe is always evolving and each restaurant has its own interpretation—but all have eliminated mayonnaise. This particular recipe uses a truffle dressing along with red and green apples and celeriac.

Serves 8

For candied walnuts:

2 cups raw walnut halves (pecans can be used as a substitute)

1 egg white

1 tablespoon spice mixture (such as a combination of paprika, cayenne, ground fennel seed, and ground coriander)

1 cup sugar

For dressing:

¼ cup Dijon mustard

1 egg yolk

¾ cup Champagne vinegar

2 tablespoons white truffle oil

3 cups olive oil

Salt to taste

For salad:

2 large Granny Smith apples, unpeeled

2 large Gala apples, unpeeled

½ cup celery root (celeriac), peeled (if not available you may substitute regular peeled celery)

½ cup micro arugula or celery leaves

1 dozen seedless red grapes, halved lengthwise

1 tablespoon chopped chives

Make candied walnuts: *Preheat oven to 350°F. In a large bowl, combine walnuts and egg white; add spice mixture and sugar and mix until evenly coated. Spread walnuts into one even layer on a nonstick baking sheet lined with parchment paper; roast in the oven until browned, about 20 minutes. (The nuts can be prepared ahead of time and stored in an airtight container. Store-bought candied walnuts can also be used as a shortcut).*

Prepare dressing: *In a medium bowl, combine mustard, egg yolk, vinegar, and truffle oil. Whisk in olive oil in a steady stream, whisking briskly to emulsify. Season to taste and set aside.*

Make salad: *Using a mandoline on the fine-comb setting (or a sharp knife), julienne the apples into matchstick-size strips, being careful to avoid the seeds and the core. Separately cut the celeriac into a brunoise of small cubes. Transfer all to a mixing bowl. Gently fold the dressing into the apple mixture until well combined, then add the arugula, grapes and chives. Be sure to not overdress the salad or more apples will need to be julienned! (You will likely have dressing left over.)*

Assemble salad: *Divide the salad among chilled serving plates. Garnish if desired with dried apple chips.*

Recipe courtesy of the Waldorf Astoria New York

"Top of the Waldorf" Rooftop Honey Ice Cream

The Waldorf Astoria New York

More and more New York restaurateurs have become rooftop gardeners, growing many of the herbs and vegetables they use in their dishes on-site. The Waldorf Astoria has a rooftop garden that includes six active beehives, and the "Top of the Waldorf" honey that is produced shows up on the Waldorf restaurants' menus in all sorts of creative and interesting ways. This delicious honey ice cream is made from the honey harvested from the Waldorf's rooftop hives.

Serves 20–30

2500 grams heavy cream
150 grams sugar
550 grams honey

600 grams egg yolks (approx. 2 dozen egg yolks)

In a large sauce pot bring cream, sugar, and honey to a boil, then lower the heat. Take some of the hot cream and slowly add it to the yolks to temper them. Place the egg yolk mixture back into the hot cream and cook, stirring constantly on low heat until the mix slightly thickens enough to coat the back of a spoon. Once the mixture has thickened, take it off the stove and immediately cool down in an ice bath with cubes and water. Cover and chill in a refrigerator. The ice cream base is best the next day, so cover and chill in a refrigerator or cooler overnight. Prepare in an ice-cream maker per manufacturer's instructions.

Recipe courtesy of the Waldorf Astoria New York

Fettuccine with Gulf Shrimp, Louisiana Crawfish & Sungold Tomatoes

Chef Dave Pasternack, Esca

James Beard Award–winning chef and ardent fisherman Dave Pasternack over-sees the bustling kitchen at Esca, a Southern Italian restaurant in the Theater District that prepares some of the best seafood dishes in town. This is a simple but elegant summer pasta, bursting with color and flavor.

1 pound dried fettuccine

3 tablespoons plus ¼ cup extra-virgin olive oil, plus high-quality extra-virgin olive oil for drizzling

1 medium pickled cherry bomb pepper, stemmed and seeded, and sliced into thin strips

½ pound Gulf shrimp, peeled and deveined

Sea salt

Freshly ground black pepper

12 Sungold cherry tomatoes

½ pound crawfish, cooked and peeled

2 cups arugula, rinsed, dried, chopped

Bring a large pot of salted water to a boil. Add the fettuccine and cook 1 minute less than the box instructs for al dente. Drain the pasta in a colander, reserving about ¼ cup of the cooking water.

While the pasta is cooking, heat 3 tablespoons olive oil over a medium flame in a deep straight-sided sauté pan. Add the cherry bomb pepper and cook until softened, about 1 minute. Season the shrimp with salt and pepper, then add to the pan. Sear the shrimp on all sides for 4–5

minutes total. Add the tomatoes, stir well to combine, and cook for about 1 minute more. Season with ½ teaspoon sea salt.

Reduce the flame to medium and add the crawfish and arugula. Stir to combine. Add the pasta and the reserved pasta water. Use tongs to combine the ingredients, and continue cooking for about 1 minute more. Season with additional salt and pepper. Use the tongs to transfer the pasta to four serving bowls, and drizzle some high-quality extra-virgin olive oil over each bowl before serving.

Recipe courtesy of Chef Dave Pasternack of Esca

Pumpkin Cheese Custard Stuffing

Chef Derrick Van Duzer,
Knickerbocker Bar & Grill

One of those storied neighborhood joints that always feels like a party, Knickerbocker Bar & Grill is a jazzy, breezy, old-school spot with some equally jazzy food on the plate. This is a lovely autumn dish, perfect to use as a Thanksgiving side dish or as part of a special-occasion meal.

Serves 6–8

6 eggs
3 egg yolks
⅔ cup sugar
2 cups heavy cream
2 cups milk
⅓ teaspoon vanilla extract
⅓ teaspoon cinnamon

⅓ teaspoon allspice
⅓ teaspoon nutmeg
2½ cups canned pumpkin
Dash of salt
Loaf of brioche bread, cubed
Crumbled feta and blue cheese (1 cup of each)

Mix all wet and dry ingredients together. Note: Use all the liquid; this is a wet mixture.

Add dehydrated or slightly toasted brioche cubes to the mixture and gently toss.

Fill 4-ounce tins or a baking dish of your choosing halfway with wet mixture, then add some crumbled cheese. Remember: Very wet is good. Top with cheese crumbles (amount of cheese is to your liking).

Place in 350°F oven for about 30 to 40 minutes. Test doneness by pressing down on top; no liquid should ooze out.

Recipe courtesy of Chef Derrick Van Duzer of Knickerbocker Bar & Grill

Appendices

Appendix A:
Eateries by Cuisine

American
Bluebell Cafe (Midtown), 112
Bridge Cafe (Downtown), 24
Carlyle, The/Bemelmans Bar
  (UES), 129
Good Enough to Eat (UWS), 137
Harry's (Downtown), 23
Henry's (UWS), 137, 250
Odeon, The (Downtown), 34, 250
Ouest (UWS), 139
P.J. Clarke's on the Hudson
  (Downtown), 22
Red Rooster (UWS), 141, 148
Tir na nÓg (Midtown), 105
"21" Club, The (Midtown), 107, 210
Westville Hudson (Downtown), 43

Barbecue
Daisy May's BBQ (Midtown), 100
Hill Country (Downtown), 89
Mighty Quinns BBQ (Downtown), 53

Bosnian
Saro (Downtown), 55, 246

British
Breslin, The (Downtown), 86, 131
Spotted Pig, The (Downtown),
  75, 259

Cambodian
Num Pang (Downtown), 72, 252

Chinese
Han Dynasty (Downtown), 51
Mission Chinese (Downtown), 53
Nom Wah Tea Parlor
  (Downtown), 20
Oriental Garden (Downtown), 21
Peking Duck House
  (Downtown), 21
Prosperity Dumpling
  (Downtown), 21, 244
Royal, The (Downtown), 22
Shun Lee West (UWS), 142
Szechuan Gourmet (Midtown), 105

Chophouse
Keens (Midtown), 106

Pizza

Co. (Downtown), 66
Farinella Italian Bakery, Pizza &
   Panini (UES), 126
Forcella Pizza (Midtown), 113
John's Pizzeria (Downtown), 78
Motorino (Downtown), 54
Patsy's Pizzeria (UWS), 139
Phil's Pizza (Downtown), 44
Ribalta (Downtown), 175
San Matteo Pizza (UES), 128

Ramen

Ippudo (Downtown), 52
Totto Ramen (Midtown), 106, 245

Raw Foods

Pure Food & Wine (Downtown), 92

Salads

City Bakery, The (Downtown), 87,
   177, 249
sweetgreen (Downtown), 93

Seafood

Ai Fiori (Midtown), 112
Esca (Midtown), 100, 228
Grand Central Oyster Bar
   (Midtown), 117
Le Bernardin (Midtown), 102
Marea (Midtown), 103

Soul Food

Red Rooster (UWS), 141, 148
Sylvia's (UWS), 143, 148

Spanish/Tapas

Tertulia (Downtown), 76
Tía Pol (Downtown), 77

Steak House

Costata (Downtown), 40
Harry's (Downtown), 23
Knickerbocker Bar & Grill
   (Downtown), 70, 230
Wolfgang's Steakhouse
   (Midtown), 116

Thai

Kin Shop (Downtown), 69

Vegetarian/Vegan/Organic

Angelika Kitchen (Downtown), 48
Butcher's Daughter, The
   (Downtown), 20
Dirt Candy (Downtown), 49

Viennese

Wallsé (Downtown), 77

Appendix B: Specialty Stores & Producers

Appendix C: Best of Manhattan

Best Food Experiences in Manhattan

Starting the Day with a Bagel & Lox. The quintessential Noo Yawk staple, the bagel—basically, a chewy yeast roll shaped like a plump-cheeked doughnut—is a ubiquitous presence in the daily lives of city folks, showing up in at morning office meetings, grab-and-go carts at train stations and bus stops, and piled high in every deli and coffee shop in town. Why, New York babies even teethe on them! In the great tradition of old-time Jewish delis, order your bagel with lox or nova (smoked salmon), a schmear (cream cheese, flavored if you like), and maybe a sprinkling of sliced red onions. For the city's very best bagel and lox, made to order, head uptown to **Zabar's** (zabars.com) (see p. 193) or downtown to **Russ & Daughters** (russanddaughters.com) (see p. 61, 192). But bagels are delicious all by themselves. Our favorites are found on upper Broadway at **Absolute Bagels** (absolutebagels .com; see p. 144).

Dining in a Classic New York Haunt. New York is not Rome; it's old but hardly ancient. But as the world rockets light-years into tomorrow, even the Jazz Age feels far, far away. Some of our favorite spots to dine are those that conjure up bygone eras, faded zeitgeists, and the wonderfully languid cadences of old-school romance. In other words, we're suckers for an old joint with lots of interesting stories to tell. Go to "Landmarks & Old-School Faves," in each chapter for our favorites in every neighborhood.

Paying a Dollar for Five (Tasty!) Dumplings. Who says you can't find a bargain in New York? Here on the fringes of Chinatown are a few simple storefronts serving hot and tasty fried pork-and-chive dumplings (aka potstickers) in plastic containers to dumpling cognoscenti and hungry locals. Cost: $1 for five dumplings. The profit margins are all about volume, so join the queue. One of the best is the aspirationally named **Prosperity Dumpling,** at 46 Eldridge St., between Canal and Hester streets (prosperitydumpling.com; see. p. 21).

Celebrating the Seasons at the Union Square Greenmarket. It's heartening to know that the city's biggest Greenmarket is open and bustling the whole year long. In winter, regional farmers and food purveyors arrive at dawn bearing root-cellar crops, fresh-laid eggs, creamy milk, and home-baked breads. Springtime arrives in bundles of fresh ramps and bright green fiddleheads, trailed by asparagus, sugarsnaps, and May peas. In the peak growing season, from late June through the month of September, the market sings with color and fragrance; heirloom tomatoes come in all shapes and hues and just-picked melons perfume the air. Fresh corn is available deep into October, when the autumn chill brings orange pumpkins, big stalks of Brussels sprouts, and ripe, juicy apples. (See. p. 184.)

Slurping Ramen Noodles on a Blustery Day. What, are we in Japan? It sometimes feels that way, with Japanese rustic-style ramen noodle restaurants popping up all over the city. And why not? Ramen is perfectly suited to the temper and temperament of a city that respects flavor and fleetness—you can sit down, order up, and have a

fat bowl of steaming noodles plopped in front of you in a matter of minutes. This being New York, of course, the competition is stiff. That's good news for diners, who reap the rewards of a hotly contested market: delicious hand-pulled noodles, rich, flavorful broth, and savory accoutrements. Truth be told, we have deep love for **Totto Ramen,** 366 West 56th Street, between Eighth and Ninth avenues (tottoramen.com; see. p. 106).

Sampling Haute Cuisine During Restaurant Week.

Scores of top restaurants—including many of the city's vaunted culinary temples—offer reasonably priced three-course prix-fixe menus during the city's twice-yearly Restaurant Weeks, held, no uncoincidentally, in the laggard and often haggard months of January and August. Yet we are here today to testify that if you happen to be in town for NYC Restaurant Week, give a hooray. It's a great way to sample the food (and soak up the ambience) of some of the city's best (and often most chillingly expensive) restaurants for a mere fraction of the cost. Our experience: Participating restaurants make truly thoughtful efforts to serve dishes that are not only delicious but emblematic of the restaurant's culinary philosophy (see. p. 14).

Learning about the Elemental Power of Pizza.

Manhattan's best food tours are up there on our list of the city's top attractions, memorably fun and full of rich cultural insight and historical context. But buyer beware: Don't sign up for just any neighborhood "food tour"—lamentably, plenty out there simply don't measure up. We can guarantee a fabulous time when you sign up for one of **Scott's Pizza Tours** (scottspizzatours.com; see p. 157)—especially those led by the pizza Ph.D. himself, Scott Wiener. Equally enlightening are the **Enthusiastic Gourmet** tours led by Susan Rosenbaum (enthusiasticgourmet .com; see p. 156). Check out the "Resources" section (see p. 160) for recommended food tours.

Plotting Your Own Neighborhood Food Crawl. Don't limit yourself to one restaurant on your big night on the town. Create a customized food crawl, where you kamikaze into a handful of spots of disparate cuisines and atmospheres for an appropriately multi-textured evening out in the Big Apple. One recent sultry summer night we swept into the Lower East Side, kicking off the evening amid the wallpapered English-tearoom decor of **Saro** (sarobistro.com; see. p. 55) with chilled Slovakian beers and the signature Saro Slaw, here with toasted sesame seeds and sauerkraut. Then it was on to sunny Provence at **Antibes** (antibesbistro.com; see. p. 48) for grilled shrimp in a tomato compote and truffle-roasted asparagus. We ended the night in the vampy hothouse vibe at **Spur Tree** (spurtreelounge.com; see. p. 56), digging into Jamaican jerk chicken, Caribbean-style rice and peas, and a neat Mojito.

Best Rooms with a View

For an island surrounded by water, Manhattan has a sorry lack of waterside restaurants. Along its outer edges an inelegant ribbon of beltways shuttles car traffic in and out of the city. Where there *is* prime waterfront property, like the South Street Seaport, or along the Battery City promenade, the choices are often uninspiring. But there are waterside views, and then there are urban panoramas, of which several aeries in the sky deliver splendidly. Here are our recommendations for the city's best dining views.

Boat Basin Cafe, W. 79th St. at the Hudson River, in Riverside Park; boatbasincafe.com. A true harbinger of summer, the Boat Basin has one of the city's most enviable perches: The open-air restaurant overlooks Riverside Park, the blue-black Hudson River, and the 79th

Street Boat Basin, a jumble of pleasure yachts, houseboats, and zippy skiffs. Try it at lunch or get there before the happy-hour crowd, and ask for a table (no reservations) right along the front rails, for unencumbered waterside views. (See. p. 143.)

Gigino, 20 Battery Place, in Wagner Park; gigino-wagnerpark .com. Facing the mighty maw of the New York Harbor, with little between you and Scotland but the high seas, this Italian trattoria is a fine place to dine and admire Manhattan's southernmost tip, with the sea-sprayed Statue of Liberty trained in your sights from the comfort of a linen-draped table. Sit outdoors if you can; it's much more pleasant than the indoor space, and you don't want to miss a second of that panoramic eye candy.

Hudson River Park, Pier 26. At press time, a still-unnamed restaurant was in construction in a beautiful, glass-filled space right on the Hudson River in Hudson River Park. The restaurant has dining options inside and out, including a spectacular 4,458-square-foot roof-top terrace. If it's done right, this could be the most breathtaking waterside dining in the city.

Loeb Boathouse, Central Park, E. 72nd St., at Park Drive N.; the centralparkboathouse.com. Every time we find our way to this circa-1923 structure, we wonder why we don't come more often. Well, for one thing, dinner in the open-air section is seasonal, and for another, the food is not really the point. It's not a foodie destination, per se, but it does have dreamy views of the Central Park Lake, clouds of mature trees, and stately buildings crowning the edges of the park. It's really pretty, and it's in the middle of the park, with birdsong instead of taxis honking. And they do make a fine-dining effort, with flickering candles and crisp white linens. So by all means let's go again. Lunch and brunch served year-round; dinner only April through November. (See p. 127.)

Per Se, 10 Columbus Circle, at 60th St.; perseny.com. On the fourth floor of the Time Warner mall on Columbus Circle, vaunted chef Thomas Keller has set up shop at Per Se. Yes, the food is great, but the views are nothing to sniff at. Long windows overlook Columbus Circle and the glistening green of Central Park, with 57th Street marching crosstown to Fifth Avenue. Swellelegant you'll feel as you survey the hoi polloi below. (See p. 139.)

Riverpark, 450 E. 29th St., at East River; riverparknyc.com. High enough above the rumbling FDR to dull the traffic sounds below, this Tom Colicchio restaurant stretches out on a spacious concrete plaza, the newish home of the NYU Biosciences Center. Running along the north side of the plaza is the Farm, where seasonal plantings of heir-loom vegetables and herbs give this restaurant farm-to-table bonafides few other urban eateries can claim. In good weather, you can dine on the restaurant's outdoor terrace and admire the East River views, but even inside you can catch the shadows of tugboats skimming the water through floor-to-ceiling glass. (See p. 114.)

Best Family Friendly Dining

Don't think that just because you have kids in tow in one of the world's top culinary capitals that you have to spend your mealtimes in a purgatory of chicken fingers and French fries. Yes, Manhattan has its fair share of cuddly kid-centric theme restaurants, but those will find you. These days plenty of sophisticated kitchens are welcoming well-behaved families. No, this does not mean that you should breeze into on a Friday night with a passel of cranky toddlers. If you want to sample Manhattan fine dining or enjoy the sizzling restaurant du jour, consider these tips: 1) Go for early-bird seatings. 2) Book on a less-busy evening (Sunday, in fact, has become a sort of a de facto family night out in New York). 3) Pick a place where you can dine outdoors, where any unruliness will be less of a nuisance. 4) Visit in summer, when many locals head to the hills (the Hamptons) and tables to the city's most vaunted eateries magically open up.

Benihana, **47 W. 56th St., nr. Sixth Ave.; benihana.com.** Do the teppanyaki chefs seem slightly bored, even as they juggle eggs and deftly catapult shrimp tails into pockets? Are there an inordinate number of tourists in the house? Yes and yes, but the table show is still a hoot at the flagship of this pioneering Japanese steakhouse, which has gotten a needed makeover.

Bubby's, **120 Hudson St.; bubbys.com.** This place is so family-friendly you're almost a pariah if you come in without some kind of pipsqueak in tow. Bubby's has terrific, wholesome food and serves breakfast until 4pm daily, something our daughter would sign up for in perpetuity; rub elbows with the hood's deep-pocketed moguls when daddies take over at weekend brunches. (See p. 31.)

Carmine's, **200 W. 44th St., at 7th Ave.; or 2450 Broadway, nr. W. 91st St.; carminesnyc.com.** "Family-style" means food served on great big platters to share—and when said food is lusty Southern Italian–style pasta, meatballs, and more, well, that's amore! Everything is remarkably tasty and the ambience is properly clamorous, meaning kids can be their boisterous selves. It's quite an efficient assembly line. (See p. 101.)

City Bakery, **3 W. 18th St., btw. Fifth and Sixth Aves.; thecitybakery.com.** You may not think a place touting healthy, organic, and sustainable would draw kids by the barrelful—but when the place includes seriously fabulous versions of fried chicken, mac 'n' cheese, Old Bay chicken wings, and quesadilla, why wouldn't they? Fresh-made hot chocolate (with homemade marshmallows), and gigantic, chewy chocolate chip cookies don't hurt either. (See pp. 87 and 177.)

Chelsea Market, 75 Ninth Ave.; chelseamarket.com. Such a cool place, set in an old biscuit factory with a waterfall here, castle torches there. The food is great, from the meatloaf sandwiches at Dickson's Farmstand Meats to Hale & Hearty's soups to Buon Italia's frittatas to Fat Witch's rich brownies. And if the weather's nice, you can take your food to a table along the High Line (right above the market) with Hudson river views. (See p. 167.)

Eataly, 200 Fifth Ave. at 23rd St., eataly.com. This is a bustling emporium of all things authentically Italian, from fresh-baked foccaccia to house-made gelato. It's got plenty of tables to sit down and eat, too. (See p. 168.)

Henry's, 2745 Broadway, at 105th St.; henrysnyc.com: This friendly spot serves all-American standards in a sunny, spacious, Arts-and-Crafts-inspired space that draws Upper West Side families in droves. (See p. 137.)

The Odeon, 145 W. Broadway, at Thomas St.; theodeonrestaurant .com. For further proof that this truly is the golden age of children in NYC, witness as more and more grownup city restaurants develop kid-friendly menus and attitudes. The Odeon has grown from its wild-child 1970s past into a great neighborhood *boîte,* with solid food but no cutesy kids' menu, thank you. (See p. 34.)

Shake Shack, shakeshack.com. From its somewhat humble origins as a retro "shack" selling premium-quality drive-in favorites (burgers, fries, shakes) in Madison Park, Shake Shack has muscled into Midtown and points north and south, spreading its insanely popular menu to the rest of Manhattan, with locations on the Upper East Side (154 E. 86th

St., btw. Lexington and Third Aves.), the Upper West Side (366 Columbus Ave., at 77th St.), Theater District (300 W. 44th St., at Eighth Ave., at 44th St.), Battery Park (215 Murray St., btw. West St. and North End Ave.), and the Grand Central Dining Concourse (Grand Central Station).

Best Local Chains

Yes, Manhattan has its share of international chain brand eateries, including a smattering of locations for such fast-food titans as Mcdonald's, KFC, Subway, Wendy's, and Taco Bell, among others. Manhattan even has two Olive Garden franchises (696 Ave. of the Americas/22nd St. and 2 Times Square/47th St.); one Red Lobster (5 Times Square/41st St.); and four IHOP locations, uptown and down (ihop.com). But eating the same fast food you can find anywhere is a little beat, in our minds. Being the hyper-competitive entity that it is, Manhattan has a number of homegrown chains that promise fast food but also pretty darned *good* fast food, often sustainably and seasonally sourced, full of nutritious ingredients—in other words, food that bears little resemblance to industrial fast food. Here are our faves.

Chop't, 11 Manhattan locations; choptsalad.com. Conceptualizing a shop offering fresh, customized (and chopped) salads to order, two college buddies opened the first Chop't store on 17th Street in Manhattan in 2001. Today Chop't is a mini empire of some 11 Manhattan locations and the menu has expanded to include raw kale, fresh beets, Niman Ranch bacon, and soy-marinated tofu, among scores of other healthful ingredients.

Hale and Hearty Soups, 26 Manhattan locations; haleand hearty.com. The lone survivor of the soup frenzy that hit New York around the Seinfeld "Soup Nazi" episode, Hale and Hearty outlasted the competition for a number of reasons, not least because it makes really good—and often terrific—soup. Standouts include mulligatawny, Charleston crab, white bean and escarole. Sandwiches are pretty terrific too. Hale and Hearty shops are set up largely as takeouts, but most offer limited seating. Hale and Hearty enjoys some prime Manhattan locations, including the food courts at Chelsea Market, Rockefeller Center, and the Grand Central Dining Concourse.

Luke's Lobster, 5 Manhattan locations; lukeslobster.com. Luke, a Maine native, has been an entreprenurial type since high school, and his authentic Maine lobster rolls come on a buttery New England griddled bun with barely a whisper of anything but sweet lobster meat. Luke's also serves exemplary shrimp and crab rolls, as well as a satisfyingly unfussy New England–style clam chowder. You can find Luke's Lobster in five Manhattan locations, including the Plaza Food Hall (1 W. 59th St.) and a mobile food cart, Nauti Mobile—check its Twitter site (twitter.com/nautimobile) for current locations.

Nanoosh, 3 Manhattan locations; nanoosh.com. Healthy Mediterranean food (is that a redundancy?) is the focus at these warm and attractive little restaurants, serving an all-organic menu of stellar hummus, babaganoush, falafel, wraps, soups (lentil with carrots and onions; organic tomato with a dollop of basil pesto); and healthy salads.

Num Pang, 4 Manhattan locations; numpangnyc.com. Bred and born right here in the Big Apple, these little takeout shops specialize in made-to-order gourmet Cambodian sandwiches. The first location at 21 E. 12th Street (btw. University Place and Fifth Ave.) is still a popular stop—at lunch, the line snakes out the door down 12th Street. (It has limited seating upstairs.) The big, baguette-style sandwiches are high quality and absolutely delicious, sourced locally and sustainably whenever possible. We love the peppercorn catfish, a minxy blast of pepper balanced by a sweet soy sauce, and the hoisin meatballs is a home run. Num Pang is now in Chelsea Market. (See p. 72.)

Shake Shack, 6 Manhattan locations; shakeshack.com. For a fast-food burger joint, this Danny Meyer phenom cranks out top-quality product. The burgers are made from an original top-secret blend devised by celebrated meat purveyor Pat LaFrieda, and the shakes are state of the art. Add a dream drive-in trifecta of hot dogs, fries, and frozen custard, and you can see why Shake Shack now has 25 locations all over the globe. Shake Shack most recently opened up on the lower-level Dining Concourse at Grand Central.

'wichcraft, 14 Manhattan locations; wichcraftnyc.com. Top Chef Tom Colicchio's Craft empire is class all the way. Even the low man on the totem pole, the casual little sandwich chain known as 'wichcraft, serves up thoughtfully sourced and consistently flavorful dishes to take out or eat in. The range of artisanal, seasonal sandwiches include a free-range chicken salad with kale, walnuts, and red onions; a slow-roasted Berkshire pork. 'wichcraft has some of the best cookies around, topped by a peanut butter cream'wich that's in the upper echelons of Manhattan dessert treats

Best Soup Spots

Immortalized in the classic *Seinfeld* episode, the Soup Nazi was no figment of anyone's imagination—he was the real deal. Many a cold winter's day we waited in line for a cup of seafood bisque, rich and thick and meticulously ladled out of a big cast-iron soup pot. If you were good, ordering briskly, moving methodically to the left, cash money at the ready, above all no monkey business, then you were rewarded with a container of soup. If you were bad, well... These days the Soup Nazi—aka Al Yeganeh—and his curmudgeonly peculiarities are gone, and we are much the worse for the loss—his soups were indeed miraculous. Yeganeh cashed in on a "Soupman" franchise, and now you can find some version of his soups in freezer counters all over the country. You can even find them, rather forlornly, in the little window front shop where the Soup Nazi himself once ladled his original recipes. People who love the *Seinfeld* episode find their way here. We suggest you head elsewhere for good soup. The following should do nicely.

Cafe Medina, 9 E. 17th St., btw. Fifth Ave. and Broadway; (212) 242-2777; cafemedina.com. This little cafe off Union Square offers a daily menu of eight to 10 hearty, flavorful homemade soups, many with a Mediterranean/Middle Eastern bent, from curried eggplant and green lentil to African chicken peanut to fava bean and spinach. A good number of the daily soups are vegan. Go ahead, ask for a taste; soup sampling is part of the gestalt here. (See p. 87.)

CC's Cafe, 496 Hudson St., btw. Christopher and Grove Sts.; (646) 638-2800; Subway: 1, 9 to Christopher St. This "New American Bistro" is in fact little more than a sunny little takeout joint with a smattering of marble-topped cafe tables. But size is no issue, what with the big-hearted soups, wraps, and smoothies made fresh here. We love the split pea, thick with carrots and onions, and the cream of tomato and curried lentil are also spot-on.

Eli's Vinegar Factory, 431 E. 91st St., btw. First and York Aves.; (212) 987-0885; elizabar.com; Subway: 4, 5, 6 to 86th or 96th St. Practically the whole food pyramid in a soup, Eli's chicken noodle is also delicious. (See pp. 132, 165.)

Eva's Health Food, 11 W. 8th St, btw. Fifth and Sixth Aves.; (212) 677-3496; evashealthfood.com; Subway: N, R to Broadway/8th St. In the off-the-radar department, Eva's is a quasi-health-food store with muscle powders and a faux tin ceiling. It also makes awesome, nutritious soups—its vegetable soup is power-meets-flavor in a proletarian cardboard cup. Meg Ryan was recently spotted sipping soup here recently, and although she wasn't pounding the table, she looked content.

Grand Central Oyster Bar Takeout Window, Grand Central Oyster Bar, Grand Central Station. Serving some of the best seafood soups in town, this little takeout window is open from 11:30 a.m. to 5:30 p.m. Either of the two chowders—Manhattan or New England—will more than satisfy, but the Maryland crab is a one-way ticket to the divine church of lump crabmeat, cream, and sherry. (See p. 117.)

Shopsin's, 120 Essex St., at Delancey St.; shopsins.com; Subway: F, J, M, Z to Delancey St./Essex St. To find the soup section you must scythe your way through the breathtakingly exhaustive menu. But once there, you won't go wrong with anything you order, from beef pepperpot to African green curry to pecan duck wild-rice cream, cause the Shopsins are real good at making delicious things to eat.

Soup Spot, 220 W. 31st St., btw. 7th and 8th Aves.; (212) 643-8623; soupspot.com; Subway: A, C, E, 1, 2, 3, to 34th St./Penn Station. Steaming soup, and lots of it—some 17 varieties a day—is the engine that runs this cramped little takeout store next to Penn Station. If you love soup, this it the mother lode—they make 37 different varieties of chicken soup alone! And even though one could argue that superior versions of individual soups can be had elsewhere, most folks will find something to love here.

And you thought Seattle was a coffee town: The 24-hour assembly line that is Manhattan positively *requires* a worker population of overcaffeinated superachievers. Luckily, you can't throw a cat without hitting a coffee bar in New York these days, touting everything from fresh roasts to Fair Trade to French press. The biggest presence is that ubiquitous Seattle franchise, **Starbucks,** which currently has some 160 Manhattan locations, many in some pretty strategic spots. Go to starbucks.com to find the one nearest you. Other very solid artisanal-style coffee-bar chains include **Think Coffee** (thinkcoffeenyc.com), **Oren's Daily Roast** (orensdailyroast.com), **Joe Coffee** (joenewyork.com), **Cafe Grumpy** (cafegrumpy.com) and the **Coffee Bean and Tea Leaf** (coffeebean.com).

Abraco, 86 E. 7th St., at First Ave.; abraconyc.com/#home; no phone. We were alerted to this sweet little East Village espresso bar by an Australian tourist, here on his honeymoon in an Airbnb East Village rental and a voracious coffee drinker. "Best I ever had," he said. Abraco is tiny, but the product is flavorful, and you can get savories like housemade frittata and olive oil cake.

Au Breve, 51 Cooper Square, btw. 6th and 7th Sts.; (212) 533-1864; aubreve.com. Serving quality seasonal brews coffee roasted by the Brooklyn Roasting Company, this Cooper Union brew bar also has a sampling of nibbles and looseleaf teas.

Bluebird Coffee Shop, 72 E. 1st St. at Second Ave., (212) 260-1879; bluebirdcoffeeshop.com. Terrific Counter Culture brew in a warm East Village spot, with savories and sweets to keep you hanging around.

Cafe Sabarsky, Neue Galerie, 1048 Fifth Ave., at E. 86th St.; (212) 288-0665; cafesabarsky.com. Sip Viennese espresso and imagine you've been transported to Vienna, circa 1912, in this atmospheric cafe in the Neue Galerie museum.

East Harlem Cafe, 1651 Lexington Ave., at 104th St.; (212) 996-2080; eastharlemcafe.com. This colorful spot has dreamy Cuban espresso, cappuccino, and a menu that includes banana walnut pancakes for breakfast and tapas and tuna salad sandwiches for lunch.

Nespresso Boutique, 92 Prince Street, at Mercer St.; nespresso -us.com. It took one steaming cup of Vivalto Lungo, brewed by our friend Robin, to bring us out of a 10-year coffee hibernation—the stuff is that good. Lots of folks love their Nespresso espresso, and now with this free-standing Nespresso boutique/restaurant in Manhattan, you can get your Nespresso fix in a cafe environment.

Porto Rico, 201 Bleecker St., btw. MacDougal St. and Sixth Ave.; (212) 477-5421; portorico.com. Established in 1907, this longtime family-owned and –operated coffee importer sells a wide range of brewed and bagged coffee blends from all over the world out of its Bleecker Street storefront. (It now has locations at Essex Market on the Lower East Side, St. Mark's Place, and Brooklyn). The coffee is kosher-certified. (See p. 199.)

Stumptown, 30 W. 8th St., at MacDougal St.; stumptowncoffee .com. This legendary Portland outfit finally opened a small Manhattan location in 2009 in the Ace Hotel, but its Manhattan "flagship," opened in the summer of 2013, in a handsome, exposed-brick space in a vintage storefront on newly revived 8th Street in the Village. It has both a traditional espresso bar and a brew bar. Baristas wear old-time newsboys' caps and vests, and the coffee has a savory burn. (See p. 83.)

Third Rail Coffee, 240 Sullivan St., btw. Bleecker and W. 3rd St.; no phone; thirdrailcoffee.com. It's also recently opened a second location in the East Village (159 Second Ave., at 10th St.).

Best Big Apple Burgers

It's easy to find a good burger in Manhattan, and most every bistro and cafe has its own version of the all-American burger on the menu. Here are some of our favorites.

BLT Burger, 470 6th Ave., at 12th St.; (212) 243-8226; e2hospitality .com. Chef Laurent Tourondel's BLT ("Bistro Laurent Tourondel") brands include this casual West Village spot. Order the Classic (5 oz. of 100% Black Angus beef), the Steakhouse (custom blend of 30-day dry-aged prime beef), or a salmon burger topped with avocado and arugula.

Burger Joint, Le Parker Meridien Hotel, 119 W. 57th St., btw. Sixth and Seventh Aves.; (212) 708-7414; burgerjointny.com. Look for a neon burger sign hung discreetly near the concierge desk, and follow it off the hotel's hushed marble-columned lobby to this dimly lit, clearly downscale burger joint. The menu is bare bones—burgers, fries, drinks—and ordering is Soup Nazi no-nonsense. What more do you want? Well, another location, and now there's a Burger Joint downtown (33 W. 8th St.; 212-432-1400).

Corner Bistro, 331 W. 4th St., btw. Jane St. and Eighth Ave.; (212) 242-9502; cornerbistrony.com. This place is a bar, with wooden booths, a jukebox, and a certain frat-house ferality. It also has legendarily delicious burgers and fine fries.

The Spotted Pig, 314 W. 11th St., at Greenwich St.; (212) 620-0393; thespottedpig.com. We think the Spotted Pig burger is one of the city's best; it's big and juicy and slightly wild, with a hint of lamb. (See p. 75.)

Steak 'n Shake, 1695 Broadway, at W. 53rd St.; (212) 247-6584; steaknshake.com. Burger made from prime steak cuts. This Midwest burger chain opened its first location in New York in 2012, with burgers made from 100% organic meat. Seating is limited, but burgers are solid.

Umami Burger, 432 Sixth Ave., btw. 9th and 10 Sts.; (212) 677-8626; umami.com. When the first Umami Burger opened in Manhattan in the summer of 2013, the lines snaked outside the door. For weeks. The legendary Los Angeles franchise, created through some kind of mad-scientist food alchemy by some guy named Adam Fleischman, who was looking for that flavor sweet spot known as umami, has many fans. The Original comes with caramelized onions, tomato, shiitake mushrooms, and a Parmesan crisp, but

Best Ice Cream and Gelato

Manhattan has greedily coopted Italian pizza; why not gelato? In the last 10 years, gelaterias have mushroomed, overtaking the corner ice-cream shop as the frozen treat du jour. Yes, the big (Ben and Jerry's, Haagen-Dazs) and local chains (Carvel) still have strategic locations around the city, but custom-made Italian imports and their American counterparts rule the streets. Here are some of our favorite places in the city for ice cream and gelato.

Amorino, 60 University Place, at 10th St.; (212) 253-5599; amorino .com. This sinfully rich (with prices to match), high-quality gelato comes artfully sculpted in the shape of a flower.

Chinatown Ice Cream Factory, 65 Bayard St., at Mott St.; (212) 608-4170; chinatownicecreamfactory.com. With flavors ranging from classic American to Asian exotic (lychee, red bean, durian), this Chinatown ice-cream store has satisfying ice-cream lovers since 1978.

Ciao Bella, 285 Mott St., near Houston St.; (212) 431-3591; ciao bellagelato.com. What started out as a simple storefront gelato and sorbet shop on Mott Street has mushroomed into a ubiquitous presence in stores all over the city. To whit, the ice cream is plenty good.

Emack and Bolio's, 389 Amsterdam Ave.; (212) 362-2747; emackandbolios.com. Predating Ben and Jerry's by 3 years, with a similar hippie whimsicality and eco-consciousness, this Boston-based ice cream chain only uses milk from hormone-free cows and has three locations in New York.

Grom, 233 Bleecker St., at Carmine St.; (212) 206-1738; grom.it/eng. Imported straight out of Turin, Italy, this gelato shop has been a hit since it opened in 2007. Made with all-natural Italian ingredients, Grom's gelato is creamy and rich.

Il Laboratorio del Gelato, 188 Ludlow St., at Houston St.; (212) 343-9922; laboratoriodelgelato.com. The college student who founded and eventually sold Ciao Bella (see above) later created this gelato "lab" making small-batch, hand-crafted gelato. (See p. 60.)

L'Arte del Gelato, Chelsea Market, 75 Ninth Ave., btw 15th and 16th Sts.; (212) 924-0803; lartedelgelato.com. Selling artisanal gelato made in traditional Italian style, L'Arte del Gelato offers flavors ranging from Amaretto to Nutella to chocolate with raspberry to butterscotch.

Serendipity 3, 225 E. 60th St., btw. Second and Third Aves.; (212) 838-3531; serendipity3.com. It's a full-service restaurant, with creamy white walls, Tiffany lamps, and rococo styling, but Serendipity is best known for its classic ice-cream concoctions: "drugstore" ice-cream sundaes, banana splits, and a "Forbidden Broadway" sundae with Serendipity's own Chocolate Blackout cake, ice cream, and chocolate fudge.

Sundaes and Cones, 95 E. 10th St., btw. Third and Fourth Aves.; (212) 979-9398; sundaescones.com. Big windows and white wainscoting give this place an eternal summer feel. Sundaes and Cones is a popular stop for local schoo lkids for its home-made ice cream in classic flavors and more.

Van Leeuwen Ice Cream, 48 1/2 7th St., at Second Ave.; (718) 701-1630; vanleeuwenicecream.com. Made with fresh hormone- and antibiotic-free dairy products, this terrific ice cream is crafted in Greenpoint, Brooklyn. It's also available via food truck (four locations in Manhattan, including on the High Line).

Vivoli at Macy's, Sixth Floor, Macy's, 151 W. 34th St.; (212) 967-9251; vivoli.it. The biggest gelato news of late is the opening of the first New York outpost of that high temple of gelato, Vivoli, imported from Florence, Italy, where it has been owned and operated by the same family since 1929. It's worth fighting the Macy's crowds for a scoop of this rich and delicious gelato, sold at a simple marble counter near the Stella 34 trattoria.

Best Chocolate

From Hershey's classics to hand-crafted designer truffles, Manhattan is chocolate city. Here are a few of our favorite spots to satisfy your chocolate cravings.

Black Hound, 170 Second Ave., (212) 979-9505; blackhoundny .com. One glance in the window of this gourmet dessert shop reveals exquisitely made cakes and chocolates. (See p. 57.)

Chocolate Bar, 19 8th Ave., btw. W. 12th and Jane Sts.; (212) 366-1541; chocolatebarnyc.com. A purveyor of designer chocolate bars and smart-looking truffles, this boutique in the West Village also sells hot chocolate and Chocolate Bar tea.

Hershey's Chocolate World Times Square, 1593 Broadway, at 48th St.; (212) 581-9100; thehersheycompany.com. It's 16 stories of chocolate, candy, paraphernalia, and tie-ins, via Hershey's.

Jacques Torres Chocolate, 350 Hudson St., at King St.; (718) 875-9772; mrchocolate.com. This Hudson Square chocolate factory is the domain of pastry chef extraordinaire Jacques Torres, who makes high-quality chocolate everything. This location also has a chocolate bar, where you can order up a steaming cup of Torres' divine hot chocolate. Torres also has locations in Chelsea Market (75 Ninth Ave.; 212-414-2462); Rockefeller Center (30 Rockefeller Plaza; 212-664-1804); 285 Amsterdam Ave. (at 73rd St.; 212-787-3256); and just over the Brooklyn Bridge in DUMBO (at 66 Water St.; 718-875-1269), also home of the Jacques Torres Ice Cream Shop. (See p. 46.)

Kee's Chocolates, 80 Thompson St., near Spring St.; (212) 334-3284; keeschocolates.com. Kee Ling Tong crafts ethereal chocolates and macaroons fresh daily. Kee's also has locations inside the HSBC bank at 452 Fifth Avenue (at 40th St.; 212-525-6099) and at 315 West 39th Street (212-967-8088). (See p. 46.)

La Maison du Chocolat, 1018 Madison Ave., at 78th St.; (212) 744-7117; lamaisonduchocolat.com. The New York flagship of sells the Paris shop's signature high-quality chocolates. La Maison has several other locations in Manhattan, including 30 Rockefeller Center (212-265-9404) and the Plaza Hotel Food Hall (One W. 58th St, at Central Park South; 212-355-3436). (See p. 133.)

Li-Lac Chocolates, 40 Eighth Ave., at Jane St.; (212) 924-2280; li-lacchocolates.com. This landmark chocolatier was founded in 1923 selling delicious handmade chocolates, many in a range of whimsical shapes, including dinosaurs, fish, and New York City–centric (which makes for great gifts). It also has a location inside Grand Central Station, at the Grand Central Terminal Market (Park Ave. and 42nd St.; 212-370-4866.

MarieBelle, 484 Broome St., nr. Wooster St.; (212) 925-6999; mariebelle.com. Everything about this fanciful European-style shop is exquisite, including the silk-screened truffles and hand-painted chocolate imperial eggs, and the little Cacao Bar in back sells hot chocolate (ice chocolate in summer) and other sweet treats.

Max Brenner Chocolate by the Bald Man, 841 Broadway, nr. 14th St.; (646) 467-8803; maxbrenner.com. A full-service chocolate emporium in Union Square, where you can sit down, take out, or buy from the chocolate retail shop. It even serves chocolate pizzas!

Mondel Chocolates, 2913 Broadway, nr. 114th St.; (212) 864-2111; mondelchocolates.com. With an old-time "Little Shop around the Corner" feel, this vintage chocolate shop has been selling chocolates since 1943. (See p. 147.)

Neuhaus, 500 Madison Ave., at 52nd St.; (212) 644-4490; neuhauschocolates.com. Exquisite, beautifully packaged Belgian chocolates with a pedigree that goes back to 1857. Visit the New York flagship store on tony Madison Avenue and sample a chocolate praline or buy a box of chocolate biscuits. It's chocolate luxe.

Roni Sue's Chocolates, Essex Street Market, 120 Essex St., at Delancey St.; (212) 260-0421; roni-sue.com. Wonderful chocolates, including "pig candy" (chocolate-covered bacon) and homemade truffles, are sold in this little Essex Street Market stand. (See p. 168.)

Teuscher Chocolates of Switzerland, Channel Gardens, Rockefeller Center, 620 Fifth Ave.; (212) 246-4416; teuscher.com. Elegant Swiss chocolates, with meltingly fabulous champagne truffles. Teuscher's Madison Avenue location was the chocolatier's first store in the United States; it's at 25 East 61st Street (at Madison Ave.; 212-751-8482).

Best of Kosher

Observant visitors should have little trouble keeping kosher in Manhattan, which offers a wide range of kosher restaurants, from fine dining to casual. For the lowdown on all things kosher, we turned to our expert, Naomi Kraus, who also happens to be a passionate food lover. For help in finding kosher restaurants, Naomi says the go-to website for kosher-keeping diners is **Kosher Restaurants Database Shamash. org** (shamash.org/kosher). Naomi also recommends **Yeah That's Kosher,** a kosher travel/dining blog (yeahthatskosher.com), which often has news on just-opened restaurants throughout the city. Here are a few of Naomi's hot spots for dining kosher in Manhattan. *Note:* Kosher dining in the city tends to be more expensive than equivalent non-kosher spots.

Casual Kosher

Mendy's (61 E. 34th St., at Park Ave.; mendysdeli.com) "does a great burger and deli sandwiches" and **Gotham Burger** (726 Amsterdam Ave., btw. 95th and 96th Sts.; gothamburgerco.com) has good burgers.

Coffee Bar

Coffee Bean and Tea Leaf (coffeebean.com) has several locations in Manhattan; check the website for one nearest you.

Desserts

My Most Favorite Food (247 W. 72nd St., btw. Broadway and West End Ave.; mymostfavorite.com) is best known for its desserts and light fare.

Italian

For dairy kosher Roman cuisine, upscale **Va Bene** (1589 Second Ave., btw. 82nd and 83rd Sts.; vabenenyc.com) is "pricey, but the food is good." **Tevere** (155 E. 84th St., btw. Lexington and Third Aves.; teverenyc.co) serves Roman-style glatt kosher cuisine.

New American

Abigaels on Broadway (1407 Broadway, at 39th St.; abigaels .com), with a creative New American menu overseen by James Beard award winner Jeff Nathan.

Pan-Asian

Serving Chinese and Japanese food is **Eden Wok** (43 E. 34th St., btw. Madison and Park Aves.; edenwok.com).

Steakhouses

Le Maraís (150 W. 46th St., btw. Sixth and Seventh Aves.; lemarais .net), which also has a butcher shop (see p. 18); **Talia's Steakhouse** (668 Amsterdam Ave., at 93rd St.; taliassteakhouse.com); **Wolf and Lamb** (10 E. 48th St., btw. Fifth and Madison Aves.; wolfandlamb steakhouse.com), and the **Prime Grill,** which Naomi calls "probably numero uno expense account place for kosher business meals" (25 W. 56th St., nr. Fifth Ave.; theprimegrill.primehospitalityny.com).

Tapas

Ladino Tapas Bar and Grill (940 Eighth Ave., at 56th St.; ladinogrill.com).

Index